ALGARVE

Contents

the magazine 5

- ◆ Lagos: Heroes and a Villain
- ◆ The Way We Were: Algarve Memories
- ◆ Behind the Sunglasses
- ◆ Cerámica and the Celtic Connection
- ◆ A Taste of the Algarve
- ◆ Building Sights
- ◆ The Bests, Greats and Ifs of the Algarve
- ◆ Golf Courses ◆ Local Curiosities and Tall Tales

Finding Your Feet 33

- ◆ First Two Hours
- ◆ Getting Around
- ◆ Accommodation
- ◆ Food and Drink
- ◆ Shopping
- ◆ Entertainment

Faro and the East 41

Getting Your Bearings
In a Day
Don't Miss ◆ Faro Old Town ◆ Tavira
◆ Rio Guadiana ◆ Beaches
At Your Leisure ◆ 9 more places to explore
Where to... ◆ Stay ◆ Eat and Drink ◆ Shop
◆ Be Entertained

Albufeira and Central East Algarve 67

Getting Your Bearings
In a Day
Don't Miss ◆ Albufeira ◆ Vilamoura ◆ Igreja de São
◆ Loulé
At Your Leisure ◆ 7 more places to explore
Where to... ◆ Stay ◆ Eat and Drink ◆ Shop
◆ Be Entertained

Central West Algarve 93
Getting Your Bearings
In Four Days
Don't Miss ✦ Praia da Rocha ✦ Portimão
✦ Carvoeiro and surrounding beaches
At Your Leisure ✦ 8 more places to explore
Where to... ✦ Stay ✦ Eat and Drink ✦ Shop
✦ Be Entertained

The West 113
Getting Your Bearings
In Three Days
Don't Miss ✦ Lagos ✦ Lagos beaches and coves
✦ Fortaleza de Sagres and Cabo de São Vicente
At Your Leisure ✦ 6 more places to explore
Where to... ✦ Stay ✦ Eat and Drink ✦ Shop
✦ Be Entertained

The Hills 137
Getting Your Bearings
In a Day
Don't Miss ✦ Silves ✦ Caldas de Monchique **At Your Leisure** ✦ 4 more places to explore
Where to... ✦ Stay ✦ Eat and Drink ✦ Shop
✦ Be Entertained

Walks and Tours 153
✦ 1 Lagos Town
✦ 2 Caldas de Monchique ✦ 3 Boca do Rio
✦ 4 Villages and Countryside of the Barrocal
✦ 5 Tavira ✦ 6 Rio Guadiana
✦ 7 Quinta do Marim

Practicalities 71
✦ Before You Go
✦ When to Go
✦ When You Are There
✦ Useful Phrases
✦ Town Pronunciation Guide

Atlas 179

Index and Acknowledgements 187

Written by Paul Murphy
Where to sections by Susie Boulton

Copy edited by Rebecca Snelling
Page layout by Design Directions
Verified by Brian and Eileen Anderson
Indexed by Marie Lorimer

Edited, designed and produced by AA Publishing.
© Automobile Association Developments Limited 2002
Maps © Automobile Association Developments Limited 2002

Automobile Association Developments Limited retains the copyright in the original edition © 2002 and in all subsequent editions, reprints and amendments.

All rights reserved. No part of this publication may be reproduced, stored in a retrieval system, or transmitted in any form or by any means – electronic, photocopying, recording or otherwise – unless the written permission of the publishers has been obtained beforehand.

The contents of this publication are believed correct at the time of printing. Nevertheless, the publishers cannot be held responsible for any errors or omissions or for changes in the details given in this guide or for the consequences of any reliance on the information provided by the same.

Published in the United States by AAA Publishing, 1000 AAA Drive, Heathrow, Florida 32746.
Published in the United Kingdom by AA Publishing.

ISBN 1-56251-667-1

Colour separation by Leo Reprographics
Printed and bound in China by Leo Paper Products

10 9 8 7 6 5 4 3 2 1

the magazine

Take a stroll around the historic city of Lagos and you will see three statues. Two of these – Prince Henry (1394–1460) and Gil Eanes (c1400–88) – are quite conventional; they are obviously serious heroic fellows, remembered for the right reasons. But the third is an enigma. Is he an androgynous astronaut, a Flowerpot Man, or just a character in a funny hat and motorcycle gauntlets? The plaque says King Sebastião, but a less kingly sight you never saw.

Lagos Heroes and a Villain

At the turn of the 15th century, when the world was still flat, when sailors steered by the stars and when ship-swallowing sea monsters lurked just over the horizon, it was a giant step for mankind to venture forth from *O Fim do Mundo* (the End of the World) – as the westernmost point of the Algarve was then known. To do so required bravery, faith, knowledge, and a few escudos too.

Henry the Navigator

Infante Henrique, or Prince Henry – the Anglo-Portuguese son of King João I and Phillipa of Lancaster – had all of these qualities, and more. One of Portugal's first true Renaissance men, Henry distinguished himself at the age of 18 by organising a successful raiding party against the Moors in Ceuta, in North Africa. But he was not a soldier, nor even a sailor – Ceuta was as far as he ever ventured. Henry was a thinker, a planner, a motivator, an entrepreneur, a visionary and ultimately the man who launched Portugal's great Age of Discoveries.

Henry's palace was at Lagos but, for secrecy, he moved his base as far west as possible and built the town of Vila do Infante (now Sagres, ▶ 123–5, 130). It was a top-secret research base, where great minds pooled their knowledge of astronomy, cartography, ship-building, commerce and other disciplines, in pursuit of great prizes overseas. From here originated the *caravela* ship design that propelled the

Above: A court chronicler reported that Henry "inspired fear in those unaccustomed to him". Previous page: King Sebastião's reign was a disaster; many feel the same about his statue!

6 *the magazine*

Portuguese ahead of Spain and England in the Discoveries race.

But it was the second of our heroes, **Gil Eanes**, who made the first great breakthrough. In 1434 he succeeded in rounding the fearsome Cape Bojador (on the west African coast, southeast of the Canary Islands), which was then the edge of the known world. The area towards the Equator was known as the Torrid Zone, and it was thought that ships would meet a fiery end if they ventured too far south.

During Henry's time expeditions discovered Madeira, the Azores and the Cape Verde Islands, though he never lived to see the voyages of his famous pupils, Magellan, Vasco da Gama and Cabral (see box), which would establish the Portuguese Empire and bring the country to the height of its power.

King Sebastião

But less than a century after Prince Henry's reign, King Sebastião was to bring the country to its lowest ebb. Born in 1557, he acceded to the throne as a child. He is frequently described as an unstable, headstrong, idealistic, chilvalric fool who

> When four ships under Vasco da Gama successfully negotiated the Cape of Good Hope, the way was opened for Portugal to become a significant commercial power

Henry's Legacy of Discoveries
- Vasco da Gama discovered the sea route to India between 1497 and 1499.
- Pedro Alvares Cabral discovered and took possession of Brazil in 1500.
- Ferdinand Magellan's first circumnavigation of the world was between 1519 and 1522.

the magazine

took no heed of elder advisers. It was also said that feelings of inadequacy gnawed away at his soul and perhaps this was why he had to prove himself in a crusade against the Moors. Whatever, in 1578 he sailed from Meia Praia (▶ 121) to the shores of Morocco with a force of around 20,000 men. But his ships were intercepted *en route* and his supplies were lost. Ill-prepared for battle in the burning heat, outnumbered and outmanoeuvred, some 8,000 men, including Sebastião and the cream of the Portuguese nobility, were killed and over 10,000 captured at Alcacér-Quibir. Only 100 made it back to Portugal. Ransom demands for the survivors virtually bankrupted the country and in the heirless vacuum left by Sebastião, Portugal became a pawn of Spain.

Sebastianismo

Yet Sebastião's memory failed to die. For years after his débâcle, various impostors claimed to be the king and a cult of *Sebastianismo* grew up, conveniently forgetting the experience in North Africa and clutching at straws for deliverance from the Spanish. Remarkably, even though the Spanish yoke was shaken off just 60 years later, the cult continued into the 20th century, invoked during troubled times. His controversial, rather ridiculous-looking statue in Lagos has been interpreted by some as taking the cult into the space age, but to most people it is just a bizarre piece of modern art.

Below: Battleships once sailed from Lagos but now pedaloes ply the water Bottom: the *caravela* helped the Portuguese win the race to distant lands

Quote from the young Christopher Columbus:

"The Torrid Zone is not uninhabitable for the Portuguese are sailing to and fro in it every day."

8 *the magazine*

Algarve Memories

Dorothy Boulter and Sally Vincent are two of the Algarve's great pioneers and, although they may not wish to be reminded of the fact, these two long-serving hoteliers have provided board and lodgings to visitors for a combined total of nearly 70 years.

The Way We Were

Above: Beautiful beaches have always been the Algarve's main draw for tourists
Below: Dorothy: "My sum knowledge when I first arrived (in Portugal) was that it was a small country which grew grapes!"

Dorothy Boulter at the Solar Penguin

Dorothy arrived at Portimão by boat from Tanganyika (now Tanzania) in 1962, along with her husband, Royston, and seven young children. She recalls how the locals greeted them with a friendly curiosity and how they were guided proudly around Portimão's thriving sardine factories.

Convinced of the potential at neighbouring Praia da Rocha, Dorothy and Royston bought a dilapidated guesthouse in a magnificent position right on the clifftop above the beach. Built in 1918 on the site of an

the magazine

ancient castle, it had been enigmatically christened the Solar Penguin by its previous owner. They kept the name, renovated the building ("it was great fun") and Dorothy has been here ever since.

In the 1960s the seafront was lined with grand villas, a handful of hotels and a single grocery store. There was not a restaurant to be seen and the only nightlife was the casino. It was all "quite decorous, not rag-tag" remembers Dorothy wistfully. In the 1960s cars were a novelty in this region and the only public transport was the *carroça*, a horse and carriage that plied the route between Portimão and Praia da Rocha, carrying ten passengers at a time for a fare of 1.5 escudos.

Over the years, Dorothy has accommodated visitors from just about every corner of the world, but the Solar Penguin remains a very English corner of a foreign field. One of her proudest moments is the day when Field Marshall Montgomery called at the Penguin.

▶ 108 for more details about the hotel.

Sally Vincent at the Casa Grande

Sally Vincent arrived at Burgau (just west of Lagos) in 1972. An actress by profession and a great character in every sense, Sally came to the Algarve from Chicago and, like Dorothy, chose the then-underdeveloped country for a fresh start. To go from the bright lights of the USA to the Casa Grande – a large run-down manor house in a primitive village with no running water or electricity – was something of a culture shock. But Sally soon adapted and made a virtue out of necessity, buying a cow and supplying fresh milk to the villagers. As a sideline she had a "fleet" of 13 donkeys and took her guests and other tourists trekking.

"It was a wonderful place to bring up the kids, no crime and just seven cars in the whole of Lagos," Sally laughs. But medical conditions were also primitive and Sally well remembers her daughter's appendectomy administered under ether.

Initially she spoke little Portuguese and communicated with her eight staff

Sally: "We've had Jerry Hall, Bryan Ferry and the Vatican diplomat here, though not all at the same time!"

Praia da Rocha's white tower blocks are typical of the modern Algarve coast

10 *the magazine*

largely by sign language and pictograms. However, thanks largely to her bubbly character she and her husband were quickly integrated into the local community – "the Casa Grande was like a village social club in those days".

This was to be a big help when just months after their arrival the Portuguese Revolution occurred. In its immediate aftermath many foreign-owned hotels and restaurants faced hostility, even nationalisation, but for the Casa Grande it was business as usual. Two visitors Sally remembers very well in 1972 were scouts from McDonalds, the burger chain. Scared off by the revolution, they reappeared some years later further east, where they eventually set up shop and so helped accelerate the rate of commercialism in the central Algarve.

Today the Casa Grande is no longer the only guesthouse in the village and Sally's uninterrupted sea view has long disappeared, but Burgau is still a sleepy little place, and it's now enclosed in the protected Costa Vincentina National Park.

▶ 132 for more details about the hotel.

By 1965, package holiday makers were joining locals on the Algarve's beaches

the magazine 11

Behind the Sunglasses

It's midday at Gigi's restaurant in Quinta do Lago and although this isn't the first time someone has literally dropped in for lunch, the helicopter turns a head or two. "You do have a reservation sir?", asks the eponymous owner, "because today – as most days – we are full". Embarrassed looks and a few minutes later the helicopter is airbound again. With the calibre of clients that Quinta do Lago provides, Senor Gigi can afford to be choosy.

"Quinta" (▶ 83) is the place par excellence for star-spotting in the Algarve. Luxurious homes in spacious surroundings with world-class sporting facilities on the doorstep have long attracted the rich and famous. Madonna, Jon Bon Jovi and Brad Pitt have all been associated with the area, though it's often difficult to substantiate the stories that fly around. Short of actually meeting the stars you must often rely on the word of someone who has! Part of Quinta do Lago's appeal is that it manages to cloak its

George Michael, Sir Paul McCartney (above) and Prince Rainier (below) are some of the many celebrities to visit the Algarve

12 *the magazine*

Luis Figo, the most famous Portuguese sportsman of the last 30 years

stars in a very discrete veil: just try asking any hotel concierge about them and see how far you get!

Close by, at Porches, Sean Connery, Prince Rainier and Princess Caroline of Monaco have been seen shopping for ceramics, while singer Cliff Richard, who has a house near Guia, is seen regularly. Other British music stars with homes in the Algarve include Sir Paul McCartney (near Lagos) and George Michael (near Luz).

The Algarve is naturally a draw for the sports fraternity, most notably Luis Figo, the Portuguese national hero. He owns Bar 7, a restaurant-bar on the front corner of the marina at Vilamoura (▶ 76). Football fans can look at the many pictures and signed shirts of international footballers from all over the world. On a related matter, Alan Shearer, the former England football captain, has a house in Quinta do Lago.

In the fields of literature and the arts the Algarve has a lesser profile, though in the 1930s it was the haunt of many writers and intellectuals. Most notable of these was the French novelist Simone de Beauvoir, who regularly held court at the Café Aliança in Faro (▶ 63). Today the tradition is upheld by the German novelist, dramatist and poet Günter Grass, winner of the 1999 Nobel Prize for literature, who has a summer home in Portimão.

Other Good Places for Spotting the Rich and the Famous
Hotel Vilajoya, near Albufeira : former German chancellor Willy Brandt and singer Cliff Richard (▶ 87).
Hotel La Reserve, Santa Bárbara de Nexe: the Spanish royal family and the Portuguese president, Jorge Sampaio. ✚ 185 D2
Vila Lara Hotel, near Armação de Pêra. ✚ 183 F2

cerâmica and the celtic connection

Anyone who has ever shopped in the Algarve will tell you that it is a great place for ceramics and those in the know will tell you that the centre of the pottery (*olaria* or *cerâmica*) industry is the village of Porches. So, what could be more typically Portuguese than pottery from Porches? And thereby hangs a tale, of an Irishman, a Portuguese man, three daughters and a Scotsman.

The mass-produced pottery that you're likely to see along main roads is very different to the *olaria* painstakingly crafted at Porches

When the accomplished Irish artist Patrick Swift arrived in the Algarve in 1962, he was horrified to find that the pottery heritage of the region (which went back to Roman times) had all but succumbed to the new age of plastic. From what was once a thriving industry, only three small potteries remained active.

Swift joined forces with the Portuguese artist Lima de Freitas to revive the tradition. They aimed not only to create works of art but to provide employment by producing high-quality souvenirs. Local potters and painters were taken on and in 1968 the Olaria de Porches (Porches Pottery) was founded.

A Distinctive Style

Seeking to gain a distinctive style and competitive advantage over the cheap pottery of northern Portugal that was flooding the south, they went back over a thousand years to Moorish times and the majolica technique. Basically, this entails glazing the earthenware then painting directly onto the surface with oxide paints, before a second firing. It produces a deeper, brighter, longer-lasting finish than other techniques.

The two artists were primarily influenced by the designs and motifs of the Algarve, past and present. For example, the beautiful long-tailed bird so prominent in many of their pieces is of Phoenician origin, while their flamboyant flowers, fruits and foliage can be seen along any country roadside today. Look too for the Algarvian hare, and a lean hunting dog that was once used by the Moors.

Clear, free-flowing brush strokes set Olaria de Porches aside from its competitors, where mass-production techniques were rigidly employed. Only the highest quality glazes and paints were used by Swift and de Freitas, and over the next decade or so Porches became a byword for high-quality pottery (▶ 111).

The tradition lives on

Patrick Swift died in 1983, Lima da Freitas in 1998, but their techniques are kept alive by Patrick's widow, Oonagh, and her daughters, Stella and Julie, who now manage the business on a daily basis, employing 11 local people. A third daughter, Kate Swift, has left the fold to gain international repute as a ceramic painter. Kate's splendid works are free interpretations of ancient Iberian, Islamic and pre-Islamic designs. Every piece is unique and no stencils or any kind of reproductive technique is used. She is now based at Silves in the Estúdio Destra (▶ 151).

Working in a similar vein to Kate is Ian Fitzpatrick, who

Above: Julie Swift, continuing her father's legacy of high quality pottery

Below: By contrast, mass produced pottery can be found all along the N125

Magical Majolica
The majolica method is named after the island of Majorca, one of the places it originated from. It has a palette of four basic colours: blue (cobalt oxide), green (copper oxide), yellow (antimony oxide) and purple (manganese oxide).

Left: Freshly-baked pottery for sale. Below: Craftsman-quality *azulejos*

Inspired by the past – plate from Estudio Destra

also grew up under cold Celtic skies. Ian (a Scot) arrived in Porches in 1981, fresh from Dundee Art College. He came to work with Jorge Mealha, who had worked with Patrick Swift before going it alone to form Olaria Velha (the Old Pottery) on the site where Olaria de Porches began in 1968. In 1983 Jorge moved out and Ian took over the premises, rechristening it Olaria Pequena (the Little Pottery). Ian's style is vibrant, bold, simple and colourful, drawing on natural local produce for many of his designs – olives, fish, oranges and lemons are recurring themes – and producing unmistakable southern European works of art. In the spirit of the late Patrick Swift he employs a Portuguese assistant who he hopes will one day help manage the business. For more details see ▶ 111.

A Taste of the Algarve

Sardines and Other Fish

It has been said that the smell of sardines grilling on charcoal is the perfume of the Algarve and although it will never be bottled it certainly does linger in the nostrils long after the suntan has faded. Popular myth says Portimão is the only place that can grill a sardine properly, which is of course nonsense. The town's famous "Sardine Dock" (▶ 100–1) is worth a visit, where – as at a dozen other places along the coast – the fish are hauled ashore and cooked immediately for maximum freshness.

The Portuguese may like sardines but they just love *bacalhau* (pronounced "bakel-yow"), dried salt-cod (▶ 29). More popular with visitors is *caldeirada*, a robust *bouillabaisse*-like stew with tomatoes and peppers.

Cuisine of the Colonies

Culinary remnants of the empire are few in southern Portugal. In fact the only obvious reminder is the tiny bright red *piri-piri* chilli peppers (mostly from Angola), used to flavour the oil that is basted onto chicken *piri-piri*. *Piri-piri* sauce is also put on the table as a condiment and is a delicious way of spicing up soups and stews, though do treat it with caution as you don't need much to add a little fire! Both the oil and the peppers, strung like necklaces, are on sale in the local markets. Chicken *piri-piri* is now found all over the Algarve but has become associated particularly with the Monchique hills. One of the best places for sampling it is Guia, near Albufeira, where several inexpensive restaurants specialise in roast chicken.

Grilling on the dock of the bay at Portimão

The ubiquitous *piri-piri* peppers, hanging at Loulé market

the magazine 17

Curries, from Goa and Mozambique, are more elusive. Try Safari at Praia da Rocha (➤ 96) and the very individual Kudissanga at Tavira, (➤ 51), whose menu comprises dishes solely from the former African colonies.

From Brazil comes *feijoada*, a thick stew comprising various types of pork, bacon, sausage and beans. This warming peasant food is usually found in the spring or autumn at more rustic eating places. Brazil is also responsible for the popular *caipirinha* (a cocktail of white rum or cane spirit, lime and sugar) and much of Portugal's coffee.

Moorish Influences

It is common knowledge that the Moors gave the Algarve figs, oranges and lemons and their ultra-sweet egg- and-marzipan-based delicacies, but it is not so well known that they also invented the *cataplana*. This distinctive clam-shaped primitive pressure cooker may be seen in tourist shops in gleaming burnished copper but usually appears on restaurant tables in a silvery, somewhat battered form. No matter – when the hinged lid is sprung open and the steamy aroma of clams, *chouriço* (spicy sausage), wine, garlic, parsley, onions, tomato and pork bursts forth like a Moorish *djinn* to bewitch the waiting diners, it could be a rusty bucket for all they care.

Ironically, today's favourite combination – seafood and pork – was invented *after* the Moorish occupation, as a dish that only true Christians could enjoy. These ingredients were (and are still) proscribed to the resident Muslims and Jews, who had been expelled from the Algarve in the late 15th century.

White Port and Green Wine

The very last time and place that you would want to drink sweet, dark sticky port is on a balmy summer Algarve evening. Which is precisely why white port was invented. Made in exactly the same way as dark port, but from white grapes (of course!), it can vary from bone dry, akin to a fino sherry, to a smooth sweet aperitif wine. If it is not already chilled, add some ice.

Vinho verde also originates from Minho, and translates literally as "green wine" (green in the young or immature sense). It is low in alcohol and flavour, but it's also low in price, and with a slight spritzer-like fizz. It

always comes chilled and is perfect for sipping outside a bar in the Algarve heat.

An Algarve feast: marzipan sweets, fresh red peppers, ethnic squashes, plump sardines, rustic bread, crisp *vinho verde* and *cataplana*. Enjoy!

BUILDING Sights

An A–Z of the Algarvian architectural heritage; where to find its best (and worst) examples.

Azulejos are the ubiquitous painted tiles of the Iberian Peninsula. The most important historical examples are to be found in churches, such as the Igreja de São Lourenço in Almancil (➤ 77–8). However, *azulejos* can be found almost anywhere, from homes and restaurants to public gardens (see ***Jardins*** below).

Bridges span the centuries from "Roman" to late 20th-century masterpieces. The mighty steel road bridges at Portimão (➤ 100–1, pictured above) and Castro Marim (➤ 53) are reckoned to be the finest of their kind in Europe.

Chimneys (*chaminés*), filigreed (such as the one pictured) and decorated in a hundred different styles, have become one of the Algarve's unofficial trademarks. The basic design is Moorish and it used to be said that the more elaborate and bigger the chimney the wealthier the owner was likely to be.

The **Discoveries** (*Descobrimentos*) of exotic lands by Portuguese sailors in the 15th century began a frenzy of architectural frippery, manifested in maritime themes such as knotted ropes, sails and anchors, and newly discovered flora and fauna. This style, known as Manueline architecture (see below), is best seen on church portals and windows at Monchique, Alvor, Silves and Luz de Tavira village.

Estói Palace (➤ 58), pretty in pink with fantasy flourishes, is a baroque gem, although you can view only the exterior.

Ferragudo (➤ 104) boasts the finest *fortaleza* (sea fortress) in the Algarve. There's another opposite at Praia da Rocha (➤ 98–9), and one at Lagos (➤ 118–19).

Gilded wood-carving (*talha dourada*) is

The spectacular interior of the church of São Lourenço

a Portuguese speciality found in many churches.

Houses in the Algarve generally look like plain white boxes, and are decorated with coloured bands around the doors and windows. This style, like many others, originally came from North Africa.

Igreja matriz means parish church and is often the finest building in the community – it's usually worth taking a look inside.

Jardins (public gardens). Tavira (➤ 49–51) has the prettiest, both north and south of the river, and the majestic Mosteiro dos Jerónimos (Jerónimos Monastery) and the exquisite Torre de Belém.

The **Moorish** influence is omnipresent in the Algarve from Old Town Albufeira to Olhão and many a mock-Moorish hotel and apartment development.

The **neolithic** tomb site of Alcalar, near Portimão, dating back over 5,000 years, is the oldest structure in the Algarve.

Olhão (➤ 57) is famous for its *açoteias*, the flat terraces on its brilliant white cubist fishermen's houses, linked by external flights of steps.

Window dressing in the Algarve is a vibrant if simple art

Portimão also has a couple of restful spaces, including the Largo 1 Dezembro by the old town hall, which is notable for its *azulejo* benches.

King Manuel I's reign (1495–1521) saw Portuguese architecture reach its zenith, hence the name Manueline style.

Lisbon is the place for the best Portuguese architecture – if you're on a day-trip to Portugal's capital, don't miss

Palheiros, primitive round straw-topped huts, were still in use in the wilder parts of the Algarve in the 19th century. You can see a reconstruction of one at the Parque Mineiro Cova dos Mouros (➤ 168).

Quinta do Marim (➤ 169–70) has one of the last surviving tidemills in Portugal.

Roman villa remains are to be found at Milreu (➤ 58) and Vilamoura (➤ 75–6), but

the magazine 21

the "Roman" bridges elsewhere have been much rebuilt.

Silves (▶ 142–4) boasts the best-preserved castle in the Algarve.

Tavira (▶ 49–51) is the region's most beautiful architectural ensemble, effortlessly blending over 30 churches, a Roman bridge, riverside gardens and handsome 18th- and 19th-century houses.

U is for "ugly duckling", a term often applied to Quarteira (▶ 83) because of its 1970s high-rise blocks.

Vilamoura (▶ 75–6) and **Vale de Lobo** (▶ 83–4) are examples of the new face of the Algarve; expensive neo-Moorish apartments and manicured lawns.

Wells (*noras*), distinguished by waterwheels with attached cups, are all over the Algarve.

X-rated are the chapels housing human bones at Faro (▶ 28, 56) and Alcantarilha!

The **Youth Hostel** at Alcoutim (▶ 36), is the best in the south, set in a white circular building overlooking the river.

Z is for **Casa do Zé**, a ubiquitous name sign. Often applied to cheaper restaurants, Zé is a diminutive of José.

Rather Moorish: from traditional *platibandas* (above) to modern designs (below)

A wealth of detail in the Manueline carving at the Igreja Mattriz, Alvor

THE BESTS, GREATS AND IFS
of the Algarve

Best Place to Watch the Sunset
As Europe's westernmost land there are a number of contenders for this crown, the most obvious being *O Fim do Mundo* itself, **Cape St Vincent** (➤ 123–5).

However, almost anywhere facing westwards within a few miles of here is spectacular. The views from the **Ponta da Piedade** at Lagos (➤ 122) and over **Faro lagoon** are particularly good.

Great Views
Go west – to the cliffs of **Arrifana** (➤ 127) and the **Miradouro da Cordama** (➤ 126). Words alone cannot do justice to these breathtaking cliffs and seascapes.

Great Meal, Great View
It is hard to beat the panorama from the cliff tops of Albufeira – try **O Cabaz do Praia** (gourmet French, ➤ 89) or **A Ruina** (classic Algarvian fish menu, ➤ 88). Alternatively, the tree-top views from the **Restaurant Florestal** (➤ 134) at Barão de São João near Luz are unique in the region. The food is top-notch mid-price American fare and the views are more reminiscent of Asia or Africa than the Algarve.

You don't have to go to the end of the earth (*O Fim do Mundo*) for a great sunset, but in this case it definitely helps!

the magazine

Great Beaches

How can you compare travel-poster coves such as **Dona Ana** at Lagos, or **Benagil**, near Carvoeiro, to the wild beauty of the west coast at **Arrifana**, **Amados**, or **Bordeira**? You don't, you just enjoy them.

You could also try **Marinha** (Lagos), **Ingrina**, **Cabanas Velhas** (Salema), **Castelo** (Albufeira) and **Praia da Rocha**, but this is of course very subjective and you will no doubt find your own favourites.

If You Only Visit One Museum…

… make it the **Museu Municipal** at Lagos (➤ 119–20). This is a real jackdaw's nest – from menhirs and mosaics to pickled freak animals, weaponry, folklore, and just when you think it is all over, you'll come across a gilded chapel that will make your jaw drop.

The best museum setting, however, is the tranquil **Convento de Nossa Senhora da Assunção** in Faro (➤ 47).

If You Are Only Impressed by One Chimney…

… it will be the superb example in the centre of **Porches** (➤ 105).

If You Only Visit One Village…

… make it **Querença**, near Loulé (➤ 161).

And if you only visit two villages, **Cacela Velha**, near Tavira (➤ 60), is also worth the detour.

Best Markets

For genuine atmosphere, visit one of the everyday *mercados*. **Loulé** (➤ 79–81) on a Saturday has all the local colour, sounds and smells you could wish for.

Top marks also to **Olhão's market halls**, (➤ 65) which, despite modernisation and gentrification, have retained their down-to-earth character.

Best Places for People-Watching

• **Albufeira by night:** the main square and The Strip at Montechoro – holidaymakers of all nationalities in all colours, sizes and fashions.
• **Portimão gardens by the dockside:** domestic and foreign tourists looking slightly lost, heading to and from sardine feasts.
• **Any fresh produce market:** to see the locals.

Best Ceramics

The Algarve is full of pottery, much of it cheap and mass

Top: Praia de Beliche is another great beach to fall in love with.
Above: Eating by the beach always tastes better

produced. But the individually crafted wares at **Olaria de Porches** and **Pequena Olaria** in Porches (➤ 14–16, 111); **Estúdio Destra** in Silves (➤ 151); and **Olaria Nova** in Lagos (➤ 135) would grace any house.

Best Outdoor Café

Waste an hour or so with coffee and cakes on the terrace of the **Café Inglês** (➤ 144, 150), on the steps below Silves Castle. On a Sunday at 3 pm you can hear traditional Brazilian guitar music dating from the 1930s.

Best Radio Station

If it's not already pre-set on your hire car, tune into **Radio Comercial**, 96.1 FM – hard-driving rockin' music from Led Zep, Stones, REM, U2, Oasis, Lenny Kravitz and so on. Too loud? Move along the dial to 106.1, **Radio Nostalgie**.

Happy as a sand boy on the beach

Best Set-price Meal

Normally these are to be avoided, but for a culinary Portuguese-international treat at a ridiculously low price, beat a path to **Anna's** (Rua Nova 7, tel: 289 513558) in Albufeira.

Best *Bifana*

You'll find the best pork steak sandwich at the friendly all-Portuguese **Bar Ferradura** in Lagos (➤ 120). Take two slices of perfectly textured fresh white bread, one just-cooked pork steak, add a good squirt of mustard, then drizzle on just a few drops of *piri-piri*.

The king of Algarve chimneys, at Porches

GOLF COURSES

So, you've just arrived in the Algarve, you play golf most weekends and you want to know which are the best courses that won't scare you to death *or* cost you an arm and a leg. There are plenty to choose from. These recommendations are from east to west.

Vilamoura Laguna
Fairly flat layout (length 6,100m) but lots of water hazards and tight bunkers. *Watch out for*: the fifth (par four), trees, bunkers, lake, sloping green.
☎ 289 310180;
www.vilamoura.net

Gramacho (Carvoeiro)
Cleverly crafted double-nine course (18 tees and greens, nine fairways), measuring 5,900m, which proves a real challenge for a good score. *Watch out for*: the second (par five) – you'll need *two* very good approach shots to make par here.
☎ 282 340900

Alto Golf (Alvor)
Measuring 6,100m and set in rolling countryside with lots of trees, bushes and bunkers ready to punish wayward shots. *Watch out for*: the 16th (par five) – a mere 604m!
☎ 282 416913

Palmares (Lagos)
This 6,000m course offers links-style golf on the first nine holes with spectacular views over the Bay of Lagos, and a parkland course on the back nine with panoramas of the Monchique hills and the sea. *Watch out for*: the first (par four), one of the most impressive holes in the Algarve with an elevated tee looking out to sea and a steep dropping fairway with the green tucked out of sight.
☎ 282 762953

Parque da Floresta (Budens)
Attractive hilly course with spectacular views. At 5,700m it is slightly shorter than the courses above. *Watch out for*: the 14th (par four); do you shoot for the bunkers, or go out of bounds? Do you go for the stream or the tree? The green – when you get there – is a rollercoaster ride.
☎ 282 690055;
www.vigiasa.com

Best in the west: Parque da Floresta (top) and Palmares (above)

Left: Try tackling the 16th hole on the Royal Course at Vale do Lobo

Top League Courses

San Lorenzo (tel: 289 396522) is rated one of the best courses in Europe. The setting, amid the Reserva Natural da Ria Formosa (➤ 57), is magnificent. Just a short distance away, in a very similar setting, is the world-famous **Quinta do Lago** course (➤ 91, tel: 289 390700). You will have to play your best golf to get away with a respectable score on either of these masterpieces.

The most famous hole in the Algarve – and perhaps the most photographed in the world – is the 16th on the **Royal Course** at Vale do Lobo (➤ 91, tel: 289 393939), yet another of the Algarve's truly memorable golf experiences.

Family Favourite
At Parque da Floresta there's also archery, bowls, horse-riding, mountain biking, tennis, outdoor and indoor swimming pools, a sauna, a gym and a Jacuzzi. The elevated clubhouse is excellent for lunch.

Need to Know
All courses (except for Parque da Floresta) require a handicap certificate and most have a dress code.
Check your tee-off time when booking.

Local Curiosities and Tall Tales

A Shaggy Dog Tale

You might say the Algarve *cão d'agua* (water dog) is the original sea dog. With webbed feet to enable it to walk on shifting sands and thick shaggy hair to keep out the cold, in times past it was the Algarve fisherman's best friend, retrieving nets and fishing gear, barking like a fog horn, swimming from boat to boat with messages, even diving into bubbling seas to round up tuna and pull out drowning men – so they say. Although no longer gainfully employed, the breed has been preserved and you can see the dogs in kennels at Quinta do Marim (➤ 57, 169–70) in the Reserva Natural da Ria Formosa.

Skulduggery in the Chapel

There's a tiny chapel in Faro where even on the warmest day you'll find a chill in the air. Attached to the Igreja do Carmo (though easily overlooked), it is called the Capela dos Ossos (Chapel of the Bones, ➤ 56). As you enter it you come face to face with the grinning skulls, tibias, fibulas, femurs and other bones of around 1,000 former parishioners and monks, literally supporting the chapel walls. The inscription "*Nós ossos, que aqui estamos, Pelos vossos esperamos*" means "Our bones

Web-like membranes between the toes of this shaggy leonine poodle make it at home in the water and on shifting sands

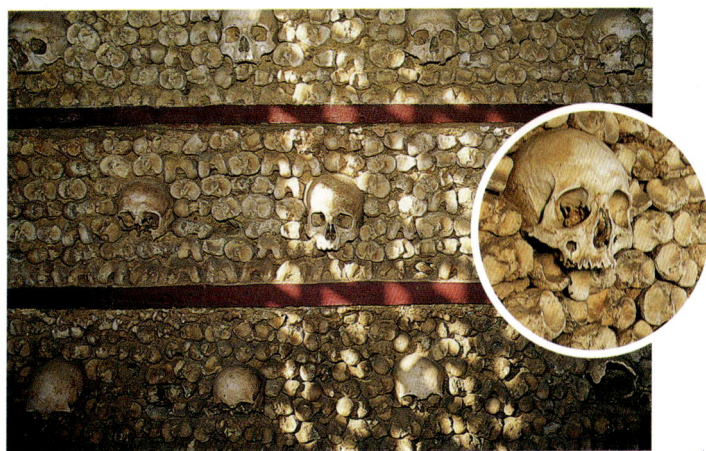

Grim reminders of mortality at Faro's Capela dos Ossos

standing here are waiting for yours".

Bone chapels are a Portuguese speciality and there's a very similar example at Alcantarilha, the scant remains of one at Faro Cathedral (▶ 47), and at Evora, in the Alentejo area, is the largest of all, housing the bones of around 5,000 monks.

Cardboard Fish

Now why would a country with over 800km of its own coastline and goodness knows how many varieties of tasty, local, ocean-fresh fish choose as its national dish *bacalhau*, dried salt-cod imported from Scandinavia? *Bacalhau* (▶ 17) first got onto the Portuguese menu in the 14th century when large fleets went hunting for cod in Newfoundland, and for some reason has stayed there ever since. Look in old-fashioned grocers and you will see it on sale. Resembling fossilised grey cardboard, it is cut with a saw, then soaked for several hours to get rid of the preserving salt and to rehydrate it. It is said there are 365 ways to cook it but foreigners don't usually make it past the first or second tasting.

The Enchanted Algarve

The Algarve is romantically called "The Land of the Enchanted Moor", after the work *As Mouras Encantadas e os Encantamentos do Algarve* (The Enchanted Moorish Women and the Enchantments of the Algarve), written by Dr Francisco de Ataide Oliveira in 1898. Dealing with Moorish legends and the supernatural, one of its recurring themes is that of a Moorish maiden left behind in a state of enchanted limbo after her people were expelled back to North Africa (see box on ▶ 30). She appears in ghostly form in many places around the Algarve, accosting passers-by on dark nights and asking them to perform certain tasks that will release her from the spell and allow her to return home.

Probably the best-known story, however, is that of a Moorish lord who falls in love with Gilda, a beautiful slave from the north. They marry but she falls into deep

Algarve almond blossom – the only kind of "snow" that most people will ever see in this balmy land

the magazine 29

despondency, pining for the snow of her homeland, and her life starts slipping away. Fortunately a wise old man advises the Arab to plant almond trees throughout the kingdom. In the spring the falling almond blossom resembles snow and Gilda is cured.

Hot Chestnuts in the Sun
One of the Algarve's more incongruous sights is that of hot-chestnut sellers – an icon of northern winter – plying their trade in October and November while tourists walk by in T-shirts and shorts.

The Reconquest
The Moors of North Africa invaded the Iberian Peninsula early in the 8th century and had a profound cultural influence, particularly on southern Portugal. The "Reconquest" of the country began early in the 11th century when the Moors were driven from the north, but they remained entrenched in the south for another 200 years. King Afonso III won decisive victories in the Algarve between 1239 and 1249 and by the end of the 13th century the Christian Reconquest of Portugal was complete.

Above: You'll find many unexpected delights while exploring the Algarve's countryside.
Left: Hot stuff – chestnuts in the sun from a Faro street vendor

Finding Your Feet

First Two Hours

Faro airport is the only terminal serving the Algarve and is just 6km from the town centre. A desk in Arrivals (tel: 289 808080) provides general flight information. For flight arrival and departure times, tel: 289 800801.

Tourist Information
- There's a **desk in Arrivals** (open 8 am to midnight, personal callers only).
- There's also a tourist information office in the **centre of Faro** (tel: 289 803604).

Getting into Faro
- Faro is a 15–20-minute bus ride away, and in summer (mid-May to October) a **complimentary bus** shuttles to and fro, 8–8, daily except Tuesday.
- Alternatively, **public buses No 16** and **No 18** run a regular service into town.

Further Afield
- If you want to proceed any further by bus, take the No 16 or No 18 to the Faro terminal and change. **Long-distance buses** serve the whole of the Algarve from there.
- The **train station** is about 200m west of the bus station, and it's located right on the seafront.

Taxi Fares
- **Average taxi fares** to all resorts are posted on a board in Arrivals though you should, as a safeguard, agree the price before you set off.
- **Prices include baggage** but it is an extra 15–20 per cent if you travel between 10 pm and 6 am at weekends or holidays.
- To pre-book a taxi call the **Associação Taxistas** (Taxi Drivers Association, tel: 289 800860).
- If you have any **queries** as to the price of taxis or any other transport from the airport, ask at the general information desk in the main hall.

Orientation
- If you have **pre-booked a hire car** the chances are that your operator will meet you at the airport and take you to pick it up. Their depot is a five-minute drive away on the main road leading from the airport (there is only one road in and out).
- **Navigation** from here is simple. Continue on the same road then turn right onto the N125 for Faro, left onto the same road for Quinta do Lago or Vale do Lobo, or take the E01 motorway for all other points west and east.

...And The Last Two Hours

Standby and Last-minute Flights
- If you haven't got a return ticket or want to change your plans, pick up a copy of the *Algarve Resident* (on sale every Thursday at most news-stands) and contact any of the advertised agents, under Flights, for **cheap late-availability offers**.
- For **standby tickets** go to the airport on the day (in summer there are several daily flights throughout the day to Britain and other European countries) and go to the ASAP desk in Arrivals. They will tell you flight times, the cost

of the ticket and ask you to arrive around 45 minutes before your chosen flight is due to take off.
- **If there is space** on the next flight – and even in high season there is usually a seat or two – you will be sold a ticket there and then, and hurried through check-in and the departure lounge to board immediately.
- The **cost of a standby ticket** depends on season and availability but is often very reasonable.

Delays
- In the peak season, delays are inevitable. The best plan is to **stay landside as long as possible** and (as long as the weather is good) to use the outdoor public terrace bar, which has an excellent view not only of the planes but across the lagoon to the beach. It's on the upper floor of Arrivals.
- If the **delay is more than an hour or two** and your bags are already checked in you could take a taxi to the Praia de Faro beach, if not to bathe, then to sit at one of the restaurants and enjoy a few last solar rays. Ask the taxi driver to turn left at the beach and drop you at the O Paquete restaurant, which has a very pleasant beachside terrace.

Getting Around

The Algarve is a small place – only 150km from Sagres to Spain, and some 30–40km from the southern shores to the Alentejo region – so getting from A to B is simple, although in peak periods traffic congestion is a problem. Inexpensive car-hire rates and the obvious freedom a car gives make this the favoured method of getting around.

Driving

Roads
- In general, the **roads** in the Algarve are of a high quality and in many instances EU funding has helped to spread a good network well into the countryside. Roads that are marked as secondary or minor roads on maps may now be well surfaced.
- The **best map** is by Hildebrand, though do make sure you get the latest edition (available in the UK from Stanford's, tel: 020 7836 1321).
- The Algarve's **principal road** is the notorious **N125**, in peak season always overloaded and one of the most dangerous routes in Europe. However, it's hard to avoid if you want to explore the Algarve as it runs all the way along the coast and is the artery for every resort and main town.
- The **E01 (also known as the Via do Infante IP1) motorway** runs for around two-thirds of the length of the Algarve from the Spanish border to just beyond Alcantarilha (8km west of Albufeira). Recent improvements mean that it should continue as far as Lagos by 2002. It is an excellent motorway, often underused, and is a better option than the N125.
- A new motorway, stretching from the Algarve to Lisbon is currently under construction. Named the **A2**, the route will begin just north of Albufeira and section from there to Castro Verde. The motorway is expected to be open by summer 2002.
- Speed limit on motorways: **120 kph**.
- Speed limit on main roads: **90 kph**.
- Speed limits on urban roads: **40 or 60 kph**.

Driving Standards

- **Driving** in Portugal is of a poor standard and the accident fatality rate per number of drivers is one of the highest in Europe.
- In general, you should **drive as defensively as possible**. Try to be stoical and just accept the fact that you will be cut up, forced to slow down to let overtaking cars squeeze in and frequently have a driver up against your rear bumper.
- **Drinking and driving** should be avoided. In 1999/2000 an ongoing zero-tolerance campaign was launched on the N125.
- One peculiarity of the N125 is its **wide hard shoulder** that slower-moving vehicles often move into to allow overtaking. It's fine to do this for a moment (particularly if it gets a speed merchant off your tail) but do not drive along here for any length of time as you may well encounter a parked or stopped vehicle.

Car-hire Operators

- **Local operators** offer a comparable service to the international companies, usually at a lower price.
- To hire a car **you must be at least 21**, and for some operators 23.
- **Booking though a broker** at home is not generally necessary as even at the height of the season there are enough cars to go around and anyway, it is a more expensive option.
- **Shop around** and look for special offers.
- A small knock or scrape is always possible so to be on the safe side look for **"no excess to pay"** deals.
- Your **driving licence** is the only motoring document you need.

Delays

- During the summer months and holiday periods the **N125 is often bumper to bumper** between Alcantarilha (where the motorway finishes) and Lagos. The roundabout at Lagoa is a particularly congested point. Unfortunately, other than taking a long, long diversion via Caldas de Monchique and Aljezur, there is no way around this. This situation is unlikely to change much before **2004**, when the motorway extension to the far west is scheduled for completion.

Buses

- **Local buses** are fine for short hops around town or the resort, but no more than that.
- To get from town to town the **regional and long-distance bus operators** in the Algarve provide an acceptable service.
- Modern **high-speed buses** run from west to east Algarve and beyond, to Seville and Lisbon, in just a few hours; you can get from Albufeira to Lisbon or Sagres to Seville in around four hours.
- Ask at the **local tourist office** or **bus terminal** for details.

Train

- Rail travel is the **slowest** way to get around the Algarve.
- The **line runs east–west** shadowing the N125 for much of its length; from Lagos to Vila Real de Santo António takes 4 to 4½ hours.

Admission Prices

The cost of admission for places of interest is indicated by price categories:

Inexpensive under €2.5   **Moderate** €2.5–5   **Expensive** over €5

Accommodation

Accommodation in the Algarve caters for all budgets, from hostels and simple guesthouses to luxury hotels and villas. Although the majority of tourists arrive as part of a package holiday, there are plenty of attractive options for independent travellers.

During high season, particularly in July and August, advance booking is essential if you are not travelling as part of a package deal. Also be aware that accommodation is most expensive during these months. Off-season (November to March) prices plummet by up to 50 per cent, with January and February being the cheapest times to find a room.

Portuguese tourist offices abroad can supply details of hotels and a list of tour operators who specialise in hotel and self-catering accommodation in southern Portugal.

Hotels

- Portuguese hotels are **officially graded** from one to five stars. The categories tend to indicate facilities offered rather than quality or cost, and standards vary considerably within each star rating.
- The majority are mid-range, catering largely for British or German **package tours** and many are block booked for the summer months. Typically they are medium to large, fairly impersonal places with noisy pools and uninspiring dining rooms, but are fine if all you want is a simple beach holiday.
- At the top end of the market are the **beach resort hotels**, complete with the usual choice of restaurants, pools, sporting facilities, health clubs and other luxury mod-cons.
- Displayed in every bedroom should be an **authorised price list**, and there are usually discounts for young children.
- Those seeking authentic Portuguese character should opt for one of the privately run *estalagens* or *albergarias* (roughly translated as "inns"), which have fewer facilities than their equivalent grade hotels but are generally better value.

Pousadas

- *Pousadas* are state-run hotels, either converted from **historic properties** or purpose-built in locations of **outstanding natural beauty**. By their very nature, they are often situated away from touristy areas in order promote the appreciation of local traditions, handicrafts and food.
- Although there are more than 40 *pousadas* in Portugal, the Algarve has two, both falling into the second category: the Pousada de São Brás de Alporte (➤ 62) and the Pousada do Infante (with its related annexe the Forteleza do Beliche) at Sagres (➤ 134). A third *pousada* is currently under construction in Tavira.
- All *pousadas* have **restaurants** that serve food specific to the region. These are usually open to non-residents. The quality of the food is usually high.
- Many people believe that *pousadas* offer the most attractive accommodation in Portugal, so make sure you **book well in advance**.

Pensões and Residenciais

- A *pensão* or *residencial* offers **simple rooms for rent**.
- If you want **breakfast** too there is more chance of getting it at a *residenciai*.
- In recent years, **standards have risen** and nowadays, in the better establishments, you can get a room furnished to the level of one in a mid-range hotel, with its own bathroom and TV, at a fraction of a hotel price.

Solares de Portugal (previously *Turismo de Habitação*)

- This is a successful state scheme for renovating and converting rustic and old properties into **comfortable and usually characterful tourist accommodation**. These are normally in the countryside or just outside a town or resort.
- Prices vary greatly according to location and degree of comfort, but if you prize character above cosseting, this is probably the best way to **get a feel of the "true Portugal"**.
- **Properties are graded** from A (most expensive) to C (least expensive).
- **Specialist operators** generally feature a handful of *Solares de Portugal* in their brochures (even if they are not referred to as such), and local tourist offices keep a full list.

Youth Hostels

- The Algarve has never been on the backpackers' trail and as the trend is for accommodation to go upmarket so crash pads become more scarce, but there are **a few decent youth hostels** so a bed need never cost more than a few euros.
- The best youth hostel is at **Alcoutim** and offers round 50 beds.
- Also try the youth hostels at **Lagos** (Rua Lançarote Freitas 50); **Vila Real de Santo António** (Rua Dr Sousa Martins 40) and **Portimão** (Lugar de Coca Maravillas; this is the largest, with about 180 beds).
- **Spaces are limited**, so book ahead for most times of year.
- **For more information** on youth hostelling in Portugal, contact: Associação de Pousadas de Juventude (Avenida Duque de Ávila 137, 1000 Lisbon; tel: 21 355 9081).

Camping

- There are **plenty of campsites** in the Algarve, many of which are fairly inexpensive to use.
- Campsites are usually found **along the coast – near beaches or wooded areas**. Some are very basic, but others have facilities such as swimming pools and supermarkets. Many also provide pitches for motorhomes and caravans as well as tents.
- **For more information** on camping in Portugal, contact: Federação Portuguesa de Campismo (Rua da Vaz do Operário I, 1010 Lisbon; tel: 21 812 6890; www.roteiro-campista.pt).

Self-catering

- Villas and self-catering apartments **proliferate** along the coast.
- **Anonymous apartment blocks**, often with hotel facilities such as pools, restaurants and shops, offer units of varying standards of comfort, location and space.
- Like hotels, however, they may be **block booked** during peak season.
- **Villas** range from small units within a cluster of properties sharing facilities to grand detached residences with a private pool, manicured gardens and marble bathrooms.
- In addition to **cooking facilities** (usually a gas cooker and small fridge), there may be a maid service at least once a week.
- **Try booking privately** rather than through a tour operator for better price and, often, a higher standard of accommodation.

Accommodation Prices

The price of accommodation featured in the guide is indicated below.
Prices are for a double room per night.

£ under €50   ££ €50–125   £££ over €125

Food and Drink

A plate of grilled fish and salad is still the quintessential Algarve meal. In fact leaving without tasting barbecued sardines is as unthinkable as leaving New York without trying a hotdog.

Dining Options
- In most restaurants **you don't have to worry about dress codes**. Some of the **best-value meals** are those served on paper tablecloths in locals' joints.
- At the other end of the scale are **the few elegant and relatively expensive restaurants** where you can dine in style. Although typically these are international restaurants, charging for ambience and service, a small number serve cuisine of exceptional quality (see Where to Eat sections).

Unsolicited Appetisers
- Soon after you are seated the waiter will automatically bring a **basket of bread and a plate of appetisers**. The usual trio is sardine paste and cheese spread (pre-packed in small plastic tubs), and a dish of olives.
- In better quality places you may get homemade sardine pâté, slices of flambéed spicy sausage, pickled vegetables, marinated olives and cheese. These are **not complimentary** and will appear on your bill (though they are cheap). If you do not want them just say "*não obrigado*" (no thanks).

Main Courses
- Wherever you go, **fish** is likely to dominate the menu. Watch out for the price, especially for fresh fish, which is priced by the kilo.
- **Chicken and pork** are at their best when barbecued (*churrasco*).
- The *prato do dia* (dish of the day) is often excellent value and gives you a chance to sample local specialities.
- If you're **vegetarian**, opt for soup or salad followed by fish, if you eat it. Some places have a vegetarian menu, but generally strict vegetarians have to eat in international restaurants.
- Meals can be washed down with **house wine**. The main local wine is the cheap Lagoa (➤ 111); for better quality try the excellent Alentejo reds.

A Practical Guide to Eating Out
- **Lunch** is normally served from noon to 3 pm and **dinner** from 7 pm to 10 pm, or 9 pm in rural areas. A few restaurants open for dinner only.
- Restaurants rarely charge service charge. **Leave around 10 per cent** if the waiter deserves it. A cover charge is almost always added to the bill.
- **Credit cards** are accepted by many but by no means all restaurants. If you aren't sure, it's wise to take cash.
- **Portuguese portions are huge** and it's quite normal to share a dish or ask for *uma meia dose* (half portion).
- Don't worry about the language barrier. Most restaurants will provide a **menu in several languages**; if not, the waiter will at least know enough English or German to prompt you in the right direction.
- **Check menus in advance**. Some house specialities require 24 hours notice.

Restaurant Prices
Price guides in this book are based on the amount you should expect to pay per person for a three-course meal, excluding drinks and service charges.

£ under €15   ££ €15–23   £££ over €23

Shopping

Although the Algarve is not renowned for its shopping, nor for the quality of its local handicrafts, there are exceptions and bargains to be had, usually in the typically southern European areas of leather, ceramics, wood and basketware. The best centre for handicrafts is Loulé, which has a wonderful Saturday morning market and streets where you can still see local artisans making copper and brass pots and pans.

Out of North Africa
The Algarve has never lost its taste for Moorish goods and some of the best leather and wooden articles in today's shops (Lagos and Silves in particular) are made in North Africa.

In the Chair
Chairs are a speciality of Monchique. Children's chairs hand painted in bright colours in a naive style (similar to English bargeware), and folding X-shaped "scissor chairs", thought to be of Roman origin, both make portable souvenirs.

The Cock that Crowed
If there is one single item that says "I've been to Portugal", it is a little brightly painted wooden or ceramic Cock of Barcelos. This commemorates a folk tale about an innocent man from the northern town of Barcelos who was accused of murder. His final wish was to see the judge, who was in the middle of eating a roast cockerel dinner. "If I am innocent that cockerel will crow," shouted the condemned man, pointing at the dinner plate. The cock, of course, did crow and so the man was released. The cock became a national symbol and subsequently launched a whole souvenir industry.

Unusual Local Souvenirs
- a jar of homemade *piri-piri* sauce or a necklace of *piri-piri* peppers from any local market (► 17).
- a religious **statue** from an antiques shop in Lagos or Faro Old Town.
- a **scissor chair** from Monchique.
- a real *medronho* still – try Rua de Barbaca, Loulé (► 90).
- a panel of *azulejos* from Porches or Estúdio Destra, Silves (► 15, 151).
- a *cataplana*, the Algarvian cooking pot (► 18).
- a heavy-knit **woollen jumper** from Fóia (► 148) or Sagres (► 135).
- white port (► 18), *aguardente* (local brandy) or *medronho* (► 157).

Gipsy Markets
Weekly or fortnightly markets known as gipsy markets are held in all the major tourist centres. Sadly, some have sacrificed local crafts for cheap, low-quality goods, pirated brand-name articles and children's international fashion crazes. In general the fewer tourists, the less adulterated the market.

Opening Hours
Most shops close for an hour or two at lunchtime and all day Sunday. In the resorts they often open late into the evening.

Service
You will never be hassled by shop staff. Many Portuguese shop owners and staff are charming and helpful but it is also a regrettable fact that in too many places service is poor. "*Faz favor*" may get someone's attention if need be.

Entertainment

Sports enthusiasts are spoilt for choice, whether it's golf, tennis, riding or watersports. Evening entertainment mainly takes the form of bars and discos, although larger towns such as Faro and Lagos host occasional concerts and folklore evenings.

"Sportugal"

- The area between Faro and Vilamoura is sometimes referred to as "Sportugal", on account of the superb facilities in and around the resorts of **Quinta do Lago, Vale do Lobo and Vilamoura**.
- The hinterland is ribboned with some of Europe's finest **golf courses**, along with academies, driving ranges and golf shops.
- The golf **season lasts all year** and holidays devoted exclusively to golf are big business here and elsewhere in the central and central-western Algarve.
- There are currently **22 courses**, and more in the pipeline.
- A useful **booklet on golf** in the Algarve, including requirements of the various clubs, is available free from tourist offices abroad.
- Beware that some of the clubs are so **exclusive** it is almost impossible to get a game – and if you do it can be prohibitively expensive.
- **East of Faro and west of Lagos** there are fewer facilities for golfers.
- **For more details** refer to the individual resort entries and Where to be Entertained sections of this book.
- **Tennis** is another big attraction in the Algarve, with tennis academies in Vale de Lobo and Quinta do Lago, tennis clubs in the main resorts and a large number of hotels with their own courts.
- **Horse-riding** is available across the region, with riding centres catering for all standards. Treks can be organised along the beach or in the foothills of rural Algarve.

Watersports

- **Windsurfing** is the region's major watersport and boards and tuition can be found all along the coast. The rough Atlantic waters preclude waterskiing, though the usual tourist favourites – jetskiing, inflatables and parascending – can be found in major resorts. Waterskiing and windsurfing novices will find benign conditions at the lake in Quinta do Lago.
- **Divers** can take the plunge at Sagres, Lagos, Burgau, Albufeira, Armação de Pera and Tavira, all of which have diving clubs.
- **Surfers** head to the west coast to take advantage of the big Atlantic rollers.
- **Scenic cruises** along the coast are organised from main resorts.
- For **boat hire** and **big-game fishing** try Portimão or the marinas at Vilamoura and Lagos.

Highbrow and Local Entertainment

- The resorts of the Algarve tend towards the lowbrow entertainment of any tourist region but there is usually a venue or two – often large hotels – staging **fado** (typically a woman singing melancholy ballads accompanied by a guitarist or two) or **folklore** (traditional singing and dancing) on a weekly basis, and perhaps even a quiet bar with jazz or a Brazilian guitarist.
- **Faro and Lagos** are the best towns to catch local culture. Both offer a number of venues and stage a monthly programme of dance, classical musical and jazz concerts.
- **Portimão** and the churches of **Silves and Tavira** regularly echo to the strains of classical music. Pick up details of all these at the local tourist office.

What's On
The best entertainment listings are given in the front of the excellent free monthly paper *Welcome to the Algarve*. See also the monthly *Algarve Guide* magazine. Both can be picked up from tourist offices. Another option is the listings section of the glossy monthly *Essential Algarve* magazine.

Casinos
You can gamble your money away at Vilamoura, Praia da Rocha and Monte Gordo (passport or ID required). A nightly floorshow is also staged, occasionally featuring top-quality Portuguese and Brazilian acts.

Major Cultural Festivals
Fairs and festivals are held throughout the year. Towns and villages celebrate the local patron saint's day with parades, fireworks, song and dance. Some festivals are strictly religious, others are geared primarily to tourists. For information of local events ask at the nearest tourist office or look for details in local newspapers. The following are some of the main events:

February–March: Carnival celebrations begin four Saturdays before Shrove Tuesday and culminate in three days of street merriment. However, it's subdued compared to celebrations in Spain. The largest and liveliest carnival is Loulé's, with its procession of colourful floats, marching bands and dancers.
March–April: Religious processions celebrating Easter are held in Faro.
May: International film festival, various venues. Festa da Espiga, the Corn Festival, is celebrated in Salir, with a procession of floats, followed by fireworks and folk dancing.
May–June: International Music Festival. This is the highlight of the Algarve calendar: two months of classical musical events and ballet, including international stars; Jazz Festival, Portimão.
July: Motoclube Faro Festival: the biggest single event in the Algarve. This is no place for the faint-hearted as some 60,000 bikers converge near Faro airport for the biggest motorcycle rally in Europe. The festival consists of three days of bike shows and rock concerts. On the Sunday morning at 11 am a parade takes place through Faro.
July–August: International Jazz Festival at Loulé.
October: Algarve Choir Festival Performances held throughout the region.

Food Festivals
Although few visitors come to the Algarve for its cuisine, the locals take the business of food festivals very seriously. Sample sausages at Querença in January, feast on fish and seafood at Portimão in April to May; mix *mel* (honey) and *medronho* (Algarve moonshine) in Monchique in May; savour shellfish and sardines by the seashore in Olhão in August and enjoy sweet potatoes and shellfish at Aljezur in late October. If you come in mid-June you can eat at the Portuguese Gastronomy Week at Lagoa, then drive the short distance to Silves to wash it all down at the annual Beer Festival.

Bullfighting
"The bull is not killed", repeats the tannoy as vans circulate the streets of Lagos and Albufeira entreating tourists to attend the spectacle. Well, not in the ring perhaps, but later, out of sight, most are dispatched. Portuguese bullfighting differs primarily from the Spanish version in that the bull is not killed in the ring, its horns are cut and padded and the principal bullfighter is on horseback. This *cavaleiro* is a fine sight attired in his 18th-century garb but once his colourful *bandarilhas* start hammering into the bull many overseas visitors start to wonder if they have made the right decision.

Faro and the East

Getting Your Bearings 42 – 43
In Four Days 44 – 45
Don't Miss 46 – 55
At Your Leisure 56 – 60
Where to... 61 – 66

Getting Your Bearings

The eastern Algarve – the Sotavento (leeward) coast – is the lesser-known half of the region with a very different topography and character to the central and central-western Algarve. Tourist developments are scarce, the pace of life is slower and the beaches are long and flat. Serving the beaches, though separated physically and spiritually from them, are three small towns that accommodate visitors but still cling to their own way of life. These are Faro, Olhão and Tavira.

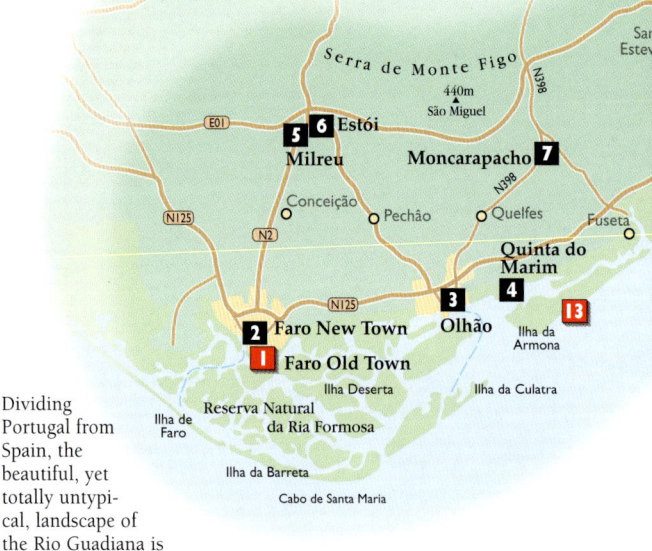

Dividing Portugal from Spain, the beautiful, yet totally untypical, landscape of the Rio Guadiana is one of the Algarve's best-kept secrets.

Faro, the capital, is the most interesting of the eastern towns with enough sightseeing, restaurants, bars and nightlife to keep curious travellers amused for a couple of days and nights. The fishing port of Olhão with its offshore beaches has an earthier atmosphere, with a bustling picturesque market, but little else to recommend to visitors. Near by, however, the Quinta do Marim reserve makes for an excellent half-day out. Tavira, frequently described as the most handsome town in

Previous page: Fishing boats at rest, Olhão
Right: entertaining the kids

Getting Your Bearings

★ Don't Miss
- **1** Faro Old Town ➤ 46–8
- **8** Tavira ➤ 49–51
- **12** Rio Guadiana ➤ 52–4
- **13** Beaches ➤ 55

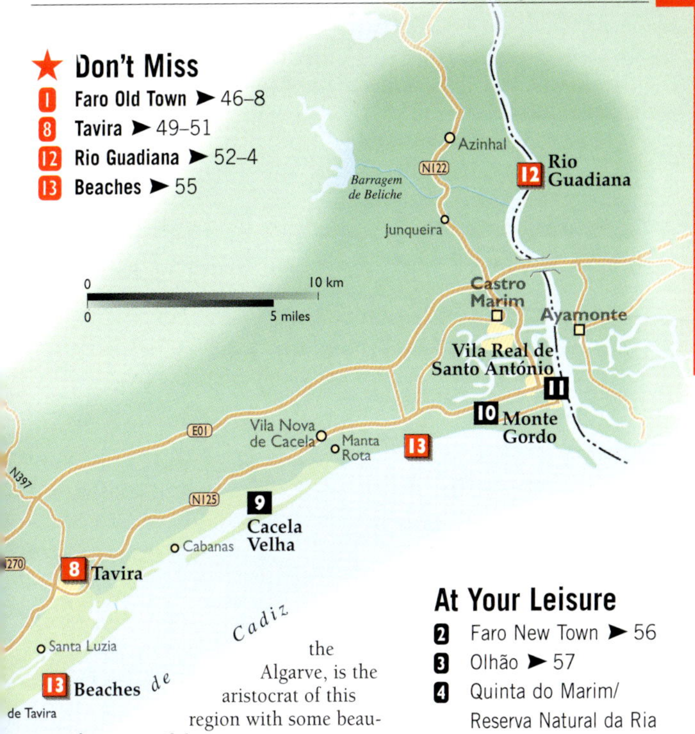

At Your Leisure
- **2** Faro New Town ➤ 56
- **3** Olhão ➤ 57
- **4** Quinta do Marim/Reserva Natural da Ria Formosa ➤ 57
- **5** Milreu ➤ 58
- **6** Estói ➤ 58
- **7** Moncarapacho ➤ 59
- **9** Cacela Velha ➤ 60
- **10** Monte Gordo ➤ 60
- **11** Vila Real de Santo António ➤ 60

the Algarve, is the aristocrat of this region with some beautiful domestic and church architecture, peaceful riverside gardens, good accommodation and several appealing restaurants. There are the beginnings of a nightlife scene here as well.

River traffic at the port of Tavira

From elegant architecture to an idyllic riverscape and rolling hills, this tour of the eastern half of the region proves that there is much more to the Algarve than busy resorts, cove beaches and golf courses.

Faro and the East in Four Days

Day One

Morning
Enter **Faro Old Town** (➤ 46–8) through the Arco da Vila, pausing to stop at the adjacent tourist office and pick up a map. The cathedral, the Museu Arqueológico and the Igreja de São Francisco are the main sights, but the real attraction of this cobbled quarter is its quiet, historic atmosphere.

Afternoon
Return through the arch and head up the pedestrianised Rua de Santo António, the main street. At the top of the street is the small **Museu Regional** (➤ 56). Walk up Rua Vasco da Gama into the Praça Ferreira de Almeida, then take the Rua José Estevão to the Largo de São Pedro and adjacent Largo Carmo where you will find the **Igreja do Carmo** (➤ 56) and its macabre bone chapel (➤ 28). Walk back straight through the Praça Ferreira de Almeida to the *doca*, Faro's small inner harbour, to watch the sunset.

Day Two

Morning
Take the N125 eastwards to **Olhão** (➤ 57) and have a coffee by the quayside while enjoying the local cornucopia (net workers pictured right). Then walk straight across the road and into the Rua do Comércio, which leads to the **parish church** (➤ 57). Have a fish lunch at the Tamboril or the Pérola de República, both on the seafront.

Afternoon
Continue east on the N125 to the **Reserva Natural da Ria Formosa** (➤ 57) visitor centre at Quinta do Marim and spend the afternoon strolling around the well-marked trail, taking in the fascinating natural history of the reserve. Spend the night at Tavira, a 20-minute drive east on the N125.

Day Three

Morning
Park as close as you can to the centre of **Tavira** (➤ 49–51; the banks of the River Gilão are pictured left), pick up a map from the tourist office and take the suggested walking tour of the town (➤ 164–5).

Afternoon
Drive the short distance to Quatro Águas, park, lunch at the Quatro Águas restaurant (➤ 55) or book a meal for the evening. Catch the ferry to the **Ilha de Tavira** (➤ 55) for an afternoon on the beach.

Day Four

Get up early and take the recommended driving tour (➤ 166–8) from Tavira to Castro Marim along the beautiful **Rio Guadiana** (➤ 52–4), and inland to the **Parque Mineiro Cova dos Mouros** (➤ 168, pictured right). Although a long day, it's worthwhile. You will have earned your dinner in Tavira by the time you return! Go African at Kudissanga (➤ 51).

Faro Old Town

Faro, particularly its Old Town (*Cidade Velha*), is one of the Algarve's most underrated attractions and most visitors bypass it completely, shuttling off left and right from the airport to beaches and golf courses. A good job too, some say, or it might not retain its workaday Portuguese atmosphere and its unhurried, historic charm.

The entrance to the Old Town is through the **Arco da Vila** (Town Gate), an elegant landmark built in the 18th century and home to a pair of nesting storks. Just inside the arch notice the horseshoe gate, a unique survival from the Moorish walls. Walk up the street into the **Largo da Sé** (Cathedral Square), a large, handsome, cobbled square lined with orange trees. If you're lucky, a busker with a Spanish guitar might be playing. Opposite the cathedral is the **old town hall** (*câmara municipal*) and the long range of buildings near to it is the 400-year-old **Paço Episcopal** (Bishop's Palace; no admittance).

The graceful gateway of the Arco da Vila has been a nesting place for storks for many years

Faro Old Town

The Cathedral

The cathedral was originally built in the late 13th and early 14th centuries though only the main doorway, the lower tower and two chapels in the transept remain from this period. The rest was rebuilt after the Earl of Essex (English Queen Elizabeth I's favourite courtier) sacked the town in 1596, and then again after the Great Earthquake of 1755 (➤ 78).

Entry to the cathedral is to the side of the main doorway, where there is a ticket kiosk. After you have paid, but just before you enter the cathedral proper, notice the scant remains of a *capela dos ossos* (bone chapel; ➤ 29) on your right.

The chapels in the cathedral are remarkable for their carvings, which are among the finest in the Algarve. On the south wall the glowing **Chapel of Nossa Senhora dos Prazeres** (Our Lady of Pleasures) is a baroque gem. The great church **organ**, decorated in red and gilt Chinese style in 1751, is no less flamboyant.

Left: The simple solid exterior of Faro Cathedral hides a wealth of interior detail such as this cherubic marble flourish (top left)

Below: The Largo da Sé is a popular convening point

Convento de Nossa Senhora da Assunção

After the gaudy excess of the cathedral, the airy cloisters of the Convent of Our Lady of the Ascension come as a relief. The convent was built in the 16th century but abandoned in the 19th century and used as a cork factory. Now it is home to the **Museu Arqueológico** and provides a beautiful setting for the small collection of exhibits. Of particular note is the **"Ocean mosaic"**, showing part of King Neptune's face. It dates from the 3rd century and was found a few hundred metres from here. From the Roman villa of Milreu (➤ 58) come **two busts**, of Emperor Hadrian and of Aggripina, wife of Claudius.

TAKING A BREAK

Take a coffee break at the **Taverna do Sé** (just off Praça Dom Afonso III) and lunch on the terrace of the **Mesa dos Mouros** (Largo da Sé, tel: 289 878 873), which you'll find next to the entrance of the cathedral.

Sé
🗺 180 B2 ✉ Largo da Sé 🕙 Mon–Fri 10–noon; 2–5 💰 Inexpensive

Museu Arqueológico
🗺 180 C1 ✉ Praça Dom Afonso III ☎ 289 824 085 🕙 Mon–Fri 9–noon; 2–5

Galeria do Trem
🗺 180 C1 ✉ Rua do Trem ☎ 289 804197

Galeria do Arco
🗺 180 C1 ✉ Rua do Arco ☎ 289 801037

For Kids
In the cloister of the **Convento de Nossa Senhora da Assunção** are wooden cut-out figures for visitors to put their heads through and have their pictures taken. They represent the city liberator, King Afonso III (the mighty statue in front of the convent would please him more), a Moorish woman and a Roman.
• Note too the various horrible **grotesques** and **gargoyles** that dot the inside of the cloister.

Also worth seeing
Temporary exhibits of modern art in the **Galeria do Trem** and the **Galeria do Arco** (signposted).
• The **workshop** (unmarked) to the right of the Mesa dos Mouros restaurant, where religious figures and large-scale antiques are restored.
• **Galeria Vila Adentro** antiques shop, next to the Taverna do Sé.

Turn a corner in the Old Town and find traditional Portugal still thriving

FARO OLD TOWN: INSIDE INFO

Top tips When you buy your **cathedral ticket** ask if one of the staff can give you a tour. It's free, though a tip won't go amiss.
• Your ticket includes access to the **church tower**. Take advantage of this because there are only 68 steps and the views across the rooftops and out across the lagoon to the airport are wonderful.
• Some of the chapels in the cathedral have their own **lights**, which you can turn on if you can't see inside clearly.
• **Parking in Faro** can be very difficult, but there is usually space right beside the cathedral in the Largo de São Francisco.

Hidden gem The **Igreja de São Francisco** is actually just outside the Old Town walls, across the Largo de São Francisco, even though it is signposted from within. Push the bell to gain access (late afternoon is the best time). Despite undergoing major restoration, this atmospheric 17th-century church is still a riot of colour thanks to its multicoloured tiles depicting scenes from the life of St Francis.

Tavira

Look in any Algarve guidebook and you'll find Tavira referred to as the most "attractive", "elegant", "handsome", "noble", "aristocratic" town in the region, and indeed it is all of these. Its heyday was between the 16th and 18th centuries when it accrued great wealth, largely thanks to its enormous tuna catches, and became the most populous city in the Algarve as well as a port of great strategic importance.

The pace of life in Tavira is still laid back

Fortunately, the 20th century wreaked little architectural havoc on Tavira and it is probably one of the few Algarve towns that the early 19th-century traveller Robert Southey would still recognise. "Clean and opulent" is how he described it some 200 years ago, and though the days of opulence have passed, it is still very clean, with many of its handsome 18th- and 19th-century buildings remarkably well preserved. Nowadays, host to a steady stream of visitors, Tavira is no longer "undiscovered Algarve", but neither has it embraced mass-market tourism. In fact it is almost conspicuous for what it lacks: there are no international food joints, pubs, kiss-me-quick souvenir shops, large hotels and apartments, or noisy disco bars. If you want these facilities go to the nearby resort of Cabanas.

City Sights

The best place to start a walking tour of the town (▶ 164–5) is the tourist office, conveniently sited close to the castle and two of Tavira's finest churches. The town has a remarkable number of churches (estimates vary from 26 to well over 30) though at any one time you will find only a handful open (see box opposite for opening times).

As you climb the steps to the tourist office you'll see the fine portal of the **Igreja da Misericórdia** (Church of Mercy) right in front of you. The church is regarded by some critics as the finest 16th-century building in the Algarve, and if you are lucky enough to get inside you can enjoy its splendid blue-and-white *azulejos* and finely carved altar.

Just around the corner is the lovely **Igreja de Santa Maria do Castelo**. This church's main claim to fame is the tombs to either side of the altar. On the right-hand side, seven crosses represent the resting place of the seven Christian knights who were ambushed and slain by Moors – then in control of the city – in 1239. This was the catalyst for the people of Tavira to rise up and reconquer their town. They were led by Dom Paio Peres Correa, whose

Above: The fine Igreja do Santa Maria do Castelo. Below: A plaque on Igreja de Santiago showing St James the Moor Slayer

Tavira

Tavira's Roman bridge still spans the Gilão River

tomb lies opposite that of the knights.

The **Castelo dos Mouros** (castle ruins), which lie in immaculately kept gardens, date from the reign of King Dinis (1261–1325). The best views of Tavira's distinctive hip-gabled (triangular sloping) 18th- and 19th-century rooftops and its church towers are to be had from its rampart walks. (Do beware of its unfenced, sudden drops.)

Another of the town's elegant structures is the **Ponte Romana** (Roman Bridge), but although this low, seven-arched river crossing has Roman foundations, what you see today dates mostly from the 17th century.

TAKING A BREAK

There is a clutch of cafés in the **Praça da República** by the bridge, of which the **Veneza** is the best. Fish is the speciality of Tavira; on the riverfront, try the long-standing **Imperial** (tel: 281 322234) or **O Canecão** (tel: 281 325260), which immodestly claims "the world's greatest *cataplana*", and certainly does a good range. Or go for something completely different on the other side of the river at the **Kudissanga** African restaurant (tel: 281 321670).

Igreja de Santa Maria do Castelo
✚ 186 A2
✉ Calçada de Paio Peres Correia
🕐 Mon–Sat 10–12.30, 2–6

Castelo dos Mouros
✚ 186 A2
✉ Calçada de Paio Peres Correia
🕐 Mon–Fri 8–5, Sun 9–5.30

Above right: One that didn't get away – an espada *at Tavira's fish market*

Church Opening Times

Locked churches with no posted opening times are a source of frustration to Tavira visitors. Ask at the tourist office which ones are currently open. One way of getting in for a quick look round is to visit just before or after Mass.
Times are as follows:
São Tiago, Sat 4.30 pm, Sun 6 pm
São Paulo, Sat 5.30 pm, Sun 9 am
Santa Luzia, Sun 9 pm
Santa Maria do Castelo, Sun 11 am.
Churches may be opened specially for walking tour groups for concerts and for exhibitions.

TAVIRA: INSIDE INFO

Top tips If you want to **stay in style** in the heart of Tavira keep your eyes peeled for the opening of its new *pousada* (▶ 35).
• Tavira is also building a **shopping and cultural centre** in the old fish market.

Rio Guadiana

The Rio Guadiana is a river that rises far from the Algarve, in the province of Albacete in southwest Spain, and flows for 780km to meet the Atlantic, where it divides the Portuguese town of Vila Real de Santo António and the Spanish town of Ayamonte. It is only navigable for the last 48km, up to Pomarão in the Alentejo region, and even then can only accommodate relatively small craft. For the last 40km it forms the border that divides Portugal from Spain.

The Fort of São Sebastião hasn't seen action for centuries

The Guadiana became the national divide in the 14th to 15th century after the Christian Reconquest of Iberia (➤ 30) and was guarded by castles such as those at Castro Marim, Alcoutim and, on the Spanish side, San Lúcar. By the late 20th century, however, it had become a peaceful backwater. In the early 1990s the first road bridge linking the Algarve to Andalucía was built and a few years later Spain and Portugal abolished all border formalities.

Castro Marim

The nearest settlement to the bridge is Castro Marim, but the new crossing has brought little change. Castro Marim's principal **castelo** (castle) was built in the 13th and 14th centuries, enclosing a 10th- to 12th-century Moorish castle that is still quite intact and houses a small **archaeological museum**. There's not much to see in the grounds or the museum but the views are excellent.

The **wetlands** below are protected as part of the Reserva Natural do Sapal de Castro Marim and attract a large number of birds. The saltpans within the reserve are centuries old and still worked today. On the hill opposite, the unrestored 17th-century **Fort of São Sebastião** (open at any time) offers panoramic views.

Little egret in the Castro Marim wetlands sanctuary

Alcoutim

Alcoutim enjoys an idyllic setting on one of the prettiest stretches of the river and is perfectly set off by the equally attractive Spanish village of San Lúcar directly across the water. A ferry plies between the two and small boats are for hire up and down the river. In summer Alcoutim has a definite bustle with boat owners and young travellers from the youth hostel (in the adjacent new part of town) hanging out at the riverfront cafés and messing about in small boats.

Spain is just across the river from Alcoutim

Faro and the East

The best view, taking in the castles of both villages and Alcoutim's orange-tiled rooftops, is from the former Ermida de Nossa Senhora da Conceição (Hermitage of our Lady of the Conception), nowadays the **Núcleo Museológico Arte-Sacra** (Museum of Sacred Art). You may be able to watch restoration work on statues and pictures here. On the hill beside the church is the shell of Alcoutim's **castelo**, built in the 14th century to defend the border. Today it houses tidy grassy terraces and a small new **archaeological museum**, mostly devoted to the ruins of the previous castles on this site. However, the main reason to come here is for the views.

TAKING A BREAK

The terrace of the **Café O Soeiro** (Rua do Municípo, tel: 281 546241) on the waterfront at Alcoutim is the perfect place to enjoy the river view.

From Portugal to Spain, across the Guadiana to the fort of Sanlucar

Castro Marim
✠ 186 C3
Castelo
☎ 281 510746
🕒 Daily 10–6, summer; 10–5, winter. Museum closes 1–3
💶 Castle free, museum inexpensive

Alcoutim
✠ 186 C5
Núcleo Museológico Arte-Sacra
🕒 Tue–Sat 9–12:30, 2–5:30
💶 Inexpensive

Castelo
☎ 281 546104
🕒 Castle: daily 9–5:30; archaeological museum: Tue–Sat 9–12:30, 2–5:30
💶 Castle free, museum inexpensive

RIO GUADIANA: INSIDE INFO

Top tips If you are popping over to **Spain** remember that it is an hour ahead of Portugal and that the Spanish still observe the siesta.
• The **stretch of the river between Castro Marim and Alcoutim** is particularly attractive, and one of the most peaceful and scenic drives in the Algarve follows its course (➤ 166–8).
• If you don't want to drive yourself, take a **boat trip** along the river, possibly combined with a **jeep safari** (➤ 66).

Hidden gem In early September **three days of medieval-themed fun**, including a banquet, are staged at Castro Marim castle.

Beaches

The beaches of the Algarve's Sotavento coast are long and low, with few, if any, natural backing features. Most of this coast falls within the protected Reserva Natural da Ria

Formosa boundaries, but there are concessions and in summer people throng the more popular stretches. But just take the time to walk a little further to find a quiet spot and the atmosphere is suddenly far from the crowded coves of the central-western part of the Algarve.

Ilha Deserta 185 D1
These sandbars are temptingly visible from the roof of Faro cathedral. There's a bar-restaurant and watersports here, however, including jetskis, so peace and quiet is not guaranteed. Ferry from Faro, just outside the Old Town.

Ilha da Armona 185 E1
Here you'll find warm shallow waters and long smooth sands, though you may have to walk a little way to escape the crowds. Ferry from República.

Ilha de Tavira 186 A1
This is the busiest of the barrier island beaches with camping and numerous restaurants and bars. The beach nearest to the Tavira ferry is the more attractive but can get crowded. Ferry from Quatro Águas, Tavira, or footbridge from Santa Luzia.

Manta Rota/Cacela Velha 186 B2/C2
This monster of a beach goes all the way to the Spanish border, via crowded, commercialised Monte Gordo. Manta Rota is quiet, with low dunes and trees; Cacela Velha is positively sleepy.

TAKING A BREAK
There are, of course, beach bars and restaurants in this area, but most are undistinguished so consider bringing a packed lunch. A notable exception is the acclaimed fish restaurant **Quatro Águas** (tel: 281 325329) on the jetty of the same name that gives access to the Ilha de Tavira.

Footsteps in the sand (above and right) at Ilha de Tavira

At Your Leisure

Modern Faro has a bustling harbour

❷ Faro New Town

Despite its name, Faro New Town dates mostly from the late 19th century and its nucleus, immediately west of the walled Old Town (➤ 46–8), is a likeable jumble of narrow residential streets and a pedestrianised shopping area centred around the Rua do Santo António. Here there are lots of thoroughly Portuguese bars, cafés and restaurants serving both visitors and locals. The most compulsive sightseeing attraction is the ghoulish **Capela dos Ossos** (Chapel of the Bones) in the **Igreja do Carmo** (➤ 28). But do also try to take in the town's two small museums. The old-fashioned **Museu Regional**, dealing with Algarvian ethnography, has the more general appeal, with evocative black-and-white photographs and curious exhibits such as the wooden water-carrier's cart that still trundled around the area until the early 1970s. On the waterside the **Museu da Marítimo** (Maritime Museum) largely comprises model boats.

On the other side of the dock a lively Faro newcomer is **Ciência Viva** (Living Science), which takes a hands-on look at how things work, with special emphasis on the solar system. It can be fun and informative for older kids and the staff are helpful, but you have to have a good working knowledge of Portuguese to make it worthwhile.

Capela dos Ossos
✚ 180 C5 ✉ Igreja do Carmo, Largo do Carmo 🕐 Mon–Fri 10–1, 3–5, Sat 10–1 💰 Inexpensive

Museu Regional
✚ 181 E3 ✉ Praça da Liberdade
☎ 289 827610 🕐 Mon–Fri 9.30–12.30, 2.30–5.30 💰 Inexpensive

Museu da Marítimo
✚ 180 A3 ✉ Doca de Faro ☎ 289 803601 🕐 Mon–Fri 9.15–noon, 2–4.30 💰 Inexpensive

Ciência Viva
✚ 180 B2 ✉ Doca de Faro ☎ 289 890920; www.ualg.pt/ccviva 🕐 Tue–Fri 10–5, Sat, Sun and public holidays 3–7, mid-Sep–Jun; Tue–Sun 4–11, Jul–mid-Sep 💰 Moderate (Wed inexpensive)

Good Places to Eat with the Locals in Faro
- **Adega Nortenha**, just off Praça Ferreira de Almeida
- **Adega Nova**, Rua Francisco Barreto
- **Adega Rocha**, Rua da Misericórdia

One to miss: Café Aliança (➤ 63), on the waterfront. Do take a peek in at this shambling, historic building, one of Portugal's oldest cafés, but eat elsewhere as the service is slow.

At Your Leisure

3 Olhão

Olhão is a no-nonsense working port, (rare in the Algarve these days) and the biggest in the region after Portimão. It is used to visitors, either exploring the fish market – the best in the Algarve (➤ 65) – or catching boats to the beaches of the Reserva Natural da Ria Formosa (➤ below). It even has a handful of places to stay and a few reasonable restaurants, but this is not a tourist town.

In More Depth
- If you want to spend more time in the Ria Formosa park, accommodation is available at Quinta do Marim.
- Take a trip on the lagoon in the reserve's restored tuna-fishing boat.

Dried octopus (and friends) at the fish market Olhão

If you like Faro you will like Olhão – it has a similar character but on a smaller scale. Wend your way from the seafront and fish market via the Rua do Comércio to the Igreja de Nossa Senhora do Rosario (Church of Our Lady of the Rosary). The tower gives fine views, including some of the town's famous açoteias (➤ 21). At the back of the church note the curious Capela dos Aflitos (Chapel of the Afflicted) with its weird collection of ex-voto offerings, including various limbs and body parts.

🕀 185 E1
Igreja de Nossa Senhora do Rosário
✉ Praça da Restauração
🕐 9.30–noon, 3–6 Tue–Sun (knock on door for key if closed) 💶 Inexpensive

4 Quinta do Marim/Reserva Natural da Ria Formosa

The Ria Formosa Natural Park stretches from Praia do Garrão/Praia d'Anção, near Quinta do Lago, to Praia da Manta Rota, just west of Monte Gordo. Ria Formosa means "beautiful river", though in fact it is a huge lagoon comprising salt marshes, five narrow sandy islands and a myriad of channels. It is the perfect home for a multitude of birds and marine life as well as boasting some popular beaches (➤ 55). By far the best introduction to the park is the informative two-hour self-guided walking tour (➤ 169–70) from Quinta do Marim, which is located 1km east of Olhão.

Quinta do Marim visitor centre
🕀 185 E1
✉ Quinta do Marim, N125
☎ 289 704134
🕐 Daily 9–12.30, 2–5

5 Milreu

A close neighbour of the Palacio d'Estói (below) are the Roman ruins of Milreu. Highlights are some fine dolphin mosaics and a part of a wall of a 4th-century early Christian sanctuary. It is uncertain whether the main building was a villa or public spa, but excavations date the ruins mostly from the 3rd century and the best finds are now in the archaeological museums of Lagos and Faro. The guide to the ruins (in English), on sale at the kiosk, is essential.

✚ 185 D2 ✉ Estói ☎ 289 997823
🕑 Tue–Sun 9.30–12.30, 2–6, May–Sep; 9.30–12.30, 2–5, Oct–Apr
💰 Inexpensive

Intricate dolphin mosaics at Milreu's pools

6 Estói

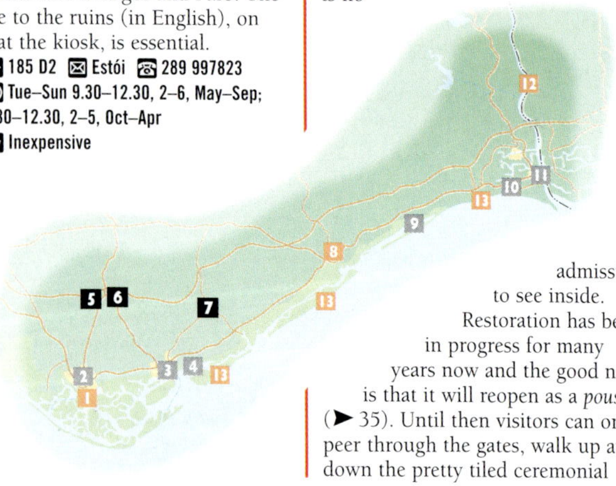

Construction of the Palacio d'Estói began in 1840 for the Conde de Cavalhal. It is a romantic pink cocktail of architectural styles (art nouveau, baroque and rococo), and is said to have the finest plaster ceilings in the Algarve – but alas, there is no admission to see inside. Restoration has been in progress for many years now and the good news is that it will reopen as a *pousada* (➤ 35). Until then visitors can only peer through the gates, walk up and down the pretty tiled ceremonial

staircases and wander in a section of its gardens. It's definitely worth the trip, however, as the views of the house are excellent and it is in a lovely setting with classical statuary, water features and formal gardens. Above all, visitors enjoy its secret, magical atmosphere. To get there park in the square in front of the church and follow the sign to the left.

🚩 185 D2 ✉ Estói 🕙 Gardens open Tue–Sat 9.30–12.30, 2–5.30 🎫 Free

❼ Moncarapacho

This pretty little hill village lies just off the N125 between Olhão and Tavira. Spend a pleasant hour or two enjoying its low-key attractions. First, find the parish church, next to the leafy main square. This is remarkable for its Renaissance façade that shows modern-looking figures scourging Christ and also for its colourful Gothic interior with columns painted

> **For Kids**
> • **Capela dos Ossos**, Faro (➤ 56).
> • Any of the **Ria Formosa barrier island beaches** (➤ 55).
> • **Fish market** at Olhão (➤ 65).
> • **Quinta do Marim visitor centre** (particularly the tidemill and Portuguese water dogs, ➤ 169–70).

The fairytale pink palace of Estói

in fading red-and-blue acanthus plant designs. As you leave the church, turn left then go immediately right to the handsome 17th-century chapel in front of you. Adjacent is the parish museu, a museum of local history and archaeology, which was established by the parish priest. The eclectic collection includes an olive press, slave shackles, tombstones, cannon balls and a charming 42-piece 18th-century Neapolitan crib scene, retrieved from a church in Faro. If the chapel is closed ask at the museum to see its *azulejo*-covered interior.

🚩 185 E2
Museu
☎ No telephone ✉ Moncarapacho
🕙 Mon, Wed, Fri 11–3

Water carrier's cart in the Museu Regional

9 Cacela Velha

Cacela Velha is no longer undiscovered Algarve, but if you do want to get away from it all on this stretch of coast, this tiny hamlet is certainly the place to come.

Uniquely on this stretch of coastline, Cacela Velha sits high on a bluff, spectacularly perched above the beach near the westernmost point of the Reserva Natural da Ria Formosa (➤ 57). It comprises a handful of houses, a handsome church, a restaurant bar, a couple of cafés and a squat 18th-century fort that takes up a fair proportion of the village "square". Unfortunately the fort has been commandeered by the government and is closed to the public. Steps lead down to the broad sandy beach which stretches all the way east to Monte Gordo. You can either hire a boat to take you the short distance to the barrier island, or walk across at low tide.

✚ 186 B2

10 Monte Gordo

This is the only major resort on the whole east coast, its thrusting high-rise structures visible from many kilometres away. A huge featureless beach with warm waters, a casino, numerous eating places of all descriptions and low prices are its main attractions to the summer crowds.

✚ 186 C2

11 Vila Real de Santo António

The death of this once thriving port at the mouth of the Rio Guadiana has been exaggerated. To be sure, the opening of the road bridge to Spain and consequential loss of ferry traffic has been a bitter blow, but to the casual visitor the town is thriving. Shops carry a few tourist fripperies and the stock-in-trade appears to be towels, soft furnishings and clothes, cheaply priced for locals and Spanish day-trippers.

The distinctive main square resembles a sundial, divided into black and white segments, with an obelisk at the centre and orange trees and handsome late 18t-century buildings and cafés around the edges. Just off the square is the beautifully renovated market hall where you will find the tourist office and the single-room Manuel Cabanas Museum featuring the woodcut works of the talented local artist Manuel Cabanas. The hall also stages temporary exhibitions.

✚ 186 C2
Museu Manuel Cabanas
☎ No telephone ⓘ Daily 10–5

Relaxing in the quiet, elegant main square of Vila Real, on the Spanish border

Where to... Stay

Prices
Expect to pay per double room per night:
£ under €50   ££ €50–125   £££ over €125

Convento de Santo António ££
Converted from a convent, this is a family-run guesthouse of exceptional charm and character. It's only 500m from Tavira centre, but behind the portal are tropical gardens, peaceful cloisters and whitewashed walls. The ambience of a convent has been preserved; there are rosaries above the beds and candles light the corridors. Large, well-equipped apartments open onto a courtyard; or there are small, simple rooms converted from monks' cells. Breakfasts of brioche, smoked hams and cheese are served outside or, off-season, in the delightful salon, full of antiques. Book in advance. The minimum stay is two to four nights depending on the season.

✚ 186 A2 ✉ Atalaia 56, 8800 Tavira ☎ 281 325632; fax: 281 325632

Estalagem do Guadiana £££
Alcoutim's only hotel was built in the 1990s to cater for the increasing number of visitors to the village. A whitewashed two-storey building with 31 rooms, the hotel is located in the newer part of Alcoutim, overlooking the river. Bedrooms are simply furnished with tiled floors, floral fabrics and dark-wood furniture. In the restaurant, the emphasis is on fresh local ingredients, particularly fish from the River Guadiana. Other amenities include a pool, a terrace and two tennis courts.

✚ 186 C5 ✉ Alcoutim 8970 ☎ 281 540120; fax: 281 546647

Eva £££
Although geared primarily for business travellers, this is a comfortable base for a night or two in Faro. It has a prime location with easy access to the airport and fine views over the harbour and Ria Formosa. Décor is modern and unexciting, but the rooms are well equipped, with air conditioning, satellite TV, mini-bar and safe. The roof-top pool and spacious fifth-floor restaurant make the most of the views, while the ground-floor café/bar has a pleasant outdoor terrace and serves freshly made cakes and pastries.

✚ 180 B3 ✉ Avenida da República 1, 8000–078 Faro ☎ 289 803354; fax: 289 802304

Guadiana ££
Unlike most hotels in the Algarve, this one has been here since the early 20th century. Over the years it has been a meeting place of politicians and statesmen, Franco and Salazar among them. Not only does it occupy a key location, overlooking the River Guadiana, but it is a fine *belle-époque* building with traditional rooms and touches of grandeur. There is no restaurant, but the hotel is next door to the excellent Caves do Guadiana (➤ 63).

✚ 186 C2 ✉ Avenida da República, 94–96, 8900–206 Vila Real de Santo António ☎ 281 511482; fax: 281 511478

Hotel La Réserve £££
If price is no obstacle, you can't do better than La Réserve. The haunt of celebrities, it nonetheless maintains a friendly and unintimidating atmosphere. There are 20 apartments, each facing south and overlooking the subtropical gardens and, 10km away, Faro and the coast. The whitewashed apartments are luxuriously appointed. The excellent breakfast under the bougainvillea by the

Faro and the East

lovely pool is a wonderful way to start the day and the restaurant here is first class.

⊞ 185 D2 ☒ Santa Bárbara de Nexe, 8000 Faro ☎ 289 999474; fax: 289 999402

Monte do Casal £££

"The most picturesque hotel in the Algarve" is how the English-run Monte do Casal describes itself and it's hard to argue. Secluded in the hills north of Faro, with views over the palms and pool to the sea, this 18th-century house is set amid a riot of flowering shrubs and citrus trees. There are 13 comfortable rooms (five are suites), with access to the heated pool and garden. Delicious breakfasts of croissants and freshly baked rolls arrive on private terraces each morning while the restaurant (▶ 63) serves some of the best cuisine in the region.

⊞ 185 D2 ☒ Cerro do Lobo, Estói, 8000 Faro ☎ 289 991503; fax: 289 991341; e-mail: montecasal@mail.telepac.pt; www.montedocasal.pt

O Pequeno Castelo £

Tucked away off dirt tracks in the hills above the little village of Santo Estêvão, O Pequeno Castelo is a perfect getaway within easy reach of Tavira. The house is modern and rooms are spacious with tasteful antiques, ethnic furnishings and traditional decor. (Note however that you may have to share the bathroom.) The breakfast, featuring fresh fruit, warm bread and pastries, is superb and you can watch the sea from the terrace as you eat it. A small pool allays the summer heat.

⊞ 185 F2 ☒ Poço das Bruxas, Apartado 107, 8800 Tavira ☎ 281 961692; fax: 281 961692

Pousada de São Brás de Alportel ££

State-run pousadas are located in sites of outstanding natural beauty and this one is no exception. Perched serenely above the small town of São Brás between the sea and the mountains, the hotel enjoys stunning views across the hills to the coast. Built in 1944, it has expanded from its original five rooms to 33. Despite this development, the style remains distinctly Portuguese and the modernised bedrooms retain their regional furnishings. Attractive features include a panoramic pool and terrace area (where meals are served in summer) and a rustic restaurant serving excellent Portuguese cuisine.

⊞ 185 D2 ☒ São Brás de Alportel, 8150 Faro ☎ 289 842305; fax: 289 841726; www.pousadas.pt

Quinta da Lua £

If you are looking for quiet, reasonably priced accommodation near Tavira, the Quinta da Lua fits the bill nicely. It is a friendly, Dutch-Portuguese-run guesthouse, set attractively and peacefully among orange trees and vineyards, and boasting its own large pool. There are just nine rooms, each furnished in a different style. Two are suites with large bathrooms attached. There is no official restaurant but on the frequent occasions the owners are cooking a meal for themselves, they'll probably cook you one too.

⊞ 185 F2 ☒ Bernardinheiro, 8800–513 Tavira ☎ 281 961070; fax: 281 961070

Quinta do Caracol ££

A blue-and-white portal and a garden of lemon, palm and pomegranate trees herald the charming Quinta do Caracol. Converted from an ancient farmhouse and stables, it comprises seven apartments separated by bougainvillea-strewn terraces. Each one is named after a flower and is attractively furnished in regional style with antiques, old fireplaces and beams. Guests have the use of a large barbecue in the garden, a swimming pool with floodlighting, a tennis court and table tennis. There is no official restaurant but with a day or two's notice you can have a meal prepared.

⊞ 186 A2 ☒ Bairro de São Pedro, 8800–405 Tavira ☎ 281 322475; fax: 281 323175

Where to...
Eat and Drink

Prices
Expect to pay per person for a meal, excluding drinks and service
£ under €15   ££ €15–23   £££ over €23

Bica £
Tucked down a narrow street on the north side of the River Gilão, the Bica is a favourite with the locals for inexpensive, wholesome meals. Don't dress up – it's a basic place with paper tablecloths and a TV in the corner. The house speciality, served daily, is *bife de atum cebolada* (fillet of tuna fish with onion sauce). Other favourites here are sole with orange sauce, crayfish rice, squid kebabs with prawns or *porco à Alentejana* (pork with clams).

🏠 186 A2 ☒ Rua Almirante Cândido dos Reis, 24–28, Tavira ☎ 281 323843 ⏰ Daily lunch and dinner

Café Aliança £
Notable for being a historic café, an ex-haunt of the literati, it has an interesting if gloomy interior with tiled scenes and a timbered ceiling. Tourists tend to prefer the spacious terrace on the Rua Francisco Gomes, which is a good spot to watch the world go by. Breakfast is available and foreign newspapers can be bought inside the café. Run-of-the-mill snacks, such as burgers, salads and omelettes, are offered all day but beware of slow service.

🏠 180 C3 ☒ Praça Francisco Gomes 6–11, Faro ☎ 289 901621 ⏰ Daily 8 am–midnight

Camané £££
The teeming Praia de Faro may not be the most desirable beach in the Algarve, but it is certainly worth a detour for what is arguably the best restaurant in Faro. It is also one of the most expensive, so save it for a special occasion – maybe before your flight back home as it's only 3km from Faro airport. The fresh fish and seafood are outstanding, as are the risottos. Try monkfish with clam rice, mixed fried fish or the lobster or crayfish rice.

🏠 185 D1 ☒ Avenida Nascente, Praia de Faro ☎ 289 817539 ⏰ Tue–Sun lunch and dinner

Caves do Guadiana ££
On the borders of the river dividing Portugal and Spain (▶ 52–4), this restaurant serves good Portuguese cuisine and excellent wines. Sit outside overlooking the river or inside where locals gather for the *prato do dia* (dish of the day) or one of the popular cod specialities: *bacalhau dourado* (filleted cod with potatoes and eggs) or *bacalhau a Africana* (spicy cod grilled with peppers). A favourite meat dish is *caldeirada de cabrito* or kid stew.

🏠 186 C2 ☒ Avenida da República, 90, Vila Real de Santo António (next to the Hotel Guadiana) ☎ 281 544498 ⏰ Fri–Wed lunch and dinner

Centenário £
Of the many restaurants in central Faro, this is one of the friendliest and best value. You can either eat outside under the trees on the square or in the vaulted interior that buzzes at lunchtime with local workers. The no-frills menu features fish soups, simply grilled meat or fish, such as tuna and swordfish steak, regional dishes and *cataplanas*.

🏠 180 C3 ☒ Largo Terreiro do Bispo 4, Faro ☎ 289 823343 ⏰ Daily lunch and dinner

Monte do Casal £££
Forming part of the Estalagem Monte do Casal (▶ 62), the restaurant has the benefit of a beautiful

hill setting. The service is professional and the gourmet dishes elegantly prepared. *Table d'hôte* and *a la carte* menus feature house specialities such as the home-smoked potted quail mousse and the seafood Monte do Casal – tiger prawns, langoustines and monkfish set on a leek and courgette *rosti* with a champagne sauce. In summer guests can dine on the terrace under the palms; in cooler months open log fires and candlelit tables provide diners with a warm welcome.

✚ 185 D2 ⊠ Cerro do Lobo, Estoi, Faro ☎ 289 991503; fax: 289 991341 ◷ Daily lunch and dinner

O Ideal £

Cabanas is an unremarkable fishing village about 5km east of Tavira. Down a side street, O Ideal is a basic, inconspicuous café that wouldn't ordinarily merit a second glance. Yet, such is its reputation for top-quality fish at rockbottom prices, Portuguese flock from afar to eat here. Dishes likely to feature on the menu are seafood starters, grilled fish such as sea bream, scabbard fish or tuna and sole with almonds, and *cataplanas*.

✚ 186 A2 ⊠ Rua Infante D Henrique, Cabanas, Tavira ☎ 289 370232 ◷ Thu–Tue lunch and dinner

O Pátio ££

This is a cheerful, busy restaurant where clients come as much for the ambience as the food. Eat out on the rooftop terrace or inside, which is hung with flags, fishing nets, ceramics and hats. The menu features no fewer than nine different *cataplanas*, along with shellfish rice, monkfish rice, couscous and duck with orange sauce. Lobster is a speciality. With 24 hours notice you can also order fondue or stuffed squid.

✚ 186 A2 ⊠ Rua António Cabreira, 30, Tavira ☎ 281 323008 ◷ Daily lunch and dinner

Paris £

An Egyptian chef recreating Portuguese dishes in a restaurant called Paris sounds an unlikely combination, but the menu is imaginative, for Chef Mohamed likes to create his own dishes. The setting, opposite Portugal Telecom, may not have the appeal of Tavira's riverside restaurants but for value it is hard to beat. The emphasis is on dishes with herbs and spices – try the delicious seafood *cataplana* with coriander rice. There is a warm welcome from Dina, Mohamed's Portuguese wife, who speaks several languages.

✚ 186 A2 ⊠ Rua Dr Silvestre Falcão, Lote 8, Tavira ☎ 281 324996 ◷ Mon–Sat lunch and dinner, Sun dinner

Portas do Mar ££

This is one of a handful of fish restaurants at Quatro Aguas, downstream from Tavira centre. Fishing boats land the catch close by at the river port and the restaurant has fine views over the River Gilão. Splash out on lobster, prawns or crayfish, or try the shellfish *cataplana* or the monkfish, either with prawns on a spit or with green sauce. There's meat too – enjoy the fillet steak Portas do Mar, served with mushrooms and cream.

✚ 186 A2 ⊠ Sítio das Quatro Águas, Tavira ☎ 281 321255 ◷ Daily lunch and dinner

Salsa & Coentros ££

In the centre of Faro where restaurants of charm and quality are rare, this is a welcome addition. Emídio Góis has produced a menu where traditional southern Portuguese cuisine sits alongside innovative dishes such as papaya stuffed with prawns. The emphasis is on simple fresh ingredients and, as the name ("Parsley and Coriander") suggests, plenty of fresh herbs. Fish, including bass and bream, dominates the menu. Cod is cooked in a different way each day, with *cod Salsa & Coentros* (a fat piece of fish cooked with peppers and chilli sauce) permanently on the menu.

✚ 181 D3 ⊠ Travessa da Mota, 10, Faro ☎ 289 826918/289 863142 ◷ Daily lunch and dinner

Where to...
Shop

MARKETS

Look out for details of the large regional markets in the local English-language magazines. Known as **gipsy markets**, they sell everything from fresh mountain cheese to antique liquor stills, and are a good source of Portuguese pottery, baskets and other crafts.

Olhão has the best **fish market** in the Algarve, held daily except Sunday alongside the fruit and vegetable market in distinctive, turreted redbrick buildings. It has been modernised to comply with EU regulations but its character has not been lost. There's a huge variety here from crabs and crayfish to whole conger eel and huge chunks of tuna. You'll see them hanging up outside and sizzling on sardine barbecues as you wander round.

Several of the coastal towns have colourful **summer fairs**, with live bands, food and wine tasting. The Handicrafts Fair in Tavira, the Art, Handicrafts, Agriculture and Recreation Show in Moncarapacho, the Sardine and Seafood Festival in Olhão and the Tuna Festival in Vila Real de Santo António all take place in August. Faro and Alcoutim hold handicraft festivals in July.

FARO

In the centre of town the main shopping area is the pedestrianised Rua Santo António and the streets running off it. Clothes shops proliferate, many of them selling designer wares, though you can also find shoes, leather, lace, ceramics and other handicrafts. **Casa Branca** (Rua Santo António Nos 10, 21 and 29) specialises in pottery, lace and leather. **Martinez**, just off the Rua Santo António (Rua Tenente Valdim, tel: 289 890090), is a stylish clothes shop with three floors of fashions for women, men and children. South of the Rua Santo António, **Sapatearia Hera** (Travessa Rebelo da Silva, 13, tel: 289 812413) has a good selection of attractive shoes for women and children.

For a great choice of port try the **Supermercado Garrafeira** (Praça de Almeida 28, tel: 289 822803), whose owner, Rui, will help you choose from the many vintages. In the Old Town area of Faro, near the cathedral, **Vila Adentro** (Largo Afonso III, tel: 289 821777) exhibits a fascinating range of antiques from all over Portugal.

The **Faro Shopping Center** (N125, Sítio das Figuras), located on the outskirts of town, has 62 shops, a hypermarket, three cinemas and a restaurant. It's useful if you want a wide variety of shops under one roof, but there is nothing very Portuguese about it and prices tend to be higher than those of the shops in the centre.

TAVIRA

Most shops of interest are craft-orientated. To see the range of regional skills, from miniature boat-making to basketry and weaving, visit the **Casa do Artesanato de Tavira** (Rua D Marcelino Franco 23). The **Artesanato Regional Bazar** (Rua José Pires Padhina) is the place to buy baskets and occasionally you can see weavers in action. Try **Alart** (Rua de Caleria) near the tourist office for pottery and other crafts, or **Artesanato Regional Casa Matias** at the Mercado Municipal (daily market at Rua do Cais). The market is worth visiting to see the morning's catch and the fresh fruits from the Sotavento's lush farmlands. Tavira's large **monthly market** is held on the third Saturday of the month at Campo da Feira. Like all the best traditional markets, it sells local produce that has been cultivated in the surrounding farmlands or freshly hauled from the sea.

Where to...
Be Entertained

OUTDOOR ACTIVITIES

The main activities for visitors are river trips, walking, cycling, golf and beach life. The long sandy beaches of the *ilhas* (islands) are ideal for swimming and sunbathing, though some can only be reached by ferry. Waters are warmer than those west of Faro, but there are fewer watersports and no surfing.

Aquataxis (tel: 964 515073) can organise fishing, diving or Ria Formosa trips, or transport you to any of the islands.

Biking or walking tours of the Ria Formosa can be organised through **Rent-a-Bike** (Rua do Forno, 22, Tavira, tel: 919 338226). For boat tours of the nature reserve, as well as jeep safaris of the northeast, contact **Viagens Cebola** (Rua Antero de Quental 117, Faro, tel: 289 827822). In Alcoutim, **Alcatia Domus** (Rua Notra Senhora da Conceição, Apt 2, tel: 966 381001) organises river-boat trips, canoeing, trekking, biking and other outdoor pursuits. **Benamor Golf** (Quinta de Benamor, tel: 281 320880) was the first golf course to open to the east of Faro. An 18-hole course, it is set scenically between the Tavira coast and the uplands of the Serra do Caldeirão.

Young children can be kept amused at the **Quinta Alegre**, near Tavira (Cabanas, Tavira, tel: 966 321021) – an ostrich ranch with activities such as a mini zoo, an 18-hole crazy-golf course, donkey rides, a bouncy castle, bumper boats and electric cars.

RIVER TRIPS

To see some of the least spoilt scenery in the Algarve, take a boat trip along the River Guadiana. These depart three times a week from Vila Real de Santo António and anchor upstream at Foz de Odeleite. Day trips include lunch and an opportunity for a swim. A river cruise can be combined with a jeep safari through the mountains and a visit to the nature reserve of Castro Marim (➤ 53). For information, contact tourist offices or **Riosul** (Rua Tristão Vaz Teixeira, Monte Gordo, tel 281 510201). For river trips that go all the way to Alcoutim, contact **Turismar** (tel: 281 513504).

NIGHTLIFE

Faro's nightlife is concentrated in the streets north of Praça Francisco Gomes. Rua do Prior is the liveliest, with late-night bars, live bands and two discos: **Emporium** (No 23), and **24 de Julho** (No 38).

The town stages regular programmes of classical music and jazz concerts, July being the best month for music, choral and dance performances. The **Câmara Municipal de Tavira** (tel: 281 320500) hosts occasional concerts, and in summer the town is the scene of a jazz festival featuring local and international musicians as well as performances of *fado* (➤ 39), folk and classical music.

The only disco in Tavira is **Ubi** (Antiga Fábrica Balsense, Rua Almirante Cândido dos Reis, tel: 281 324577), which you'll find in a warehouse on the outskirts of town, open until 6 am in summer.

Monte Gordo's nightlife centres on the beach **Casino** (tel: 281 512224), which has a floorshow with optional dinner and dancing as well as the usual roulette, blackjack and baccarat. Remember that passports or ID cards are required. For more information, enquire at your hotel, any travel agency or directly to the casino.

Albufeira and Central East Algarve

Getting Your Bearings 68 – 69
In Four Days 70 – 71
Don't Miss 72 – 81
At Your Leisure 82 – 85
Where to... 86 – 92

Getting Your Bearings

The stretch of coast between Faro and Albufeira covers the two extremes of the Algarve's tourist industry; from some of the highest density resorts in the country (most notably Albufeira's eastern suburbs) to what is claimed to be the lowest density living area in Europe, at Quinta do Lago. While wealthy clients drop in by private helicopter for caviar at "Quinta", traditional fish 'n' chips in English pubs are the order of the day in certain parts of Albufeira.

It may not be the Portugal you were expecting – Quinta do Lago, Vale do Lobo and Vilamoura represent the Nouveau Algarve, the International Golfing Zone of "Sportugal", sharing more in common with Florida in the United States or Wentworth in England. Similarly, some suburbs of Albufeira and Quarteira resemble many a faceless resort in the Mediterranean or Canary Islands.

Of course it's not all like that. Albufeira has an Old Town that retains higgledy-piggledy streets, local characters, some excellent inexpensive restaurants with marvellous views, great beaches and, out of high season, a relaxed atmosphere. And who would *really* object to relaxing in the lap of luxury in a beautiful villa in Quinta – as long as they could afford it? But for a taste of the Algarve before tourism arrived you have to leave this coast. The Rubicon is the N125. Across it you will find Loulé, Paderne, Salir and Alte – a bustling market town and three small hill villages respectively – with bags of character, colour and culture.

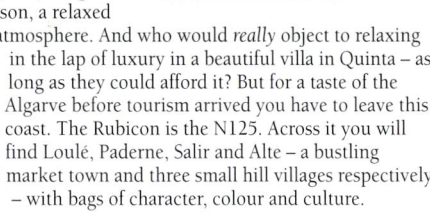

On the rocks: previous page: Praia do São Rafael, Albufeira and, above, a quiet corner of Vilamoura marina.
Left: The elaborately carved doorway of the Igreja de São Sebastião, Albufeira

Getting Your Bearings

★ Don't Miss

- **1** Albufeira ➤ 72–4
- **3** Vilamoura ➤ 75–6
- **7** Igreja de São Lourenço ➤ 77–8
- **8** Loulé ➤ 79–81

At Your Leisure

- **2** Albufeira Beaches and Satellites ➤ 82
- **4** Quarteira ➤ 83
- **5** Vale do Lobo ➤ 83
- **6** Quinta do Lago ➤ 83
- **9** Salir ➤ 84
- **10** Alte ➤ 84
- **11** Paderne ➤ 85

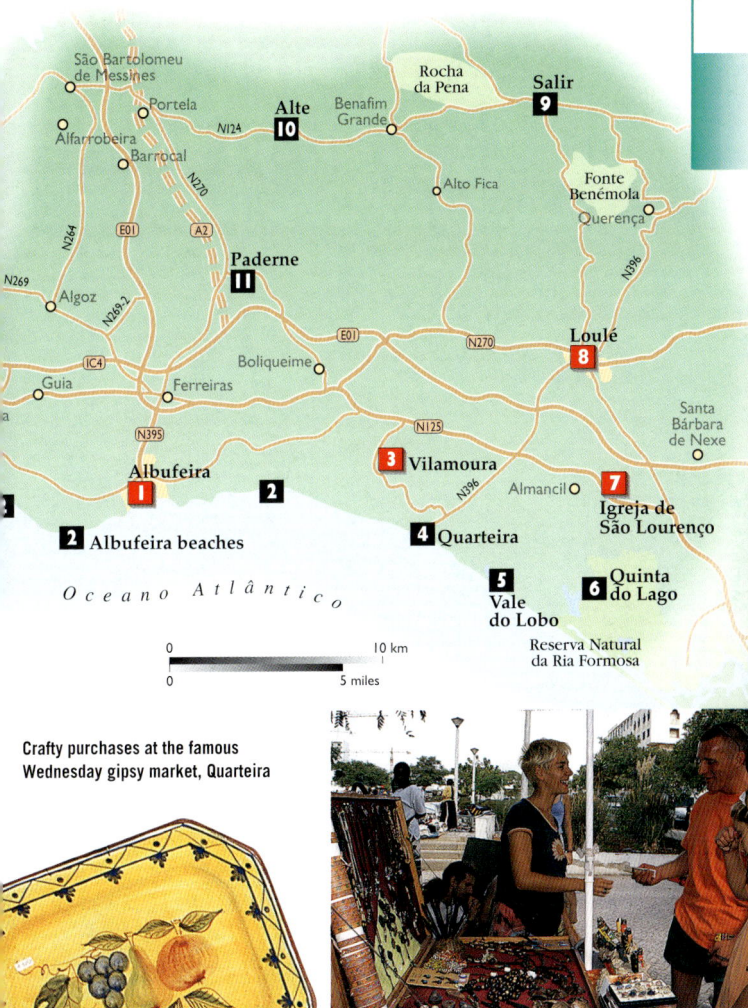

Crafty purchases at the famous Wednesday gipsy market, Quarteira

Albufeira and Central East Algarve

Depending on which days you are in this area, amend the following itinerary to include the Wednesday gipsy market at Quarteira (then lunch at a restaurant near the fish market) and the folk dancing at the Pequena Fonte restaurant in Alte on Tuesday and Wednesday nights. Saturday morning is the best time to visit Loulé. Distances are small and Albufeira and Vilamoura are interchangeable as overnight bases.

Albufeira and Central East Algarve in Four Days

Day One

Morning
The marina at **Vilamoura** (pictured above, ➤ 75–6) is slow to warm up in the morning so spend half an hour in the **Cerro da Vila Museum** (➤ 76) and Roman archaeological site, then play Roman-themed crazy golf next door. Spend a while boat-gazing and pick a place for an early lunch (➤ 76).

Afternoon
Be as active as you like; go fishing for marlin, jetski, play a round of golf, visit Quarteira's gipsy market (pictured right) or ride on the Vista Flyer tethered balloon and sunbathe on the adjacent Falésia beach. Spend the night in Vilamoura and for dinner try somewhere else on the marina, or go native at one of Quarteira's fish restaurants.

Day Two

Morning
Take the N125 west, via Boliqueime, to visit the village of Alte (▶ 84) and the castle of **Paderne** (▶ 85). Have lunch at the Pequena Fonte in Alte.

Afternoon
Return by the same route and visit the **Igreja de São Lourenço** (▶ 77–8 and pictured above) in Almancil (last tour around 5.30), and the adjacent cultural centre (closes at 7). Move on to dinner at one of Almancil's many fine restaurants then spend the night in Vilamoura or Albufeira.

Day Three

Morning
Take the N125 east and follow the signs to **Loulé** (▶ 79–81, its modern fountain is pictured left). To prepare for the recommended drive and walk ▶ 161–3, spend the morning in Loulé, shopping for a picnic in its general market, then head for the Fonte de Benémola with your local goodies.

Afternoon
Walk the Fonte de Benémola trail (▶ 163) and have your picnic by the stream. If you have time, call in at Querença before heading back to base.

Day Four

Morning
Visit Albufeira's **Old Town** (▶ 73). Lunch on the clifftop.

Afternoon
Flake out on the town beach or seek out one of the quieter beaches immediately west – they are worth the effort. Finally, go back into Albufeira for a night on the town.

Albufeira

The recent history of Albufeira is similar to that of scores of seaside fishing villages around the Mediterranean: its beautiful beach, backed by picturesque cliffs, and an Old Town of narrow alleyways and quaint stone houses never had a hope of holding out against the tide of tourism. So, the town reasoned, if you can't beat them, why not join them? Albufeira embraced mass-market tourism, grew at an alarming rate, and in a few years became Portugal's most popular resort.

Today, Albufeira is accused of being over-commercialised, but if you come out of high season, stay to the west of the Old Town and avoid the new suburbs of the east, then you can still get a sense of the place and understand why it was so appealing to travellers and holidaymakers back in the 1960s and early 1970s.

The beach is the key to
Albufeira's success, and the
eastern section, Fishermen's
Beach, still lined with boats, is
probably the most
photographed stretch of coast
in the whole Algarve. The best
time to be here is early morning when you can watch the
fishermen hauling in their
catch. By the beach, tucked
among the disco bars and "real
British pubs", there are small cafés and *adegas* where fishermen
and locals sit and chew the fat.

Above: Fishermen's Beach

The Old Town

Quite remarkably, the very heart of the Old Town,
high on the cliff above the main town beach, has
survived the tourism boom almost unscathed. Aside
from one or two restaurants, this area is a
purely residential, whitewashed warren of
cobbled alleyways. There are three
entrances: one on the east
side, the old St Anne's Gate, up
the stairs past the restaurants of
A Ruina and Anna's; one on the
west side, behind the
Museo Arqueologico; and one on the north
side by the old ramparts in Rua Joaquim Pedro Samora
(to the south is the sheer cliff face).

The area comprises just half a dozen streets, the highlight being the romantic Moorish arch and its
characteristic lantern in the Travessa da Igreja
Velha. The view, straight through to the sea,
hasn't changed in centuries. The arch is one of the few
reminders that the town once fell under Moorish control, when
it was named Al-buhera after the castle (*buhera*) that stood
close to the site of the old town hall, now home to the
Museo Arqueológico. The museum, modern and
small, makes a brave stab at local history,
showing off 5,000-year-old menhirs,
Roman capitals and mosaics, Visigothic
tombs and medieval Manueline-style
(▶ 21) church fragments.

Left: The town beach in high season. Below: Sunbather's-eye-view of Old Town clifftop houses

Albufeira and Central East Algarve

Cobbled café-lined streets in central Albufeira

TAKING A BREAK

Escape the mayhem of Albufeira's central square upstairs at the **Garrafeira Soares** shop (➤ 89). In the quiet bar area you can sit and sample aged ports and *medronhos* while nibbling cuts of local *enchido* (cold meats).

🕂 184 A2
Museu Arqueológico
✉ Praça da República
🕐 Tue–Sun 10.30–5, Oct–May; 2.30–8, Jun–Sep

Albufeira's Most Famous Son

Jacinto d'Ayet, born in Albufeira in 1590, was by all accounts quite a guy – an accomplished singer, guitarist, scholar of classical languages, medical student, dancer and swordsman. Unfortunately – as it turned out – he chose to become a missionary in pagan Japan. After refusing to renounce the Christian faith, he was imprisoned and tortured for two years in Nagasaki and eventually martyred in a burning cage in 1632. His statue stands in the Largo Jacinto d'Ayet just west of the town centre.

ALBUFEIRA: INSIDE INFO

Top tips **Watch the sunset** from the cliffs immediately to the west of the Old Town at Bizarro's Bar or O Penedo restaurant (both on Rua Latino Coelho), or around the corner at one of the clifftop restaurants on Praça Miguel Bombarda.
• **Tours**: either pick up a copy of *Historial* (sic) *and Monumental Tours of the City of Albufeira* from the Museu Arqueológico and do your own thing, or join a free walking tour of the town. These take place at 10.30 am Wednesday to Friday, February until June. Ask at the tourist office for details.

One to miss Montechoro, aka **The Strip**, to the east of town, is notorious for its rowdy nightlife.

Vilamoura

Vilamoura, begun from scratch in 1974, is one of the largest leisure complexes in Europe. At its heart is a 1,000-berth marina surrounded by large hotels, the Vilamoura Casino, luxury holiday homes and manicured golf courses. It also has two beaches on its doorstep – Praia da Falésia (the more scenic of the two) and Praia da Marina – and with many other sporty diversions is a good place to unwind. It may be short on local character but it's long on comfort.

Above: Vilamoura Marina from the tethered Vista Flyer balloon ride

Right: Modern art from old Vilamoura – sculpture at Cerro de Vil

The Sporting Life

The main attraction in Vilamoura is **golf**. It has four championship courses – five if you count the neighbouring Vila Sol course – and at least one more on the drawing board. Your choice will depend upon your budget and your ability; a handicap certificate is required for all courses (men 24, ladies 28 for the Old Course and Millennium Course). The best and most prestigious is the **Old Course**, while a great future is predicted for the **Millennium Course**. The choice between Pinhal and Laguna courses depends largely upon your predilection for *pinheiros* (pine trees), or *lagoas* (lagoons, and other water hazards). The Old Course and the Millennium are almost twice the price of the others.

Albufeira and Central East Algarve

Watersports, including big-game fishing, are another draw. Go to the huddle of kiosks at the far corner of the marina to try your hand. Strung up here is a stuffed world-record black marlin, weighing 743kg, caught from a boat out of the marina. You can also book jetskiing and parascending, or take various cruises from these kiosks.

TAKING A BREAK

Akavit (Loja 7, tel: 289 380712) is possibly the most attractive front-row marina restaurant and puts a successful Modern European and Swedish spin on Algarvian seafood. Football fans should call in at **Bar 7** (➤ 13).

Vista Flyer
✚ 184 B2
✉ Road to Praia da Falésia
☎ 289 316576/7
🕐 Daily 10–10, flights every 15 minutes (weather permitting)
💰 Expensive (20 per cent discount for return flight)

Cerro da Vila
✚ 184 C2
✉ Avenida do Cerro da Vila
☎ 289 312153
🕐 9.30–12.30, 2–6, Nov–Apr; 10–1, 4–9, May–Oct
💰 Inexpensive

Golf Clubs
Old Course
☎ 289 322650
Laguna, Pinhal, Millennium
☎ 289 310180
Vila Sol
☎ 289 300505

Left: Record black marlin at Vilamoura Marina. Below: Teeing off at Vilamoura's Old Course

VILAMOURA: INSIDE INFO

Top tips To see the bright lights of Vilamoura take a night flight on the **Vista Flyer**, a landmark tethered balloon that soars up to 122m. Views stretch from Carvoeiro to Faro. Take a warm top and your camera.
• **Hire a car**, even if you're not going outside the resort. Despite the fact that Vilamoura is a self-contained complex, distances between places within it are so great that you have to drive almost everywhere.

Hidden gem Right next to the marina are the remains of a site known to the Romans as **Cerro da Vila**. The finds, mostly small-scale items, are exhibited inside the Cerro da Vila Museum and with the aid of the plan you can trace the adjacent scant remains of a villa, public baths, a necropolis, the port and other areas.

Igreja de São Lourenço

Every part of the church interior is covered in paintings or blue-and-white 18th-century *azulejos*

The Church of São Lourenço sits serenely on a hill in its own tiny hamlet, incongruously trapped between the crawling traffic of the old N125 and the motorway rush of the new E01. Don't let that put you off, however. Its interior, covered from floor to ceiling in beautiful blue *azulejos*, has been described by Dr Santos Simões, an expert in the field, as "the most notable in the Algarve and one of the most extraordinary in Portugal". Today it is the Algarve's most visited church.

Its story goes back to 1722, when the region was suffering a drought. As the inhabitants of São Lourenço were digging for water, they struck a spring and in gratitude vowed to build a new church in place of the existing, almost ruinous, hermitage. The project assumed greater importance when one of the region's highest dignitaries, Dr Manuel de Sousa Teixeira, offered his support. He in turn influenced the top craftsmen of the region – the Borges brothers and Master Manuel Martins – to supply the *azulejos* and the woodwork respectively. Having survived the Great Earthquake of 1755 (see box ►78) practically intact (just five tiles were dislodged), the church remains as it was some 280 years ago.

St Lawrence

The *azulejos* tell the story of the life of St Lawrence: handing alms to the poor; restoring the eyesight of two blind men; being accused of possessing riches by the Emperor Valeriano; being threatened to renounce his faith; and finally (in the year 258) being roasted alive on a grid-iron during his martyrdom. The tiled scene on the left of the altar shows Lawrence in a distressed state because he has just learned that the Pope is to be martyred and he wants to join him. However, he is comforted on being told that within a few days this will be his fate, too.

Centro Cultural de São Lourenço

A few yards from the church is the Cultural Centre, beautifully converted from traditional 200-year-old houses. A small exhibition of international modern and contemporary art changes every few weeks and a regular programme of concerts – usually classical music – is staged (see the local newspapers for details). The highlight of this charming haven is its delightful sculpture garden. An oversized, naked Samson greets visitors and the small but luxuriant sub-tropical grounds are "inhabited" by large, ingeniously created scrap-metal insects and other recycled beasts.

Don't bug this metre-long scrap metal ant at the Centro Cultural!

TAKING A BREAK

There is a café opposite the **Centro Cultural de São Lourenço** but the nearest restaurants are in Almancil, a five-minute drive away. **Pequeno Mundo** (tel: 289 399866) and **Aux Bons Enfants** (tel: 289 396840) are two of the many excellent high-class establishments to be found here. Nearly all Almancil's quality restaurants are open for dinner only.

Igreja de São Lourenço
🕀 184 C2
✉ São Lourenço, Almancil
🕐 Tours: Mon 2.30–6, Tue–Sat 10–1, 2.30–6 (5 in winter) 💷 Inexpensive

Centro Cultural de São Lourenço
🕀 184 C2
✉ São Lourenço, Almancil
☎ 289 395475
🕐 Mon 2.30–6, Tue–Sat 10–1, 2.30–6 (5 in winter)

The Great Earthquake

The Great Earthquake of 1755 – in which the Algarve was particularly hard hit – was the worst natural disaster ever to befall the country. Its epicentre is thought to have been just off the coast somewhere between Tavira and Faro and the resultant tidal wave swept 6.5km inland, killing thousands and flattening almost every building in its wake.

IGREJA DE SÃO LOURENÇO: INSIDE INFO

Top tips Before you visit the Algarve call the **Centro Cultural de São Lourenço** for concert dates as tickets sell out quickly.
• The **church is usually open for tours only**, so if you are visiting it independently you will have to tag along on the next coach tour, hoping it is in your language. If there is no tour the custodian may allow you in by yourself.

Loulé

Loulé is the central Algarve's main market town; a bustling mix of old alleyways, ancient churches, castle remains, a neo-Moorish market hall, modern pedestrianised streets and a broad boulevard. For six days of the week it is quiet and mostly oblivious to tourism, but on Saturdays its gipsy market draws visitors from miles around.

Despite the crowds, Saturday is definitely the best day to come to town because this is when the local produce market is at its biggest, busiest and best. Stalls manned by wizened local characters in trilby hats and aprons overflow from the onion-topped central market hall (built in the 1900s) onto the surrounding alleys, and the heady mix of sights and sounds and smells – herbs, peppers, olives and sausages, vegetables, cheeses, meat, dried cod and live chicks – is purely Portugal.

From Muslim to Christian – the bell tower of São Clemente was once the minaret for the town mosque

Old Town

Conveniently, the tourist office is next to the market, set in the courtyard of Loulé's medieval castle remains. Here you can pick up a map to navigate through the warren-like back streets of the Old Town. An atmospherically lit small archaeological museum, the **Museu Municipal**, featuring a handful of prehistoric, Roman and medieval relics, occupies part of the lower castle. Climb the stairs for good views from the ramparts.

Almost opposite the entrance to the courtyard (just to the left) is the tiny hermitage of **Nossa Senhora da Conceição** (Our Lady of the Conception). Built in the mid-17th century, it is remarkable for its mid-18th century *azulejos* and its gilt altarpiece. Sadly the church is in very poor condition so tread carefully as in places it actually feels as if you may go through the floorboards!

Directly opposite the courtyard entrance, on Rua Vice Almirante Cândido dos Reis, the former convent of Espírito Santo has been converted into a gleaming white **Municipal Art Gallery** where the rotating exhibitions usually feature modern art.

The main parish church, **São Clemente**, a three-minute walk away, is an architectural treat. It was rebuilt in the 16th and 18th centuries but retains its late 13th-century Gothic arches and old stone windows. The landmark separate bell-tower is the only remaining part of the city's main mosque, built in the 12th century and converted after the Christian Reconquest (➤ 30).

Nossa Senhora da Piedade

By contrast, just outside the centre of town on a hill high above the main Albufeira road, is Loulé's newest church, Nossa Senhora da Piedade (Our Lady of Piety) – a startling white rocket-shaped structure that looks as if it is just about to blast off. Alongside is the church's small 18th-century chapel. The views from here stretching down to the coast are excellent.

Nossa Senhora da Piedade is probably the Algarve's most startling church design

Loulé

TAKING A BREAK
Set in an ancient building on Rua Vice Almirante Cândido dos Reis, opposite the former convent of Espírito Santo, the courtyard of the beautifully converted **Bar Carlindos** (tel: 289 417632) makes for a good coffee break from the crowds. Alternatively, for a full meal in another pretty garden courtyard go to **A Muralha** (Rua Martim Moniz, tel: 289 412629, ➤ 88).

184 C2
Museu Municipal
✉ Rua de Paio Peres Correia
☎ 289 415000 (ext 211)
🕒 Mon–Sat 9–5.30

Ermida de Nossa Senhora da Conceição
✉ Rua de Paio Peres Correia
🕒 Irregular; mornings are best, enquire at tourist office. If closed, key at No 27, opposite

Galleria Municipal
✉ Convent of Espírito Santo, Rua Vice Almirante Cândido dos Reis
🕒 Mon–Sat 10–5

São Clemente
✉ Largo Bataláo dos Sapadores do Caminho
🕒 Daily 10–1, 2–7. If closed, key at No 19 Calçada dos Sapateiros, just off the square

Above: Find a bargain at the market.
Left: Top brass on Rua da Barbacá

Crafts on the Brink
Loulé's craft heritage of basket-weaving, lace-making, copper-beating, leather-working and pottery dates back to the Moors, but is now a dying business as the last of the artisans cease to be replaced by their sons or daughters. Individual workshops are scattered round the town but the sole surviving concentration is on Rua da Barbacá, below the castle wall.

LOULÉ: INSIDE INFO

Top tips If you want a **parking place** in town on Saturday morning get here by 9 at the latest.
• In late February or early March each year Loulé stages the Algarve's best **carnival**. It may be tame by Latin or Spanish standards but it's still good fun.
• In July there is an international **festival of jazz** featuring about ten concerts around the town.

At Your Leisure

Santa Eulália is one of eastern Albufeira's best beaches

❷ Albufeira Beaches and Satellites

Much of Albufeira's holiday accommodation is centred in Praia d'Oura and Montechoro, Areias de São João or perhaps Santa Eulália, rather than in Albufeira town. These eastern suburbs are devoted to hotels, apartments and time-share complexes, restaurants and bars (most at the cheap end of the scale) and a frequently raucous nightlife.

The area immediately west of Albufeira is not quite so heavily developed, given more to private villas and urbanisations than large hotels, and it has prettier and quieter beaches than the eastern satellites – though in high season nowhere around Albufeira is quiet.

🞢 184 A2/B2

Six of the Best Beaches Around Albufeira

West
  São Rafael: a long beach with rock-stacks and coves at the eastern end.
  Castelo: a series of small cove beaches interspersed by curiously shaped cliffs, stacks and blowholes. Wonderful for scrambling and exploring.
  Coelha: a charming, small, sheltered beach that is really an extension of Castelo. Can get very busy.
  Galé: the eastern side of this beach is composed of small cosy coves with large rocks for children to scramble over; the west is long and open, heading all the way to Armação de Pêra.

East
  Santa Eulalia: a long, broad beach attractively backed by low cliffs and pines.
  Olhos de Água: a small, pretty beach with fishing boats and eroded rock formations – but it can get very busy.

Sporting Activities at Quinta do Lago and Vale do Lobo

Golf Clubs
- **Quinta do Lago** (Quinta do Lago course, Ria Formosa course, tel: 289 390700).
- **Vale do Lobo** (Royal Course, Atlantic Course, tel: 289 393939; www.valedolobo.pt).
- **San Lorenzo** (tel: 289 396522, 289 396534).
- **Pinheiros Altos** (tel: 289 359910).

Tennis and Horse-riding
- **Jim Stewart Tennis Academy** (Quinta do Lago, tel: 289 398848)
- **Vale do Lobo Tennis Academy** (tel: 289 396991).
- **Centro Hípico Horse-riding School** (Quinta dos Amigos, Almancil, tel: 289 399339).

Villas overlooking the Royal Course at Vale do Lobo

❹ Quarteira

Quarteira is no beauty. In the 1970s it was in the vanguard of Algarve development, but today its high-rise, Costa-style frontage is regarded as an aberration.

However, it does have a long, gently shelving, rock-free beach with breakwaters (perfect for young children), authentic, inexpensive fish restaurants and a relaxed family atmosphere attracting Portuguese holidaymakers. Each Wednesday it stages the Algarve's biggest and busiest gipsy market.

Vilamoura marina (➤ 75–6) is just a 15-minute walk along the beach, so its shops, restaurants and watersports are also on tap to Quarteira's visitors.

Just outside Quarteira is Atlantic Park, the smallest of the Algarve's waterparks but still plenty of fun for younger children. It also has junior quad-bikes and bouncy castles.

Quarteira Tourist Office
✚ 184 C2 ✉ Corner of Via Infante de Sagres and rua Dioga Cao

Atlantic Park
✚ 184 C2 ✉ N125, Quatro Estradas, Loulé road ☎ 289 397282, 800 204767 ⓘ 10–6, Apr–Jun and Sep; 10–7, Jul–Aug 🅿 Moderate

❺ & ❻ Vale do Lobo/Quinta do Lago

Although these two neighbouring, purpose-built resorts are quite disinct, their ethos and character is virtually identical and they have more in common with an American country club than the rest of the Algarve.

Quite simply they provide luxury accommodation, in secluded, sprinkler-fed grounds, to guests who want privacy, the quiet life and immediate access to the best golf courses in the Algarve. (Day visitors

The scant remains of a Moorish stronghold at Salir

should note that these courses are rather exclusive; some are very expensive and must be booked well ahead.)

If you're looking for other activities, tennis is also popular and horse-riding is a great way to see wilder areas. The saltwater lakes of Quinta do Lago are used for windsurfing.

Both Quinta do Lago and Vale do Lobo have excellent beaches and because many holidaymakers here are without children, or prefer their own villa swimming pool to the chilly sea, or are out on the golf course, these beaches are rarely crowded. Bird-watchers may like to note that Quinta do Lago falls just within the Reserva Natural da Ria Formosa (➤ 57).

✚ 184 C1

❾ Salir

Despite being just north of Loulé and on the same road as Alte, Salir remains largely undiscovered. One of the Algarve's prettiest villages, it is set on a steep hill, topped by an attractive church and a rather ugly water tower. From here you can look across to the site of Salir's once sizeable Castelo Mouro (Moorish Castle) on the adjacent hill. Today there is very little to see at the castle – only the bottom section of four corner turrets, encased in concrete – and houses are scattered within the outer walls. However, it is worth getting to the top of the steep hill (you can drive up most of the way) for the panoramic views across the countryside and back to Salir.

✚ 184 C3

❿ Alte

Alte has changed little in decades, if not centuries, and "prettiest", "most typical", and "best kept" in the Algarve are all epithets that are frequently applied to the village. (A fourth might be most mispronounced – it's "Alt", not "Alté".)

On the main road, the tourist information office doubles as a small exhibition area (Casa Memória d'Alte) on local crafts and history. From here, wander up the hill to Alte's lovely 16th-century *igreja* (church) whose portal, with its knotted-rope decoration, is an excellent example of Manueline architecture (➤ 21). Inside, the church has been carefully restored and features some beautiful side chapels and a glittering altarpiece. Note too its splendid 16th-century *azulejo* tiles. If you need

For Kids
- **Atlantic Water Park**, near Quarteira (➤ 83).
- The wind- and sea-carved nooks and crannies of **Castelo beach**, west of Albufeira, is a great place for older children – preferably supervised – to explore.
- **Horse-riding** for all ages at Quinta do Lago (➤ 91).
- **Vista Flyer** tethered balloon at Vilamoura (➤ 76).

Alte, nestling amid the limestone foothills known as the Barrocal

help, the custodian is usually happy to point out the main features.

From the village centre it is a five-minute walk (signposted) to the Fonte Pequena (Little Fountain or Spring) and Fonte Grande (Big Fountain or Spring). This is something of a local beauty spot, where the eponymous springs flow into shallow canals, beside which you'll find benches, grassy areas and tiled walls. Locals flock here on Sundays for barbecues and picnics, and tour groups come here on Tuesday and Wednesday evenings for folk dancing in the Pequena Fonte restaurant.

Igreja
184 B3 Mon–Sat 8–1, 3–7 (closes earlier in winter)

⓫ Paderne

Paderne's atmospheric castle ruins are set on a hill some 2 to 3km outside the village centre. Follow signs from the village entrance; go past the *fonte* (spring), now a commercial water-bottling plant, and turn right onto a bumpy track. Straight ahead and high above roars an elevated section of the Via do Infante motorway. Turn immediately left after passing under the motorway bridge and follow the road up, keeping to the right.

The castle was built by the Moors in the 12th century and conquered by Dom Paio Peres Correia in 1249. Its outer walls remain largely intact. On the other side of the castle from where you have parked, look down to see a handsome, high-arched medieval bridge with Roman origins.

Go back down the hill and turn left, following the river (dry in summer). After a short distance you'll reach a car-parking area and a stepping-stone bridge across the river. Old millstones tell of a watermill that was once here. Continue a little further and you will come to the bridge that you saw from above.

184 B3

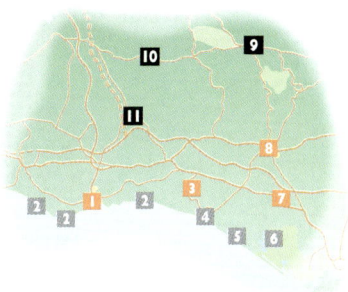

Good Places For a Picnic
- **Paderne**: beside the river or below the castle.
- Above the beaches of **Castelo** and **São Rafael**: west of Albufeira.
- **Alte**: beside the Fonte Pequena or Fonte Grande (busy on Sundays) or further upstream.
- **Fonte de Benémola** (➤ 161–3).

Where to... Stay

Prices
Expect to pay per double room per night:
£ under €50 **££** €50–125 **£££** over €125

Alte Hotel ££
This small hotel above the pretty hill village of Alte makes a good base for exploring the surrounding countryside. Facilities include a heated swimming pool, a tennis court, a games room, a TV room and a bus to the beach. The restaurant offers local dishes or fish fresh from the coast. Half or full-board terms are available.

✚ **184 B3** ✉ **Montinho, 8100-012 Alte** ☎ **289 478523/4; fax: 289 478846; email: altehotel@mail.telepac.pt**

Boa Vista ££
The hotel lives up to its name and enjoys spectacular sea and town views from the residential quarter above Albufeira's centre. The décor is quite stylish, particularly the light and airy fifth-floor restaurant which has picture windows overlooking the sea. The 86 bedrooms vary in size and price, but all rooms have sea views. Facilities include two restaurants and bars, and a good-sized pool and surrounding terrace.

✚ **184 A2** ✉ **Rua Samora Barros, 20, 8200 Albufeira** ☎ **289 589175; fax: 289 589180**

Hotel Montechoro £££
One of the landmarks of Albufeira, the Montechoro is a huge hotel 4km northeast of the centre, at the top of the bar- and restaurant-lined road known as The Strip. A regular shuttle bus links it with the nearby sandy beach of Praia da Oura and the centre of Albufeira. The hotel is modern, comfortable and spacious – if a little impersonal. Prices compare well with other hotels of its category and facilities are abundant: eight tennis courts, two squash courts, a large pool, a sauna, a gym, four bars and two restaurants, including the rooftop Amendoeiras Grill, which has stunning views.

✚ **184 A2** ✉ **Avenida Dr Fransisco Sa' Carneiru Apt 28, 8200 Albufeira** ☎ **289 589424; fax: 289 589947**

Loulé Jardim ££
Compared to its equivalent on the coast, the Loulé Jardim is excellent value. A yellow-and-white building overlooking a pretty garden square in the old part of Loulé, it was built principally in the 1990s but reconstructed from an early 20th-century residence. The plainly furnished bedrooms all have air conditioning and TV. Other hotel amenities include a rooftop swimming pool, a terrace, two bars, and a pleasant sitting room featuring a fireplace.

✚ **184 C2** ✉ **Praça Manuel de Arriaga, 8100 Loulé** ☎ **289 413094/5; fax: 289 63177**

Quinta do Lago £££
It is easy to see why the Quinta do Lago claims to be the finest hotel in the Algarve: it enjoys a magnificent setting overlooking the lagoon and sea, an interior emphasising luxury and elegance, and the best sporting facilities of any hotel in southern Portugal. You can tee off on any of three different championship golf courses, play tennis on floodlit courts, swim in indoor or outdoor pools, pamper yourself in the health club or stroll across the estuary bridge for watersports off the beach or to relax on the white sands. Choose from Italian cuisine in the intimate Ca d'Oro, or Portuguese and international food in the Navegadores Restaurant. It's not just

the facilities – no detail is overlooked in the bedrooms: on arrival you will find fresh flowers, fruit, a carafe of port and a box of chocolates waiting for you.

🏠 184 C1 ☒ Quinta do Lago, 8135-024 Almancil ☎ 289 350350; fax: 289 396393; email: info@quintadolagohotel.com; www.quintadolagohotel.com

Quinta dos Rochas ££

Situated between Almancil and Quarteira, the Quinta dos Rochas provides a peaceful rural location and a friendly relaxing atmosphere. It's a small hotel with just six comfortable and well-equipped rooms, a lounge, a library, a bar, an outside terrace and a pool. The absence of a restaurant gives you the opportunity to sample the gastronomic fare in and around Almancil – this is the best area for eating out in the Algarve, if not the cheapest. The long sandy beach is 2km away, and there are plenty of opportunities for sports enthusiasts with golf courses, tennis courts, a riding school and boating near by.

🏠 184 C2 ☒ Quinta dos Rochas, Fonte Coberta, Caixa Postal 600A, 8135-019 Almancil ☎ 289 393165; fax: 289 399198

Sheraton £££

The clifftop setting and de luxe comfort, combined with creative Moorish-style features, make the Sheraton a highly desirable hotel. Set among pines, it has access via a lift to the beautiful beach of Falésia. This is an ideal family hotel, providing children's entertainment at the Porto Pirata Village (pirate ships, mini-golf, a pool, a boat pond and basketball) which enables parents to take advantage of all the hotel facilities: a nine-hole golf course and golf academy, indoor and outdoor swimming pools, a health club, tennis courts and watersports on the beach.

🏠 184 B2 ☒ Praia da Falésia, Apartado/PO Box 644, 8200 Albufeira ☎ 289 500100; fax 289 501950; email: sheraton-algarve@sheraton.com

Vila Branca ££

Set in a quiet residential back street in the older, western part of the town, a convenient five-minute walk from the centre, the Vila Branca has been established for over 30 years and is therefore one of Albufeira's original guesthouses. Its frontage is unprepossessing but the welcome from the front desk is warm and the quality of the rooms (which include TV and air conditioning) is warm. There is also a pleasant bar area.

🏠 184 A2 ☒ Rua do Ténis 4, 8200 Albufeira ☎ 289 586804; fax: 289 586592

Vila Joya £££

The most exclusive hotel in the Algarve, the Vila Joya is set discreetly among lush gardens above a sandy bay. The entrance gate is kept closed and the ambience is more that of a private home than a hotel. Terms are unusual: the minimum stay is a week, from Saturday to Saturday, except off-season, and half-board is compulsory. As the restaurant is renowned for gastronomy this is (money aside) no hardship. The hotel is stylish and elegant and the 15 rooms enjoy stunning garden and sea views from the balcony.

🏠 184 A2 ☒ Praia de Galé, PO Box 120 8200 Albufeira ☎ 289 591795; fax: 289 591201

Villa São Vicente ££

This small hotel is a welcome addition in a resort where hotels of charm are hard to find. Opened in 2000, it is across the road from the beach, and a few minutes' walk from the resort centre. The bar/breakfast room is pretty furnished in beige and blues, with picture windows over the sea. The immaculate bedrooms vary in price according to location, the most desirable being those on the upper floor with the best sea views. Amenities include a small swimming pool and snack service at the bar.

🏠 184 A2 ☒ Largo Jacinto d'Ayet, 4, 8200 Albufeira ☎ 289 583700; fax: 289 583708

Where to...
Eat and Drink

Prices
Expect to pay per person for a meal, excluding drinks and service
£ under €15   ££ €15–23   £££ over €23

A Lagosteira ££

It's not just lobster (*lagosta*) and shellfish that feature on the menu of this popular restaurant. All tastes are catered for (including such international staples as spaghetti Bolognese, omelettes and burgers as well as more sophisticated fare) and the menu is usefully translated into ten languages. Favourite Portuguese dishes are crabs and clams brought straight from the aquarium, shellfish rice, charcoal-grilled fresh fish, succulent steaks and flambéed desserts. It's not surprisingly a bustling venue so it's worth booking in advance during the summer, particularly if you want a table on the open-air terrace.

✚ 184 B2 ✉ Açoteias, Albufeira (8km east of Albufeira, close to the Sheraton Hotel) ☎ 289 501679 ⊙ Daily 10 am–midnight

A Muralha ££

Formerly a bakery, this town restaurant has a rustic feel to it and is entered via a pretty terrace with a flourishing banana tree. Eat here or in the main restaurant where tables are laid with blue-and-white checked cloths, and walls are decorated with panels of *azulejos*. The menu changes daily and depends on the produce from the nearby market. Check the specialities on the blackboard and the daily display of fish and seafood.

✚ 184 C2 ✉ Rua Martim Moniz, 41, Loulé ☎ 289 412629 ⊙ Tue–Sat lunch & dinner, Mon dinner. Closed Jan & Feb

A Ruina ££

This long-established fish restaurant occupies a prime position, right on Fishermen's Beach. The building has four storeys and in summer you have the choice of eating on the beach, on two levels inside or on the rooftop terrace. The fish is generally dependable (it can hardly be landed any closer), but do be aware of the cost. Most of it is priced by the kilo, and you may receive a nasty shock when the bill arrives. It's best to ask to see the fish weighed before you make a firm order.

✚ 184 A2 ✉ Praia dos Pescadores, Largo Cais Herculano, Albufeira ☎ 289 512094 ⊙ Daily lunch and dinner

Aux Bons Enfants £££

This is a charming restaurant, set in a quiet country house that is located well out of Almancil. The terracotta-themed dining room is candlelit and has a pretty terrace for enjoying alfresco meals. The French cuisine created here is exceptional, with the menu featuring dishes such as *foie gras frais*, *escargots*, Châteaubriand steak in pepper sauce and homemade *confit de canard*. You are unlikely to find a better wine list in the Algarve, and as an extra touch, the end pages list a number of ports and dessert wines that you can order by the glass.

✚ 184 C2 ✉ Estrada a Quinta do Lago, Almancil ☎ 289 396840 ⊙ Mon–Sat dinner

Avenida Velha ££

Not to be confused with "O Avenida" on the same street, this is the older of the two Loulé restaurants. It is a friendly establishment, frequented by locals and crammed with pictures, plates and photographs.

There is no need to order starters here because an impressive array of appetisers arrives unsolicited: look forward to hot grilled sausage, sardines or squid, salad, cheese, olives and homemade bread. Follow these with grilled fish or meat or one of the six different *cataplanas*. If you're lucky, almond-based desserts may possibly be followed by a port or brandy on the house.

🕂 184 C2 ⊠ **Avenida José da Costa Mealha, 40, Loulé** ☎ **289 416474**
🕘 **Daily lunch and dinner**

Memories of China £££

Located at Vale do Lobo's Tennis Academy, Memories of China was founded by the late Ken Lo, author of 30 books on Chinese food and cooking. On summer evenings you can sit here with exquisite Cantonese, Peking or Sichuan cuisine and watch the tennis in action from your table. As a particularly Algarve touch, local fruits of the sea are put to good use in delicious dishes such as Cantonese deep-fried crispy squid and spiced Sichuan king prawns. A take-away service is also available.

🕂 184 C1 ⊠ **Vale do Lobo Tennis Academy, Vale do Lobo, Almancil** ☎ **289 353432, ext. 5432**
🕘 **Sun–Fri dinner**

O Cabaz de Praia £££

The "Beach Basket" is a French-run restaurant, converted from a cliffside fisherman's cottage. Prices are on the expensive side but worth it for the sea views from the rooftop terrace and arguably the best cuisine in Albufeira. The menu, a combination of French and Portuguese dishes, changes according to the daily market and is more inspiring than most. Main courses tend to come with delicious sauces such as monkfish flambéed with spicy mango sauce or duck breast with spicy quinces and honey.

🕂 184 A2 ⊠ **Praça Miguel Bombarda 7, Albufeira** ☎ **289 512137**
🕘 **Fri–Wed lunch and dinner. Closed Feb**

O Zuca £

A small, simple restaurant tucked away in a side street off the main square in Albufeira, O Zuca doesn't get a lot of passing trade but it is popular with the Portuguese (and tourists in the know) with Mr Zuca or, in season and to be ordered in advance, wild rabbit.

🕂 184 A2 ⊠ **Travessa do Malpique 6, Albufeira (off Largo Engenheiro Duarte Pacheco 7)** ☎ **289 588768**
🕘 **Mon–Sat lunch and dinner**

Soares £

Garrafeira Soares has ten off-licences in the Algarve. At this one in central Albufeira you can sit upstairs and sample Portuguese wines, ports and spirits, along with delicious tapas of smoked sausage, cheese and hams. The wines come from the Douro, Alentejo and the Douro, and there is a 40-year-old port to try as well as cherry and orange liqueurs.

🕂 184 A2 ⊠ **Largo Engenheiro Duarte Pacheco 7, Albufeira** ☎ **289 583547** 🕘 **Mon–Sat 10–7; extended hours in high season**

Vila Joya £££

Come with your pockets well-lined and enjoy some of the finest food in Portugal. Within the Vila Joya Hotel (▶ 87) the restaurant exudes warmth and elegance. Its terrace, under Moorish arches and overlooking gardens and sea, is the perfect spot for summer dining. The menu changes daily and the cuisine is one of light, aromatic Mediterranean flavours. The catch of the day is served with a creative sauce or vegetable purée. So exclusive is the Villa Joya that reservations are obligatory, and you are advised to book two weeks in advance during high season.

🕂 184 A2 ⊠ **Praia de Galé, Albufeira** ☎ **289 591795** 🕘 **Daily lunch and dinner. Closed early Jan–early Feb and mid-Nov to mid-Dec**

Where to... **89**

Where to... Shop

LOULÉ

For real shops as opposed to tourist souvenirs head inland to Loulé, where you're likely to catch a glimpse of that dying breed, the Algarve artisan, although you may have to fight through the usual tourist tat to do so. To see the town at its liveliest go early on a Saturday morning when the main **market** is in full swing (but note that market and shops close on Saturday afternoon). The streets surrounding the marketplace will be packed with stalls selling everything from buckets of olives and strings of sausages to chickens, rabbits and pottery. From the market, stroll south down **Rua Jose Fernando Guerreiro** and **Rua 9 de Abril**, where you may hear the hammers and sanders of copper and brass craftsmen. Look out for old liquor stills – a really unusual buy – and, at **Barracha** (Rua José Fernando Guerreiro), *cataplanas* for cooking Algarve-style. Near the tourist office, coppersmiths can be seen at work in **Rua da Barbaça**; and at **Correaria Moderna** you can watch saddlers and buy from the shop selling leather bags and accessories. The **Centro de Artesanato** (11/13 Rua da Barbaça) has a large display of attractive crafts, including handmade rugs, ceramics, and crafts made of cork, wood and palm-leaves. Some of the prettiest handpainted pottery in town, with large designs of fruit and flowers, can be seen at **Casa Louart** (Rua Dom Paio Peres Correia, 19, tel: 289 413794).

ALBUFEIRA

Considering its size and popularity, Albufeira is disappointing for shopping. Souvenirs are ubiquitous but there are few local handicrafts and virtually no bargains, though you could try the market on the first and third Tuesdays of each month. The main shopping streets are the **Rua 5 de Outubro**, near the seafront, and the **Rua Cândido dos Reis**. In summer, stalls set up along the most bustling streets, selling leatherware, copper, jewellery, clothes and ceramics. For good quality pottery and ceramics the best sources are **Infante Dom Henrique** (40 Rua Cândido dos Reis) or **La Lojas** (Rua Cândido dos Reis, 20/22, tel: 289 513168), which sells elegant crystal, china and porcelain. Close by, **Casa Tango** (Trav Cândido dos Reis, 3–1, tel: 289 587008) has a good selection of pottery and other crafts and gifts. For shoe bargains try **Mundo do Sapato** ("Shoe World"; Kit Market, Mestre Maco, Vale Paraiso, Albufeira, tel: 289 585485) about 2km away from the town centre. This is where Nike, Ecco, Shark and other brands are discounted by up to 40 per cent.

QUINTA DO LAGO/ALMANCIL

Appropriately for their upmarket reputations, Vale do Lobo and Almancil have some of the most elegant shops in the Algarve. **Quinta Shopping** (Quinta do Lago, tel: 289 398247), a stylish complex with designer boutiques and beauty salons surrounding a central plaza, is a favourite meeting and leisure area. Chic eateries are part of the attraction, with Italian, French and Chinese cuisine and a choice of inviting cafes and bars. Predictably, both the Quinta do Lago and the Almancil areas are well supplied with golf shops, either individually run or as part of a golfing academy or club. For golf-themed shoes, bags, accessories, books and gifts try **Florida Golf** (Vale de Eguas, N125, tel: 289 399522). On a more erudite note, in Almancil itself the **Griffin Bookshop** (Rua 5 de Outubro 206-A, tel: 289 393904) is the best shop in the Algarve for finding English-language books.

Where to...
Be Entertained

The region is a haven for sports enthusiasts. Apart from a dozen golf courses, there are tennis academies, horse-riding schools, health clubs, cycle trails, bird hides, big-game fishing trips and watersports. Larger hotels and apartment complexes provide their own sports facilities.

GOLF

The luxury resorts of Quinta do Lago and Vale do Lobo boast six scenic golf courses between them. The most famous is the **Quinta do Lago** (tel: 289 390700, ▶ 27), which has hosted the Portuguese Open seven times. It is set in undulating hills and pine forest.

Vilamoura has four golf courses, the latest addition being the 18-hole **Millennium Golf Course** (tel: 289 310333), inaugurated in 2000.

Albufeira has two courses, both of which opened in the 1990s: the 18-hole **Salgados Golf Club** (Vale Rabelho, tel: 289 591111), 6km from the town, and the nine-hole **Pine Cliffs** (Praia da Falésia, tel: 289 500113) between Albufeira and Vilamoura, commanding fine views of Falésia beach.

Soft spikes are prerequisites on some courses, handicap certificates are often required and dress code is normally strict (no jeans, T-shirts or trainers should be worn).

SPORTS CLUBS & WATERSPORTS

Vale do Lobo and Quinta do Lago are ideal (but expensive) options for sports lovers. Apart from golf courses, both resorts have a tennis academy. The one at **Vale do Lobo** (tel: 289 396691) has 14 tennis courts (six floodlit), a swimming pool, a sauna and a gym. Nearby **Barringtons** (Vale do Lobo, tel: 289 396622; www.barringtons-pt.com) offers a huge range of sports.

The excellent **Golf Academy** here has 29 driving range bays, chipping and pitching greens, bunkers, an 18-hole putting green, tuition and computer-swing analysis. Arrive for breakfast and you can get your first bucket of balls free. The Barrington Club also has a fitness centre, a health spa with indoor and outdoor heated pools, a sauna, a solarium and a daily programme of dance aerobics and water fitness at all levels. Other activities include squash, volleyball, cricket, football, rounders and a host of indoor and outdoor games.

Watersports enthusiasts are able to sail, windsurf, canoe, waterski, parasail or go on motorboat trips at **The Watersports Centre** (tel: 289 394929).

HORSE-RIDING

The **Vale do Lobo Riding Centre** (tel: 289 396099) offers treks and hacks, and holds jumping and dressage competitions throughout the year.

VILAMOURA

Vilamoura is also well endowed with sports facilities. You can play tennis, squash or badminton at the **Rock Garden Sports and Leisure Centre** (tel: 289 322740) and there are 12 courts at the **Vilamoura Tennis Centre** (tel: 289 310160). The **Cegonha Riding Centre** (tel: 289 302577) organises group treks through the Vilamoura countryside as well as lessons upon request. Keen cyclists can explore the established cycling trails, and fishing enthusiasts can hire boats or organise excursions from Vilamoura Marina. Trips include shark fishing, shark- and dolphin-watching and reef fishing; and there are also

Albufeira and Central East Algarve

leisurely sightseeing trips to beaches, rocks and grottoes – with or without a barbecue. The marina is also the place to go for information on windsurfing, waterskiing, scuba-diving, snorkelling, parasailing and trips in a hot-air balloon.

ALBUFEIRA

Albufeira offers diving at the **Montechoro Beach Club** and tennis at the **Montechoro Tennis Club**, both at Areias de São João. The finest beaches are those to the west of the resort: São Rafael, Castelo and Galé (▶ 82), Bullfights (▶ 40) take place in Albufeira's **bullring** (Areias de São João, tel: 289 510280/2). Children can be kept entertained at **Atlantic Park** (on the N125 at Quatro Estradas, near Quarteira, tel: 800 204767), which offers hours of fun with its water chutes and tunnels (▶ 83). Mini-golf enthusiasts should try **Krazy Golf** (Lagoa de Viseu, on the Guia/Algoz Messines Road, tel: 282 574134). The course is set in exotic gardens and there's also an animal farm, lakes with water-scooters, quad-bikes, a pool and a playground.

NIGHTLIFE

Albufeira is the social hot spot of the Algarve with everything from discos, clubs and karaoke to late-night bars with live music and mega-screen TVs for sports fans. If it all sounds a bit raucous, you can always go to a small bar for a quiet evening drink or find a hotel with a piano bar, live music or a folklore evening. In the centre of Albufeira the streets are lined with restaurants and lively bars. Popular venues for live music are **Harry's Bar** and **Central Station**, both on Largo Engenheiro Duarte Pacheco. The latter also has a disco, café and *gelataria*. Brasher bars, karaoke joints, shops and restaurants line the neon-lit street between the Hotel Montechoro to the Praia da Oura known as **The Strip**, but it is possible to have a pleasant drink or meal here too, at least early in the evening.

The best discos are out of town. For location you can't beat **Locomia** (Praia de Santa Eulália, tel: 289 542636) east of Albufeira, one of the smarter, more expensive discos with fantastic sea views from the terraces. Music varies from techno and rock to dance. The largest disco in the region and the last one to close (around 6–7 am) is **Kadoc** at Vilamoura on the road to Albufeira (Estrada de Vilamoura, tel: 289 360485). It caters for 7,000, has excellent music (often provided by foreign DJs), and is equipped with eight bars, a viewing terrace and a garden. For something more intimate try the **St James Club** in Almancil (tel: 289 393399), an exclusive restaurant/bar/disco (smart dress only) which offers a drive-you-home service if you've had one too many drinks.

Those who want to gamble their money away can try the **casino** (tel: 289 310000) at Vilamoura. An entrance fee is charged for the gaming tables (not the slot machines) and a passport or ID card is required. The casino has a restaurant and an (optional) nightly floor show.

The **Jazz Club** (Cinema Square, Vilamoura) hosts jazz nights on Fridays and Saturdays; and on the same square the **cinema** shows films in their original language.

Folk dancing takes place once a week at the following hotels: **Sol e Mar** (Rua José Bernardino de Sousa, Albufeira, tel: 289 580080), the **Montechoro** (Hotel Montechoro, Avenida Dr Francisco sa' Carneiro, Albufeira tel: 289 589423; fax: 289 589947), the **Quinta do Lago** (Quinta do Lago, tel: 289 396666) and **Le Meridien Dona Filipa** (Vale do Lobo, tel: 289 294141). Regular concerts – classical, contemporary and jazz – featuring international musicians are staged at the **Centro Cultural São Lourenço** (Almancil, tel: 289 395475), which is located below the church.

Central West Algarve

Getting Your Bearings 94 – 95
In Three Days 96 – 97
Don't Miss 98 – 103
At Your Leisure 104 – 107
Where to... 108 – 112

Central West Algarve

Getting Your Bearings

The area covered in this section – west of Albufeira up to the Alvor Estuary – is the essence of the Algarve's famous Barlavento (windward) coastline. What both the tiny coves of Carvoeiro and the expansive sands of Praia da Rocha and Armação de Pêra all have in common are beautiful beaches, backed by crumbling ochre cliffs and ornamented with surreally eroded rocks, arches, grottoes and stacks. Add a few fishing boats and you have a picture-postcard scene that couldn't be anywhere else in the world but the Algarve.

Previous page: Golden sunset at Praia da Rocha. Below: Big wheel at Zoomarine

Those who knew Carvoeiro and Praia da Rocha in the days before the tourist boom cry "Paradise lost!", and it is undeniable that swathes of this area – Praia da Rocha in particular – have been heavily developed. Come summer, come the crowds, most notably around Carvoeiro where the best advice is to arrive early or late in the day, or preferably at a quieter time of year. But on the larger beaches there's almost always room to be found if you just make the effort to walk that little bit further.

If Praia da Rocha and Carvoeiro are a little overdone for your liking then try Alvor or Ferragudo. Despite its moderately heavy commercialisation, Alvor retains much of its local character and its narrow whitewashed streets are a treat. Ferragudo, on the other hand, is the one that got away – a genuine Algarvian survivor, scarcely touched by all the hoo-ha going on around it.

Boat trips are popular along this coastline and the best views of the Barlavento's strange yet wonderful rock sculptures are from the sea, most notably at Algar Seco, near Carvoeiro. At Portimão, boat

Getting Your Bearings 95

excursions vary from big-game fishing charters to a quiet trip upriver to Silves (➤ 142). A half-day in either of these towns provides a welcome respite from the beach. Silves is the best bet for history while Portimão is known for its shopping and sardines, though it has much more to offer in the culinary stakes. Other alternatives to beach and sea include some of the region's finest golf

View across Praia da Rocha's new marina from the *fortaleza*

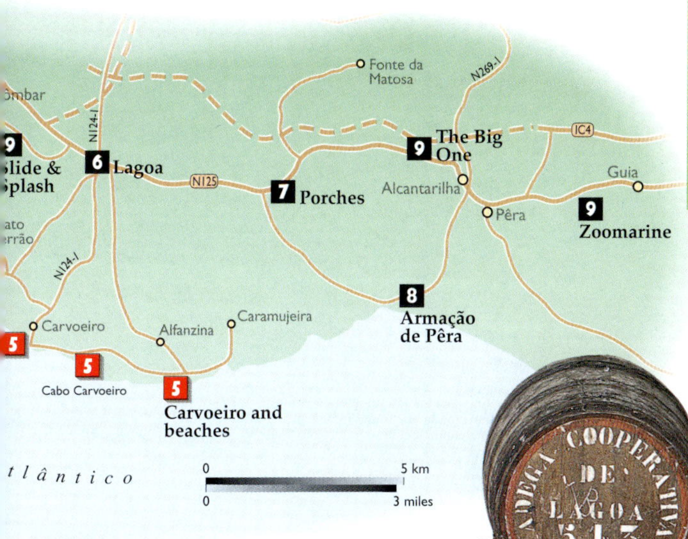

courses and tennis academies, potteries in Porches and family fun at Zoomarine and the two waterparks.

Lagoa's earthy wines pack an alcoholic punch

★ Don't Miss
- **2** Praia da Rocha ➤ 98–9
- **3** Portimão ➤ 100–1
- **5** Carvoeiro and Surrounding Beaches ➤ 102–3

At Your Leisure
- **1** Alvor ➤ 104
- **4** Ferragudo ➤ 104
- **6** Lagoa ➤ 105
- **7** Porches ➤ 105
- **8** Armação de Pêra ➤ 106
- **9** Zoomarine, Slide & Splash and The Big One ➤ 106

Seaside scenery and plump sardines are the specialities of this tour from Alvor along one of the Algarve's prettiest stretches of coast.

Central West Algarve in Three Days

Day One

Morning
Take the N125 to **Portimão** (➤ 100–1) and spend the morning either shopping or on a boat trip (a traditional gondola is pictured left). Enjoy a fish lunch at the Sardine Dock (below left).

Afternoon
Drive back along the old road by the river and stop at the **Museu Municipal** (➤ 101) before continuing on to **Praia da Rocha** (➤ 98–9). Once there, park near the fortress, enjoy the views to Ferragudo, then enjoy the beach for the rest of the day. Watch the sunset at the *miradouro*, then eat at Cabassa (➤ 109). Spend the night in Praia da Rocha.

Day Two

Morning
Make an early start and take the N125 to **Lagoa** (➤ 105). There, turn off to **Carvoeiro** (➤ 102–3). If you can get a parking place, leave your car here and take a boat to one, or more, of the idyllic cove beaches to the east (preferably Benagil – pictured above – or Marinha, ➤ 103). If you can't find somewhere to park in Carvoeiro, drive straight to the beach.

Afternoon
From the coast, return to the N125 and drive the short distance east to **Porches** (➤ 105) for pottery shopping and take afternoon tea at Olaria de Porches (➤ 14–16, 111). Drive back to **Alvor** (➤ 104), watch the sunset over the wetlands – or from the top floor of Hellman's restaurant (➤ 110) – and eat at Tony and Ria's (➤ 105) on the main street of the town, or just off it at Tasca do Guedes.

Day Three

Morning
Drive to Portimão and go over the old road bridge to Ferragudo. You may like to enjoy the beach, by the fortress, especially if you windsurf. Otherwise return to the N125 and head east to either **Zoomarine** (pictured right) or one of the water-parks, **Slide & Splash** (below) and **The Big One** (all ➤ 106), which will occupy the rest of the day.

Praia da Rocha

Star of many a tourism poster, Praia da Rocha ("Beach of the Rocks") is undoubtedly the most impressive south-facing beach in the Algarve, combining picturesque rock formations with masses of space and plenty of sporting activities. Off the beach there is little to see or do (there are no museums or cultural attractions), though Praia da Rocha does have an interesting recent history.

Praia da Rocha is the Algarve's longest-established resort, claiming holiday patronage since 1902. During the many upheavals in Europe in the 1930s it provided a fashionable refuge for writers and intellectuals and during this time was discovered by British holidaymakers. In World War II it was the backdrop for clandestine meetings between generals, political leaders and spies. When tourism in the modern sense took off in the late 1950s and early 1960s, Praia da Rocha was known as the "Queen of the Algarve". Its main street was lined with elegant villas and refined hotels, and the beach was called Aire das Rochas das Artes ("the Place of the Artistic Rocks") reflecting the type of clientele who came here.

The Beach Today

Much has changed since then, not least the beach itself, which was created in its current form in 1969 when one million cubic metres of sand were dredged from the Arade River to push the sea back some 150m. This created the widest cliff-backed beach in Europe, leaving the fantastic rock formations, which previously had their feet in the water, landlocked.

In addition, the elegant mansions of Avenida Tomás Cabreira have mostly been replaced with high-rise hotels, discos and music bars, and "home-from-home" eating joints. Behind the seafront, hotels and tower blocks spike the sky all the way back to Portimão.

It's not really so bad, however. Once you are down on the lovely beach you can easily forget the developments on the clifftop behind you and the eastern part of the avenue is still relatively quiet. The beach ends at the

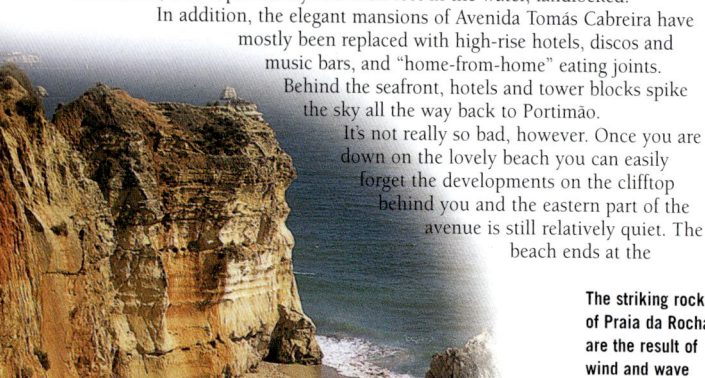

The striking rocks of Praia da Rocha are the result of wind and wave erosion

Praia da Rocha

Fortaleza de Santa Catarina (whose terrace is open to the public), which was built in 1621 along with the castle opposite at Ferragudo (➤ 104) to guard Portimão from Moorish raiders. Today, a pleasure marina below the fortress attracts a friendlier kind of visitor.

TAKING A BREAK

Praia da Rocha has a number of good-quality places to eat. These include **Casalinho** (Praia da Rocha, tel: 282 422579) and **Safari** (off Avenida Tomaz Cabreira, behind Katedral disco, tel: 282 423540).

Above: This cannon once guarded the River Arade from pirates and Moors

Left: Admire the view from the Fortaleza da Santa Catarina

PRAIA DA ROCHA: INSIDE INFO

Top tips During late afternoon or early evening, **go to the *fortaleza*** to watch the fishing boats heading back into Portimão, each one pursued by scores of screeching seagulls.

• Take a walk along the beach to the *miradouro* (lookout point) balcony and see if you can spot The Three Bears, Lion Rock, Grandma's Grotto or The Two Brothers. Sunset is a good time to be here.

• If you want to enjoy the wonderful sands of Praia da Rocha beach but you don't like the over-commercialised aspect of the resort, stay at the adjoining, quieter resort of **Praia da Vau**.

In more depth It is said that **Vasco da Gama** stayed at an earlier castle at Praia da Rocha in 1497 while charting his course around the Cape of Good Hope. It stood on the site now occupied by the Solar Penguin (➤ 9–10, 108).

Portimão

Portimão is synonymous with sardines and it is thanks largely to this humble fish that the river port here grew to become the second biggest regional town after Faro, though today its economy is dependent more upon tourism and commerce than on fishing.

The famous **Sardine Dock** by the old road bridge comprises half a dozen basic fish restaurants churning out barbecued sardines (and other fish) by the trawlerful. As part of a makeover for this part of the river frontage, the restaurants are being moved to the other side of the bridge.

Next to the Sardine Dock you can embark on one of Portimão's well-known **boat trips**. Sightseeing cruises ply the coast – eastwards towards Carvoeiro, westwards towards Lagos – while more single-minded craft pursue big-game fish. Alternatively, when tidal conditions allow, you can float upriver to Silves aboard a picturesque replica of a traditional 19th-century Portuguese gondola. The cruises are relaxing and the scenery is attractive, but do take precautions against the sun. Portimão is also a popular shopping centre (➤ 111) – typically noted for leather goods, shoes, clothes, and perhaps crystal and porcelain. The main thoroughfare is the pedestrianised Rua do Comércio.

Far left: Your visit to Portimão isn't complete unless you eat at the Sardine Dock. Left: Boat trips run throughout the summer

TAKING A BREAK

As an alternative to the Sardine Dock, duck underneath the adjacent arches to the flower-filled square of **Largo da Barca**. Here, around a re-erected red-brick chimney, cluster half a dozen top-quality fish restaurants. Or, **pick up a snack** – there is a good *croissanteria* in the Tropical Shopping Centre, off Rua do Comércio – and picnic in one of the town's small flower-filled gardens.

Museu Municipal Portimão
✉ Avenida Capitão
☎ 282 412238
🕒 Mon–Fri 9.30–12.30, 2–7, Sat 3–7

Alcalar
☎ 282 471410
🕒 Tue–Sun 9–12.30, 2–5.30
💰 Inexpensive

A key episode of Portuguese history depicted in tiles at Largo 1 Dezembro

PORTIMÃO: INSIDE INFO

In more depth At long last Portimão, the old Roman town of *Portus Hannibalis*, has got its own history museum – the **Museu Municipal Portimão**. Located on the river road between Portimão and Praia da Rocha, in an old sardine cannery, it stages temporary exhibitions.
• Another historical attraction is the 5,000-year-old neolithic, passage tomb site of **Alcalar**, between Portimão and Lagos (signposted off the N125 opposite Le Meridien Penina hotel).

Hidden gem Don't miss the cosy square of **Largo 1 de Dezembro** – you'll find it off Rua Judice Biker, between the town centre and the Sardine Dock. It features ten benches covered with beautiful *azulejo* panels depicting pivotal events in Portuguese history. The name of the square commemorates the date in 1640 when Portugal's independence from Spain was restored. The handsome 18th-century building on the square is the old town hall.

Carvoeiro and Surrounding Beaches

Pure Algarve – fishing boats beached at Carvoeiro

Carvoeiro (pronounced "carve-where-oo") lies at the head of a long, pretty, verdant valley. Irish artist Patrick Swift (➤ 14–16) first put Carvoeiro on the map in the 1960s when he made his home here and eulogised its unspoiled coves and valleys in one of the region's first guide books. Unfortunately, a decade or so later the developers moved in and began covering the area in low-rise white apartments, leaving Swift's little Eden massively oversubscribed in high season.

The single entrance road ends at a little square with a small parking area, a tourist office, restaurants, shops, bars and a small triangular cove beach that opens to a width of about 100m. Steep cliffs lined with picturesque painted houses hem it in on both sides while fishing boats ferry tourists to and from Algar Seco and beaches east of here. It's a lovely sight from above. East of Carvoeiro is a series of similar idyllic beaches and coves, most of which have also been developed, albeit to a lesser degree than Carvoeiro.

Naturally formed windows at Algar Seco

Algar Seco
The name means "dry gully" and refers to the grotto-like formations chiselled out of the soft rocks by eons of wind and waves.

Carvoeiro and Surrounding Beaches

There is no proper beach here but steps lead down to a strikingly clear lagoon, which is perfect for snorkellers to explore, as long as the waves are not too high.

Take a stroll to the picturesque Algar Seco from Carvoeiro

Praia de Vale de Centianes

Steps lead down to a long narrow beach backed by cliffs that give welcome afternoon shade, but beware, the tide comes a long way in. It's a very popular spot and has a large hotel perched above, so don't expect it to be deserted.

Praia do Carvalho

This pretty little cove is known as Smuggler's Beach, not least on account of its "secret tunnel" entrance. Like Praia das Centianes, it gets very busy because of nearby hotels. It's a good idea to park at Benagil and walk here as parking may be difficult.

Praia do Benagil

Pictured left, this could be the quintessential Algarve cove beach, with tall sun-trap cliffs, fishing boats and huts. There are a couple of restaurants and bars on the steep hairpin road above, but there are thankfully no other signs of development.

Praia da Marinha

This is the biggest and arguably the most beautiful of this stretch of beaches, with any development kept well in the background. There is a reasonably sized car park up on the cliffs so (if you get here early) even in high season you should find a space.

TAKING A BREAK

There are bars in town, but why not take a packed lunch down to the sea? Don't leave your litter there, however!

Praia da Marinha – the beaches along this stretch just keep on getting better

---

CARVOEIRO & SURROUNDING BEACHES: INSIDE INFO

Top tips Visiting other beaches by boat from Carvoeiro is fun and will save you the problem of parking.
• Another option is to take the "**land-train**" that shuttles to and from the nearest beaches (however, you do still have the problem of parking in Carvoeiro itself).

At Your Leisure

The bright yellow-trimmed Igreja Matriz at Alvor is one of the west's finest churches

❶ Alvor

Despite its many touristy restaurants, shops and bars, the little fishing village of Alvor has managed to retain a good deal of character. (Accommodation is mostly in the various large hotels to the east.) Its narrow tangle of whitewashed streets tumbles down into the Alvor Estuary, a picturesque shallow wetlands area with a lifeboat station, a fish market and dozens of boats at anchor. During the 1990s this lovely spot became a battleground between conservationists and developers but now the latter have prevailed; although the wetlands remain protected the construction of a marina has begun.

The parish church of Alvor dates back to the 16th century and is worth a look just for its extravagant Manueline portal (➤ 21). The interior is light and airy with some fine *azulejos* on show.

There are some good beaches here, notably the expansive Praia de Alvor and the coves of Três Irmãos and João de Arens.

🕂 183 D2

Alvor tourist office
✉ Rua Dr Afonso Costa 51
☎ 282 457523

❹ Ferragudo

Situated on the opposite bank of the River Arade with the high-rise towers of Portimão and Praia da Rocha clearly in sight, Ferragudo is a rare unspoiled haven on a highly developed stretch of coast. Wander through the steep picturesque streets behind the village square up to the church. Enjoy the views, then keep going until you reach the Castelo de São João de Arade. Built in the 1600s

Unspoiled Ferragudo, from across the river Arade, is a striking sight

At Your Leisure

For Kids
- **Zoomarine** (➤ 107) for its sea lions and other performing animals.
- **Slide & Splash** or **The Big One** for aqua rides and thrills in the sunshine (➤ 107).
- **Praia da Rocha beach** (➤ 98–9): let little ones run wild on this great stretch of sand, while older kids can explore the rocks or use the sports area for playing games of football, basketball or volleyball.

You can buy authentic souvenirs from roadside potteries like this one

to guard the river approach, it was added to in the 17th and 18th centuries then converted into a domestic dwelling around 100 years ago. Unfortunately it is off limits to visitors. Adjacent, Praia Grande is a popular beach for watersports.

☐ 183 E2

❻ Lagoa
Lagoa is famous locally for its wine, produced at a large co-operative plant on the main N125. You can taste and buy at its factory shop, but tours are available to pre-booked groups only. The town's other attraction is its festival grounds, used for a number of shows throughout the year. The big one is FATACIL, a trade fair featuring local agricultural and handicrafts displays, with music and food- and wine-tasting, which takes place in the third week of August. Portuguese Gastronomy week is held in June.

The main point of interest in the town is the Convento de São José, which has a pretty cloister enclosing a menhir that is thought to be between 6,000 and 7,000 years old.

☐ 183 E2

❼ Porches
Just as Portimão implies sardines, so Porches implies pottery. The craft was revived in this area in the 1960s (➤ 14–16) and has thrived ever since, prompting a rash of roadside vendors along the N125. However, it's worth turning off the main road to explore the quiet, unspoiled village itself – if only to see what is probably the Algarve's finest chimneypot. Just behind the acclaimed O Leão de Porches restaurant is a giant, plain white chimneypot, but the one you are looking for is in the square behind this. Picked out in bright yellow painted relief is a bizarre figure with the head of a man, the body of a

Five Fish Restaurants
Casa Bica (Sardine Dock, Portimão, no telephone).
Casalinho, on the beach (Praia da Rocha, tel: 282 422579).
Dona Barca (Largo da Barca, Portimão, tel: 282 484189, ➤ 109).
Taverna do Guedes (Rua dos Pescadores, Alvor, tel: 282 458528).
Tony and Ria's (Rua Dr Frederico Ramos Mendes, Alvor, tel: 282 458444).

Central West Algarve

woman, a fan in place of one hand and feet melding into a cartwheel motif. It is the unofficial symbol of the village.

✚ 183 F2

8 Armação de Pêra

From the resort's palm-lined promenade you can enjoy the sight of the biggest beach in the south. To the western end (eyes right) is the classic Algarve scene of ochre rock-stacks and cliffs, while to the east (eyes left) flat sands stretch all the way to Praia de Galé, near Albufeira (➤ 82). The boats on the beach mark the original part of town, the fishermen's quarter. Much of it has been developed but this is still the place to come for good, inexpensive fish restaurants.

There are two pretty cove beaches just west of Armação de Pêra. The first is Praia Nossa Senhora da Rocha, dotted with fishing boats and protected by two great natural cliff breakwaters that extend 100m or so out to sea. Perched on top of one of them is the hermitage of Nossa Senhora da Rocha (Our Lady of the Rocks), a curious little white hexagonal chapel with an octagonal dome. The interior dates back to the 16th century and you can see inside through a grille even when it is locked. A tunnel leads through the westernmost cliff to the beach of Praia Nova.

✚ 183 F2
Armação de Pêra tourist office
✉ Avenida Marginal ☎ 282 312145

You can spot dolphins off Sagres but they are not as well trained as those at Zoomarine

The little sanctuary of Nossa Senhora da Rocha high above the Atlantic waves

Alvor's Royal Visitor

Alvor's most famous guest was King João II, who came here in 1495 after falling ill in Monchique. The chronicles record that as he lay dying the bishop closed the monarch's eyes, at which the king gasped, "Bishop, it is not time yet!" Then he promptly passed away.

Although dropsy was the official cause of death, conspiracy theory has it that the king was poisoned by the Spanish, who wanted to seize the crown, though he was also unpopular with the Portuguese nobility for weakening their power.

At Your Leisure

Waterparks
- All three parks have their own courtesy coaches picking up from hotels as far afield as Quarteira and Lagos. Ask for a timetable at your hotel or the nearest travel agency.
- Many visitors start departing by coach for their resorts from around 4pm onwards. If you have your own transport and can arrive late, or stay until this time, queues for the most exciting rides shorten considerably.

🡒 Slide & Splash
This is the Algarve's biggest and most exciting waterpark with the usual array of spaghetti-like tubes and slides galore. The biggest lines form to take on the Black Hole, a thrilling drop in the dark.

🖶 183 E2 ✉ Vale de Deus, near Estombar, just off the N125
☎ 282 341685 ⏰ Daily Easter–Oct. Opening times vary by season. Telephone for exact dates and times
💰 Expensive

Slide 'n' splash 'n' swim 'n' surf or just get soaked by water cannons

🡒 Zoomarine
Although Zoomarine claims to take its theme from the region's links with the sea, it is doubtful that you will see many seals, sea lions, sharks, turtles, crocodiles or tropical fish swimming wild in the Algarve – nor parrots flying about the countryside. The stars of the show are the dolphins (which do live in Algarvian waters), but this park is actually all about Florida-style razzamatazz, and to this end it works well. Apart from the shows there is a tropical aquarium, a cinema, fairground rides, arcade games and swimming pools.

🖶 184 A2 ✉ N125, Guia
☎ 289 560300; www.zoomarine.com
⏰ Tue–Sun 10–5, Jan–Mar and Nov–Dec; 10–6, Apr–Jun, last two weeks Sep–Oct; 10–7.30, Jul–mid-Sep. Swimming pools close Nov–Mar
🍴 Café 💰 Expensive

🡒 The Big One
Actually Slide & Splash is the Algarve's big one, but this isn't a bad second and good for younger children, who are given their own special area. It's not for wimps though – dare you drop 23m on Banzai, the highest freefall float slide in Portugal, or slide 92m on Kamikaze, the longest speed slide in the Algarve? There are also two labyrinth (tube) slides and Raging Rapids (where you are thrown around on inflatable dinghies), plus numerous other slides and a wave pool. Beware of queues and crowds in high season.

🖶 183 F2 ✉ Alcantarilha ☎ 282 322827; www.bigone-waterpark.com
⏰ Daily Easter–Oct. Opening times vary by season. Telephone or see Website for exact dates and times
🍴 Snack kiosks and cafés
💰 Expensive

Where to... Stay

Prices
Expect to pay per double room per night:
£ under €50 **££** €50–125 **£££** over €125

Bela Vista ££
This fine clifftop mansion was one of the first hotels to be built in the Algarve; a private turn-of-the-century home converted when Praia da Rocha (the first resort in the Algarve) merely comprised a handful of villas. Décor is traditional, with fine wood panelling, stained glass and original tiled scenes decorating the dimly lit public rooms and stairway. Praia da Rocha's beach lies just below, and the large open-air seaview terrace is the perfect spot for breakfast or an evening drink.

☐ 183 D2 ✉ **Praia da Rocha, 8500-802 Portimão** ☎ **282 450480; fax: 282 415369**

Carlton Alvor £££
Formerly the Alvor Praia, this has been taken over by the Pestana chain. It has a fine location, overlooking the golden sands of Praia dos Três Irmãos. The hotel is large and modern, with facilities including an outdoor heated pool, seven tennis courts and a beauty salon. The three restaurants serve Portuguese, Italian and international cuisine. Facilities at the Dom João II Hotel (including a children's club and a golf driving range) are available to guests here.

☐ 183 D2 ✉ **Praia dos Três Irmãos, 8501 904 Alvor, Portimão** ☎ **282 400900; fax: 282 400999; email: pestana.hotels@mail.telepac.pt**

Casa Bela Moura £
If the luxury hotels in Armação de Pera are beyond your budget, this spotless 12-room guesthouse offers an attractive alternative. Built in Moorish style, it is in open countryside, set back from the road and 1.5km from the lovely beach of Nossa Senhora da Rocha (▶ 106). The hotel comprises a lounge-bar, breakfast room and bedrooms, a pool and an annexe. Rooms are decorated in local or Alentejo style, with painted furniture.

☐ 183 F2 ✉ **Estrada de Porches, 8365 Armação de Pera** ☎ **282 313422; fax: 282 313025**

Le Meridien Penina £££
Set in its own 140ha estate, with a championship golf course and Olympic-size pool, Le Meridien ranks among the most luxurious hotels in the Algarve. Established in the 1960s, it preserves a traditional décor and ambience while offering a range of amenities for all ages. In summer young children receive supervised attention at the Penguin Village, while the Junior Academy offers sporting activities for 8–15 year olds – at a price. The hotel also has a tennis and horse-riding centre, football pitch, health centre and three restaurants. In summer a shuttle bus takes guests to the hotel beach at Alvor, where there is a bar, restaurant and watersports.

☐ 183 D2 ✉ **PO Box 146 Penina, 8501-952 Portimão** ☎ **282 420200; fax: 282 420300; email: meridienalg.sm@mail.telepac.pt**

Solar Penguin £
An oasis of quiet and gentility in a resort not known for taste or restraint, the Solar Penguin is a survivor of the Algarve as it once was. It is run by Dorothy Boulter (▶ 9–10), who is a kind and attentive host. Rooms are comfortable if old-fashioned, and in need of refurbishment. There is also some early morning noise from holidaymakers falling out of nearby bars and discos. All can be forgiven, however, when you see the view from its

Where to...
Eat and Drink

Prices
Expect to pay per person for a meal, excluding drinks and service
£ under €15   ££ €15–23   £££ over €23

A Santola ££
The sea and beach views alone would justify a visit to A Santola, set near the walls of the old fort on perhaps the Algarve's longest beach. The menu caters for all tastes, from spaghetti Bolognese to fish *cataplana* or lobster live from the tank. To end the meal treat yourself to one of the house flambéed desserts.

✚ 183 F2 ☒ Largo da Fortaleza, Armação de Pêra ☎ 282 312332
☯ Daily lunch and dinner

Cabassa ££
This deservedly popular Italian restaurant is at the quieter end of Praia da Rocha, near the old fort. Across the road from the beach, it has a large open-air terrace with sea views. Choose from pizzas or home-made pastas such as tortellini with salmon, gnocchi with gorgonzola, cannelloni with *requeijão* (fresh cheese) and spinach, followed by fish or meat or a blend of the two (*frutos do mar e peito de frango*, seafood and chicken breast). Then go for the traditional Italian desserts of *tiramisu*, *zabuglione* or *gelato*.

✚ 183 D2 ☒ Avenida Tómaz Cabreira, Praia da Rocha ☎ 282 424307 ☯ Tue– Sun lunch and dinner. Closed Nov–Mar

Casa Inglesa £
The café acquired its name many years ago when the first British to buy villas in the Algarve came here to read English newspapers. You could – and still can– buy papers from the next door newsagent. The café continues to be a favourite British haunt, where gossip is swapped over coffee with cakes. The interior is a bit gloomy but there's a sunny terrace where you can watch the world go by. Snacks are served all day; you can also buy chocolates and almond sweets in the shape of fruits and fish.

✚ 183 D2 ☒ Praça Teixeira Gomes, 3, Portimão ☎ 282 416290 ☯ Daily 8 am–11 pm

Dona Barca £
One of the best-value restaurants in the Algarve, the Dona Barca lies behind the old sardine quay, through the arches under the road. Fresh fish, landed locally, is likely to be sizzling on the grill on the restaurant terrace. The *prato do dia* (dish of the

---

terrace: a magnificent panorama of Praia da Rocha beach which is worth the price of the room alone.

✚ 183 D2 ☒ Rua António Feu, off Avenida Tomas Cabreira, Praia da Rocha ☎ 282424 308; fax: 282424 308; email: residencial.penguin@mail.telepac.pt

Vila Vita Parc £££
One of the most luxurious hotels in the Algarve, the Vila Vita Parc is set among subtropical gardens sloping down to the beach. With five restaurants, seven bars, wine-tasting cellar, nightclub, tennis, squash, pitch and putt, four pools, watersports, a health centre and a kids' park, this is more of a resort than a hotel. Rooms include junior and family suites, villas with their own pools or – for the ultimate in luxury – your own 22m yacht equipped with three cabins.

✚ 183 F2 ☒ PO Box 196, 8365-911 Armação de Pêra ☎ 282 310100; fax: 282 315333; email: reservas@vilavitaparc.com; www.vilavita.com

Central West Algarve

day) is always a good bet – as is the sea bass, *cataplana* or, if you are in a group, the mixed seafood platter.

✚ 183 D2 ☒ Largo da Barca, Portimão ☎ 282 484189 ❽ Daily lunch and dinner

Hellmans ££

At the harbour in Alvor, this popular Swedish-run restaurant has breathtaking views over the estuary from its rooftop terrace. The menu combines traditional local and modern international fare. Fish options are likely to feature the grilled catch of the day (ask the waiter for size and price). Alvor clams in white wine and garlic, shellfish in a creamy saffron sauce or the irresistible seafood platter for two, combining crabs, tiger prawns, shrimps and clams.

✚ 183 D2 ☒ Alvor Harbour, Portimão ☎ 282 458208 ❽ Daily dinner. Closed Nov–Mar

O Buque ££

The reliable Portuguese cuisine here more than compensates for the uninspiring setting, in a Portimão suburb on the traffic-laden N125. Named after an old type of sardine-fishing boat, O Buque is a family run restaurant that's usually full of locals. If you have the chance, place an order a day in advance for one of their specialities: *caldeirada* (fish stew), *bouillabaisse* (fish soup) or oven-cooked wild rabbit. Fish dishes are advertised on the board outside.

✚ 183 E2 ☒ N125, Parchal (2km east of Portimão) ☎ 282 424678 ❽ Mon–Fri lunch and dinner, Sat dinner. Closed mid-Jan to mid-Feb

Sambal ££

For a change from Portuguese cuisine, try this intimate Indo-Asian restaurant in a side street up from the harbour and gardens. The menu includes Indonesian, Thai, Malaysian, Chinese or Indian dishes. A nightly buffet offers at least a dozen different Indonesian dishes (such as fresh red snapper). After dinner, sit back and enjoy live music or dance 'til the early hours of the morning. Reservations are advisable, and credit cards are not accepted.

✚ 183 D2 ☒ Rua Santa Isabel, 14–16, Portimão ☎ 282 422072 ❽ Tue–Sun 7 pm–2 am

Somewhere Else ££

A restaurant with a difference, this one lets you cook your own choice of meat or fish on hot lava stones. Choose from seven types of meat, including steak, chicken and ostrich, or opt for tuna, swordfish or salmon. The main courses are served with a choice of sauces along with chips and salad or potatoes and vegetables of the season. A vegetarian menu and children's menu are also available.

✚ 183 D2 ☒ Rua Poeta João de Deus, Alvor ☎ 282 458595 ❽ Daily lunch and dinner

Titanic £££

Save this one for a special night out. The setting, on the ground floor of a skyscraper set back some distance from the sea, is initially uninspiring but inside the restaurant lives up to its name with a shipwreck theme (and a tank of live lobsters). The menu is international, a typical meal consisting of Titanic-style prawns, fillet steak and crêpes Suzette.

✚ 183 D2 ☒ Edifício Columba, Rua Engenheiro Francisco Bivar, Praia da Rocha, Portimão ☎ 282 422371 ❽ Daily dinner. Closed late Nov–late Dec

Togi ££

Away from Carvoeiro's busy centre, the Togi has a tranquil garden setting on the road to Algar Seco. This is a Dutch-run, dinner-only restaurant. Try *corvina a Carvoeiro* (sea bass with herbs), or steak Togi (with red wine and fresh peppers), and wash them down with excellent house wine from the Alentejo. The absence of a cover charge (very rare for Portugal) is a pleasant surprise when it comes to paying the bill.

✚ 183 E2 ☒ Rua das Flores 12, Algar Seco, 8401-908 Carvoeiro ☎ 282 358517 ❽ Daily dinner. Closed Nov–Feb

Where to...
Shop

PORTIMÃO

Portimão is arguably the best shopping centre in the Algarve. Being a fishing port rather than a tourist resort, the shops are not geared for the mass tourist market and you can pick up some excellent bargains.

The town offers a wide choice of leather goods, crystal and ceramics, linen and lace, clothes and jewellery. Many of the shops are factory outlets whose prices are far cheaper than in the main Algarve resorts.

Portimão's main shopping streets are Rua do Comércio and Rua Vasco da Gama, both off the main Praça da República. **O Aquário** (Rua Vasco da Gama 42–46, also at Praça da República and Rua Direita, Edifício Delmar 10) is known for its large selection of crystal, copper, brass and porcelain, including Atlantis, a Portuguese full-lead crystal, and Vista Alegre, the finest porcelain in Portugal. **Rua Direita** is the other main shopping street in town, a busy thoroughfare with fashions, shoe shops, jewellery and some high-quality linen and lace.

For art, antiques and designerware try **Rua Santa Isabel**, where the shops occupy the ground floors of some of the town's finer houses. The **Galeria Portimão** (No 5) exhibits stylish modern art; **St James** (No 26) has reasonably priced Charles Jourdan shoes; **Louca's International Clothing** (Nos 19–23) sells designer label clothes; and **Bobi** (No 36) is a good source of unusual ceramic gifts.

POTTERY AND PORCHES

The roadside potteries on the N125 are the best source of ceramics in the Algarve. The choice is endless, from cheap models of snails and roosters to Greek and Roman-style jugs. Several of the shops lure tourists with their signs for free port and wine tasting – others have a bar or sometimes a restaurant to revive weary shoppers. However, much of what you see, including plain terracotta with white floral patterning and the attractive handpainted pieces with fish or flower designs, comes from the Alentejo. For local ceramics the best sources are the potteries at Porches (▶ 14–16, 105–6).

If you are seeking high-quality studio ceramics as opposed to mass-market pottery in Porches, Ian Fitzpatrick's studio (▶ 15–16) is the place to go. All items are individually crafted in a vibrant, bold, naturalistic southern European style and, unlike 99 per cent of the wares on sale locally, Ian's pieces are microwave and oven proof.

High-quality, handpainted majolica-style pottery at reasonable prices is the hallmark of the pioneering **Olaria de Porches** (▶ 25) on the N125. Swirling blue and green acanthus leaves, flowers, fruits and birds are typical of their naïve local-style motifs. If you would like to have a piece personalized, you must order 7–10 days ahead. Attached to the shop, the Bar Bacchus with tiled benches (naturally!) shaded by bougainvillea is a lovely spot for a light lunch or coffee and carrot cake (summer only). Just a few metres east on the other side of the N125 (set back and easy to miss) is the **Olaria Pequena** (the Little Pottery).

WINE AT LAGOA

Lagoa is the Algarve's principal wine producing area. Best known for its potent (13–13.5 per cent proof), robust red wine, local wineries also produce a Lagoan white, a rosé and *aguardente*, a golden sugar-cane spirit. The *cooperativa* on the Portimão road holds daily guided tours (book ahead; tel: 282 342181) where you can see cork-fitting and label-painting done by hand and also, for a fee, taste the wine itself.

Central West Algarve

Where to...
Be Entertained

BOAT TRIPS

Portimão is the main centre in the Algarve for **big-game fishing**. The most common species in local waters are the blue shark and the streamlined mako (prized for its speed and dramatic leaps out of the sea). Boats are equipped with fighting chairs and the latest electronic devices. For information, contact the **Big Game Fishing Centre** (Rua António Dias Cordeiro, 1, Portimão, tel: 282 425866). Alternatively, join a **ground-fishing trip** closer to shore for sea bream, conger, moray eel, octopus and squid. For details, go to the port or contact **Fred Steel** (tel: 917 433548).

Several companies offer **half-day coastal cruises**, visiting caves, grottoes and secluded beaches. Go to the fishing port, where companies vie for trade. Some, such as **Boat Tours** (tel: 282 495654), can arrange transport from hotels.

GOLF

Penina (5km west of Portimão on the N125, tel: 282 420200), designed by Henry Cotton, is a landscaped 18-hole course where the Portuguese Open has been held. Carvoeiro has three courses: the **Pinta** and the **Gramacho** are both scenic, 18-hole courses at the Pestana Golf and Resort (tel: 282 340900) and the nine-hole **Vale de Milho** (Praia do Carvoeiro, tel: 282 358502), suitable for beginners. Cotton also designed the **Alto Golfe** (between Alvor and Portimão, tel: 282 416913), the course with the longest par five in Europe (➤ 26).

WATERSPORTS

Windsurfers, sailors and waterskiers can practise at Praia do Carvoeiro, Praia da Rocha and Armação de Pêra. The **Dive Centre** (Divers Cove, Quinta do Paraíso, Praia do Carvoeiro, tel: 282 356594) runs courses for all standards and hires out diving and snorkelling equipment.

Inland, the **Slide & Splash** waterpark (N125, Vale de Deus, Estômbar, tel: 282 341685) provides entertainment for children, as does **Zoomarine** (west of Guia on the N125), with its dolphin, sea lion and parrot shows, a sea museum and a shark aquarium (➤ 107).

HORSE-RIDING

One of the best riding schools is the **Centro Hípico Vale de Ferro** (Mexilhoeira Grande, tel: 282 968444), offering scenic treks in the foothills of Monchique and a free pick-up service from the Lagos/Portimão area.

TENNIS

Tennis players have a choice of hotels with courts or the **Rocha Brava Tennis Club** (Praia do Carvoeiro, tel: 282 358856), which offers tuition and equipment for hire.

MUSIC AND NIGHTLIFE

Portimão's municipal auditorium and town hall host concerts performed by international and local groups; choral music is performed in the main church, Igreja Matriz, in the centre of town.

The most popular spot for lively nightlife is Praia da Rocha, with a casino, several discos and dozens of loud late-night bars with live music. For a more peaceful setting, try the bar and seaview terrace of the **Bela Vista Hotel** (➤ 108). At the **Hotel Algarve Casino** (Avenida Tomás Cabreira, tel: 282 415001), you can place your bets in the gaming rooms (passport or ID required) and enjoy the nightly floor show.

The West

Getting Your Bearings 114 – 115
In Three Days 116 – 117
Don't Miss 118 – 127
At Your Leisure 128 – 131
Where to… 132 – 136

Getting Your Bearings

Head west of Lagos on the N125, and, as if by magic, the snarling traffic vanishes. Your grip on the steering wheel relaxes, holiday developments fall away, the sky becomes bigger and wider. At Vila do Bispo you start to wonder where everyone, and everything, has gone.

The west is for those who want to get away from it all, and it is particularly attractive for beach lovers. The rest of the Algarve may have some great beaches but those of the west are truly magnificent. Moreover, you can often have them all to yourself – though there is a price to pay. It is the relative remoteness and the cool waters and chill winds of the western seaboard that have made tourist development here much less desirable than in the south and east. Out of season and on grey days this is indeed a place for hardy souls, but don't worry – there *are* sheltered beaches and many warm days, even on this coast. The other good news for seekers of peace and quiet is that from Burgau all the way "around the corner" to Odeceixe, at the far northwestern corner of the Algarve, this coastline is now part of the protected Parque Natural da Costa Vicentina.

★ Don't Miss

- ❶ Lagos ➤ 118–20
- ❷ Lagos Beaches and Coves ➤ 121–2
- ❽ Fortaleza de Sagres and Cabo de São Vicente ➤ 123–5
- ❾ Beaches ➤ 126–7

At Your Leisure

- ❸ Luz (Praia da Luz) ➤ 128
- ❹ Burgau ➤ 129
- ❺ Salema ➤ 129
- ❻ Vila do Bispo ➤ 129
- ❼ Sagres ➤ 130
- ❿ Aljezur ➤ 131

Getting Your Bearings 115

Surf's up at Praia de Beliche but don't forget your wetsuit in these cool Atlantic waters

The West has more to it than beaches, however. Lagos is the most characterful and historically interesting town in the Algarve, while Sagres and Cape St Vincent combine to conjure up the ghosts of Henry the Navigator, Magellan and the great days of the Discoveries. If you like the company of fellow holidaymakers and familiar international-style trappings, stay at Lagos, Luz, Burgau or Salema. But if you want to really immerse yourself in the western Algarve, there are plenty of other places where you can find your own escape far from the madding crowds of the east.

The West

Mighty beaches on a spectacular coastline haunted by the ghost of Henry the Navigator make this tour of the west a mini-epic. Do your historical homework first in Lagos and, if possible, avoid Mondays, when many attractions are closed.

The West in Three Days

Day One

Morning
Follow the walking tour of historical **Lagos** (▶ 154–5) and then choose from the many good places to lunch, or assemble a picnic from the colourful municipal market.

Afternoon
Take a boat trip from the fortress around the Lagos coastline, so that you can

view the spectacular **Ponte da Piedade** rock formations (➤ 122 and pictured opposite, top), and ask the boatman if he will drop you off on the idyllic **Dona Ana beach** (➤ 122 and pictured opposite, bottom). Or, if that is too busy, go back to the fort and use the adjacent beach, or walk across the river to **Meia Praia beach** (➤ 121). Spend the night in Lagos.

Day Two

Morning
Head west along the N125 to visit the **Fortaleza de Sagres** and **Cabo de São Vicente** (➤ 123–5) and book lunch at the Fortaleza do Beliche (➤ 134).

Afternoon
Take a boat trip spotting dolphins or catching big-game fish from Sagres harbour. If there is still an hour or two of sunshine, mop it up on one of the town beaches. Head back to Cape St Vincent to watch the sunset and stay the night at Sagres.

Day Three

Morning
Head north from Sagres along the N268, turning off at **Vila do Bispo** (➤ 129) to **Praia da Cordama** (➤ 126) and its spectacular lookout point. Continue north and check out the magnificent beach of **Amado** (➤ 126), then have lunch at neighbouring **Praia do Bordeira** (➤ 126).

Afternoon
Spend a couple of hours on either Amado or Bordeira beaches then continue north on the N268 to **Aljezur** (➤ 131). If your appetite for spectacular coastal scenery has not been sated, take a detour 6km west to Arrifana. Alternatively, take a break with a cold drink or a cup of coffee under the shady trees at Aljezur (pictured above). When you've had enough relaxation, head back south on the N268 then branch off left on the N120 to Lagos where you can spend the evening and the night.

Lagos

Still partly enclosed by medieval walls, Lagos (pronounced "lah-goosh") has more history and character than any other town in the Algarve. It's by no means uncommercialised – there are British-style bars, touristy shops, restaurants and even a couple of fast-food places – but only one large hotel (discretely tucked away), and the atmosphere is altogether different from the resorts to the east. Even the centre of town has a lived-in feel (note the old-fashioned hardware shops next to the restaurants on Rua 25 de Abril) and a bohemian atmosphere pervades the backstreets, with backpackers and independent travellers stopping a night or two, *en route* to the west. Moreover, Lagos has some excellent restaurants, good shops and nightlife, plus superb beaches on its doorstep.

Commanding the inlet to Lagos, the Forte da Ponte da Bandeira is a typical Algarvian sea fortress

The N125 runs right into the Avenida dos Descobrimentos (Avenue of the Discoveries), which runs alongside the river and separates the fishing harbour, a pleasure marina and the beach of **Meia Praia** (➤ 121) from the town.

At the end of the Avenida is the neat little 17th-century **Forte da Ponte da Bandeira**, built to guard the harbour. There's little of historical importance inside, though it's worth a quick look to see its chapel and displays on the theme of the Discoveries (captioned in Portuguese only).

Lagos

Outside the fort, fishing boats depart to view the nearby caves and grottoes to the west, including the **Ponta da Piedade** (➤ 122). Adjacent to the fort is a picturesque little cove beach.

A Tour of the Town

The history of Lagos is dominated by Prince Henry the Navigator, whose pioneering work launched Portugal as a great maritime nation (➤ 6–7). His statue (pictured right) at the top end of the Avenida, on the square of Praça da República, marks the site of his residence before it was destroyed in the Great Earthquake of 1755 (➤ 78).

A darker reminder of the past can be found in the top right-hand corner of the square, below the old custom house. Here the small arcade, now housing an art gallery, bears a plaque proclaiming that this was the Mercado dos Escravos (Slave Market). It was the first slave market in Europe, used from 1444 onwards (➤ 154, 155).

Leave the square via Rua de São Gonçalo to reach the **Igreja de Santo António**, although the entrance is around the corner via the **Museu Municipal**. Built c1710–20, and added to after the Great Earthquake, the church's high baroque interior is completely covered with gilded woodwork and is probably the finest example of its kind in Portugal. The pictures around the wall relate the many bizarre miracles of Santo António (St Anthony) and it's well worth buying the guide book on sale in the church to decipher these. Another curiosity is the prominent **floor tombstone** of Hugh ("Hugo") Beaty, d.1789, an Irish colonel who commanded the Lagos regiment in the war with Spain.

The museum's eclectic little collection begins with prehistoric menhirs and some excellent mosaics from **Milreu** (➤ 58), then continues with more ancient artefacts and pickled freak animal foetuses, including a seven-legged calf, a two-headed cat and a Cyclopean lamb's head. There's exotic weaponry from Portugal's ex-colonies, folklore items and also a quaint scale model of an *Aldeia*

A tome from the time of the Great Discoveries

The West

Imaginária (Imaginary Village), which crams in every conceivable Algarvian feature.

To continue exploring Lagos walk up the Rua 25 de Abril, the main shopping and restaurants street, then follow the recommended walking tour of the town (➤ 154–5).

Watch the world go by at a pavement café in Lagos

TAKING A BREAK

Grab a shot of espresso, a juice or a shake at trendy **Café Xpreitaqui** (Rua da Silva Lopes), or take a pot of tea in the sedate **Casa Amarela** (Rua 25 de Abril).

Forte da Ponte da Bandeira
✚ 182 C2
✉ Avenida dos Descobrimentos
🕐 Tue–Sat 10–1, 2–6; Sun 10–1
💰 Inexpensive

Museu Municipal/Igreja do Santo António
✚ 182 C2
✉ Rua General Alberto da Silveira
☎ 282 762301
🕐 Tue–Sun 9.30–12.30, 2–5
💰 Inexpensive

In amongst the gilding at São Antonio church, you'll find minature scenes of everyday life

LAGOS: INSIDE INFO

Top tips Avoid visiting Lagos on a **Monday**: the Museu Municipal, Igreja do Santo António, Forte da Ponte da Bandeira and several restaurants all close.

Hidden gem Tucked away in the backstreets on Rua 1 de Maio, **Bar Ferradura** (➤ 25) is an authentic local's bar that is also very visitor friendly.

Lagos Beaches and Coves

The delights of Lagos spread well outside its ancient city walls. Its picturesque little cove beaches, immediately west, are some of the prettiest and most photographed in Europe. Inevitably such publicity (and ease of accessibility) draws crowds, and large hotels built on top of the cliffs mean that in high season these sands are some of the busiest in the Algarve. If you're after space, you will have to come out of season or arrive early in the day. Here are the best beaches, heading from east to west.

Praia do Camilo in the early morning

Meia Praia

The town beach, as it is known, is some 4km long, mostly featureless and completely open – quite unlike the beaches due west. However, because of its size it is rarely crowded. Surfers may be able to catch a wave here, though families should beware of currents.

It's only a five-minute walk to the nearest part of the beach from the town centre and here you'll find the popular Bar Linda (see "Taking a Break") and the Lagos Watersports Centre. If you do hire from here, don't be like King Sebastião: he sailed from Meia Praia in 1578 (➤ 7–8), never to return!

Praia da Batata/Praia dos Estudantes

Next to the fort, and even closer to town than Meia Praia, is this dual-named, attractive small beach. It is partly backed by a cliff and, with a handful of stacks, arches and rock formations, it provides an appetiser for the beaches and coves just to the west. Predictably, proximity to town means it can get very busy in high season.

Praia Dona Ana

This is the beach that launched a thousand travel posters – a real beauty with high cliffs and rock formations dividing it into one larger stretch and a clutch of cosy coves. But a large hotel and other developments sit atop, and in season Dona Ana gets busy.

Praia do Camilo

A short walk west and a little less crowded, Camilo is worth trying when Dona Ana reaches overload point. Very attractive, if not as extravagantly endowed with rocky features as its neighbour.

Ponta da Piedade

The "Bridge of Piety" is the Algarve's most visited rock formation, with a series of beautiful arches, stacks and grottoes attracting boats from as far as Portimão. You can either take a boat from Lagos town (➤ 118–20) or park next to the lighthouse and walk down a series of steps to the crystal waters (no sand) where boatmen are waiting to ferry you around.

Porto de Mós

This long beach is backed with cliffs at the eastern end, fading down to ground level as it heads west. It's quite attractive and less busy than Dona Ana and Camilo, though some huge developments threaten to swamp it. The acclaimed diving school, Blue Ocean Divers (tel: 282 782 718; formerly the Luz Bay Diving Club), now operates from here.

TAKING A BREAK

Bar Linda (tel: 282 792146; closed Mondays) at the town end of Meia Praia is the closest spot for good food with sand between your toes. There are no other particularly good cafés by the beaches.

Exploring the turquoise waters of Ponta da Piedade

LAGOS BEACHES AND COVES: INSIDE INFO

Top tips Visit **Ponta da Piedade** in the morning when the sun is high and brings out the brilliant blues and glistening greens in the water.
• Return here in the evening to **watch the sunset**.
• In high summer, when the pretty little cove beaches to the west of the town centre are heaving and the traffic along the N125 is gridlocked, just stroll across the river to **Meia Praia beach**: there's always room here.

Fortaleza de Sagres and Cabo de São Vicente

The location of the Fortaleza (Fortress) de Sagres could hardly be more dramatic, or more apt as the launch pad for the 15th-century voyages of discovery sponsored by Henry the Navigator (▶ 6–8). Perched on a narrow finger of land, rising sheer 60m above the roaring waves, it prods the cold Atlantic defiantly and stares straight across to the New World. Outside the fortress perimeter local fishermen dangling lines from oversize rods dice with death on the cliff-edge, which plummets to the waters below.

The wind-rose compass points to all corners of the globe

Although modern historians may have misgivings as to the location, it has long been thought that it was at the *fortaleza* that Henry assembled his team of experts to begin the Age of Discoveries. Unfortunately, it was ransacked by Sir Francis Drake in 1587, destroying the Navigator's great library and all traces of his work, so what really happened here is mostly mere conjecture. The present structure dates from 1793 and is impressively large from the outside but the interior is a mostly empty compound, with what remains of its original walls now clad in grim modern concrete.

So, were Henry to return, would he recognise anything here? He would no doubt have prayed at the simple 14th-century chapel, and perhaps also used the white buttressed "Auditorium", which was a supplies and ammunition store, renovated in 1793 (closed to the public). But the most intriguing feature from his time is the giant, compass-like 39m diameter **Rosa dos Ventos**, or Wind Rose, laid out in the courtyard. Mount the stairs by the compound entrance and you will see a sundial looking directly down onto it. No one knows how the rose, or the rose and compass together, functioned.

The chapel of the *fortaleza*. Would the Navigator still know it today?

A **modern hall** is given over to temporary exhibitions, usually of art or photography, and upstairs you can log onto one of several computers that give you the basics on the history of the fortress, and the flora and fauna of the local area.

Cabo de São Vicente

From the *fortaleza*, the road winds around the headland for 6km to Cabo de São Vicente (Cape St Vincent). It is the westernmost point in mainland Europe, known to the ancient mariners as *O Fim do Mundo* (the End of the World). The Romans called it *Promontorium Sacrum* (Sacred Promontory) and believed that the gods slept here. It retained this holy status up until the 8th century when the remains of St Vincent were brought here in a bid to escape the invading Moors. The effort was in vain:

Fortaleza de Sagres and Cabo de São Vicente

the Moors overran the region and the body was lost. After the Reconquest (➤ 30), the king of Portugal sent a search party to find the bones, which, according to legend, was guided to the spot by ravens. St Vincent's remains were transferred to Lisbon and the ravens were adopted into the seal of the city. All traces of the shrine at Cape St Vincent have long since disappeared, though its spiritual legacy remains in the shape of the ruins of a monastery built here in the 16th century.

The ubiquitous Prince Henry is said to have lived in a house here, a bracing stroll away from his think-tank at Sagres. It's a nice twist of history that on the site of his house one of Europe's most powerful lighthouses now stands. The lighthouse keeper takes it upon himself to open up visitors – there are no set times – but if the door is closed and all is quiet, try knocking and asking "Posso visitar el faro?" Leave a tip if you are successful.

TAKING A BREAK

The *fortaleza* has an uninspiring, modern self-service café-restaurant and there are snack stalls at Cabo de São Vicente, including "Wolfgang's Wurst Machine – the last Wurst before America"! But the best place to lunch is the **Fortaleza do Beliche** (➤ 134).

Fortaleza de Sagres
✚ 182 A1
✉ Ponta de Sagres
⏲ Daily 10–6.30, Oct–Apr; 10–8.30, May–Sep
🍴 Café-restaurant
💰 Moderate

Moorish inspired rugs on sale at Cabo de São Vicente

FORTALEZA DE SAGRES/CABO DE SÃO VICENTE: INSIDE INFO

Top tips The most magical time of day to visit either of these places is sunset, when the colours are amazing.
• On a balmy summer day the cape almost feels benevolent, but at other times it can be **wild and windswept** and hostile. Don't worry if you forgot to pack your woollies; stalls by the lighthouse sell good-quality traditional chunky jumpers (and socks) at bargain prices.

Beaches

The beaches west of Sagres are unquestionably the most dramatic – and consequently the most unspoiled – in the Algarve: roaring seas and whipping winds for much of the year are hardly conducive to organised tourism. This is a coast for independent travellers and serious surf lovers – beaches are big and rarely crowded. On those summer days when the wind drops and the sea abates, these are some of the most irresistible sands in Europe.

In general, you will have to take along your own amusements though most beaches have snack bars and the occasional hardy seasonal restaurant. Beware of currents and note that there are no lifeguards.

Below are the main beaches, heading south to north. All have reasonably easy access by car, albeit involving some dirt-track driving, and are signposted off the main road.

Praia da Cordama

Follow the *miradouro* (lookout) signs up to a height of 110m then shuffle gingerly as far as the cliff edge to enjoy a stupendous, dizzying view down onto long golden Cordama beach and also of the cliffs heading north. The neighbouring, smaller Praia do Castelejo is less impressive, but it's still worth visiting. Both beaches are well and clearly signposted from Vila do Bispo.

Praia do Amado

This beautiful beach, backed by tall sheer cliffs, is many people's west coast favourite, in spite of (or perhaps because of) its lack of facilities. Surfing championships are held here.

Praia da Bordeira

Also known as Carrapateira beach after the adjacent village, this is a monster of a beach, and is backed by huge dunes and a lagoon.

Beaches

Praia de Arrifana

A classic crescent of narrow sand backed by huge cliffs, this is an excellent beach for surfing. Carry on up the road beyond the village to the ruins of the old fortress. The views north from there, of cliffs folding over like repeating mirror images, are spellbinding.

Praia de Monte Clérigo

This is the most family friendly of the west coast beaches, with a flat approach and a couple of restaurants.

Praia de Odeceixe

There is little development here and the long dark stretch of sand, backed by high cliffs, is sheltered. Nonetheless it is good for surfing.

TAKING A BREAK

Many of the old beachside restaurants – some little more than shacks – in the Costa Vicentina National Park were closed down and demolished in 1999–2000 as a result of changing hygiene regulations. A few have reopened but others will not, leaving some beaches without any refreshments. If in doubt take a picnic.

O Sítio do Rio (next to Praia da Bordeira/Carrapateira beach, tel: 282 973119), is recommended for its Portuguese-international cooking, including kebabs with ginger sauce and vegetarian specialities.

Bottom left: The striking Arrifana beach. Below: Praia de Monte Clérigo: typical wild west coast scenes

Right: The west coast is a great place for experienced surfers

WEST COAST BEACHES: INSIDE INFO

Top tips If driving to the Praia da Cordama *miradouro* **be very careful**. There are no signs or marked area to stop you driving right off the top of the cliff.

• Bear in mind that **once past Sagres** you have turned to face west and the full fury of the Atlantic. If you thought the sea was cool on the south coast, wait until you dip your toe in here!

• Except for July and August, **surfers and windsurfers** will need to wear wetsuits all year round.

At Your Leisure

Above and below: The low-key Praia da Luz

3 Luz (Praia da Luz)

Luz – also known as Praia da Luz – is the last holiday resort of any size heading west. The original village has long been submerged by neat, white, low-rise apartments and villas splashed with a profusion of bougainvillaea. British families dominate the resort and have turned it into a home from home. Tennis and watersports are the favourite pastimes here and there's a good-size golden crescent backed by cliffs at one end with large slabs at the other end.

The only bit of old Luz left is the snow-white 18th-century parish church, which boasts some fine gilded carving. Opposite is the 400-year-old *fortaleza* (fortress), now converted into a restaurant. Its interior has a rather contrived olde-worlde look but is still worth a peek. Its terrace, with fine sea views, is deservedly popular.

For a great view over Luz and inland take the well-worn pathway to the Miradouro da Atalaia (Obelisk Lookout), which peaks at 109m. The coastal path continues for another 2.2km to Porto de Mós.

🗺 182 C2

For Kids
- The **Museu Municipal at Lagos** (➤ 119), for its freak animal foetuses, model village and weapons.
- **All south coast beaches** (except Tonel at Sagres and Figueira, south of Budens). In general, the surf on the west coast beaches is too wild for young children.

At Your Leisure

Above: Fisherman's traps at Burgau
Below: Running repairs at Salema

5 Salema

This small fishing village turned resort lies at the head of a pretty valley. The road ends in a square by the beach with a few restaurants, a hotel, apartments and shops. While not as attractive nor as villagey as neighbouring Burgau, the atmosphere is similar and there is a good beach.

Between Salema and Burgau is the uncommercialised beach of Cabanas Velhas and a small but ecologically important Budens Wetlands area (➤ 158–60).

➕ 182 B2

6 Vila do Bispo

Despite its rather grand name, Vila do Bispo (Bishop's Town) is a very ordinary village and there's little to see other than the parish church. This is often locked, but behind the Manueline doorway the interior is lined with 18th-century blue *azulejos* and gilded woodwork.

A church of greater historical importance lies 2km east, at Raposeira. The simple single-nave Ermida de Nossa Senhora de Guadalupe is the oldest church in the Algarve, dating from the 13th century, and it has been sensitively restored to retain its wonderful ancient atmosphere.

Look in particular for the unusual figures (people and animals) sculptured on the tops of the villas and the roof bosses. It is recorded that Prince Henry the Navigator retreated to

4 Burgau

The picturesque little fishing village of Burgau tumbles down steep narrow streets lined with white cottages to the sea (leave your car at the top). At the bottom of the hill a much-photographed jumble of drawn-up fishing boats has become something of a village trademark. There is a handful of tourist bars and restaurants but relatively little new development and the village retains a local feel.

The sheltered crescent beach, backed by cliffs and scree, is perfect for families, and for most of the time is big enough to cope with the crowds – though in the afternoons the tide comes almost right in.

➕ 182 B2

Colourful fishing boats decorate the harbour at Sagres

Raposeira from Lagos because it was "remote from the tumult of people and propitious for the contemplation of study", and he probably prayed here. The church lies on the old road parallel to the N125 but is easily missed from the main highway – keep your eyes peeled for the small church sign: "Guadalupe".

✚ 182 A2

7 Sagres

Famous for its historic *fortaleza* (➤ 123–5), Sagres is quite literally the end of the line – the most southerly and westerly resort in the Algarve. It's not particularly attractive and it doesn't have an obvious town centre but what it does possess is some superb sandy windswept beaches.

Not long ago, only independent travellers made it this far west, and it still is quite a bohemian hang-out, though, a rash of hotel and apartment building has brought more mainstream visitors. The beaches remain generally uncrowded, however, and out of high season are often deserted.

Prince Henry built the original town in the 15th century and named it Vila do Infante (Prince's Town). Its primary function was as a first-aid station or field hospital, bandaging up the many mariners who had foundered on the dangerous rocks of the adjacent Cape St Vincent. It thrived because it was the nearest settlement to Henry's research headquarters at the *fortaleza*, but when Henry died in 1460 maritime research moved to Lisbon and Vila do Infante declined into obscurity. All traces of it were destroyed in the Great Earthquake of 1755 (➤ 78) and present-day Sagres was built in the 19th century.

The small Praça da República, at the top end of the village, is an obvious meeting point, with a handful of bars and an unofficial information centre. The main road leads off from here, past the official tourist office, and down to the harbour where a commercial fishing fleet thrives and pleasure boats take holidaymakers big-game fishing and dolphin spotting (the chances of seeing dolphin are good).

At Your Leisure

> **Four Quiet Beaches Between Luz and Sagres**
> **Ingrina:** a beautiful small cove beach south of Raposeira; popular with divers and snorkellers.
> **Zavial:** another cove beach south of Raposeira; renowned for its surfing.
> **Cabanas Velhas:** (➤ 129; 158–60).
> **Boca do Rio:** (➤ 158–60).

Beside the harbour are the broad golden sands of the Praia da Baleeira and just around the corner, east, is the Praia da Martinhal, another large sweep of sand where experts fly across the waves. It is home to the Windsurfing Club Martinhal.

A road between the Praça da República and the harbour leads south to the Pousada do Infante (➤ 134), which is now part of Portigal's chain of *pousada* inns (➤ 35). Walk out on the headland on which it is located for wonderful land's-end sea views. Below is the lovely beach of Praia da Mareta, sheltered from the wild westerly winds by the Ponta de Sagres (on which stands the Fortaleza de Sagres).

Some 3km north of Sagres, *en route* to Cabo de São Vicente, is the Fortaleza do Beliche (➤ 134). The restored remains of this small 17th-century fortress provide a pleasant place to stay and eat. Another good reason to tarry here is the beautiful little Praia do Beliche, which is charmingly secluded and sheltered in its own cove.

🖽 182 A1
Sagres Tourist Office
✉ Rua Comandante Matoso
☎ 282 624873

🔟 Aljezur
Although the Algarve extends another 17km north, as far as Odeceixe, for most visitors the region stops here. They either head east to Monchique (or have arrived from that direction) or go further west to the beaches of Arrifana and Monte Clérigo (➤ 127) or Amoreira.

The old half of Aljezur, which nestles beside the river, is the place to head for. Here, under mature trees, between two bridges, is a choice of cafés and a good restaurant. Pick up a map from the tourist office in the small adjacent car park or square. Just a couple of minutes walk away are the scant remains of a 10th-century castle (freely accessible), the Casa Museu José Cercas, featuring the canvasses and drawings of Aljezur-born Cercas and works by other local artists, and the Museu Municipal, which is devoted mostly to archaeology. You can cover them all in less than an hour.

🖽 182 A2
Aljezur Tourist Office
✉ Largo do Mercado
☎ 282 998229

Casa Museu José Cercas
✉ Rua do Castelo
🕑 Tue–Sat 10–12.30, 2–6
💰 Inexpensive

Museu Municipal
✉ Rua da Cadeia Velha
🕑 Tue–Sat 10–12.30, 2–6
💰 Inexpensive

A rustic scene at Aljezur

Where to... Stay

Prices
Expect to pay per double room per night:
£ under €50   **££** €50–125   **£££** over €125

Casa Grande £

This rambling, creaky, 100-year-old mansion set just above the fishing village of Burgau and a three-minute walk from the beach is one of the Algarve's longest established, most individual and friendliest guesthouses, owned and run by Sally Vincent (▶ 10–11), a mine of information on the local area. Ramshackle in parts, it still retains its country house feel; bedrooms are painted in pastel colours, are traditionally furnished and have high, stuccoed ceilings. Breakfast, around the large communal table, is a melting pot of nationalities from all walks of life, chatting away animatedly about how they came to arrive at such a unique establishment.

✚ 182 B2 ✉ Burgau, 8600 Lagos ☎ 282 697416; fax: 282 697825; email: casagrande@mail.telepac.pt; www.nexus-pt.com/casagrande

Casa de São Gonçalo ££

Converted from a handsome town house, full of antiques and character, this hotel feels like a private home. None of the 13 bedrooms are alike, but you won't find TVs or frigobars in any of them. In summer, breakfast is served in the delightful courtyard.

✚ 182 C2 ✉ Rua Cândido dos Reis, 73, 8600 Lagos ☎ 282 762171; fax: 282 763927 Ⓧ Closed Nov–Mar

Estalagem Infante do Mar ££

The peaceful Infante do Mar is high above the village and beach, reached by a steep road from the centre. The simply furnished guest rooms, with whitewashed walls and tiled floors, are good value. All have sea views, and some have terraces. Simple fare is served in the light, airy dining room – though Portuguese favourites such as fish *cataplana* can be ordered in advance. For a quick dip there is the hotel pool.

✚ 182 B2 ✉ Praia da Salema, 8650 Vila do Bispo ☎ 282 690100; fax: 282 690109

Hotel Belavista da Luz ££

Overlooking the beautiful bay of Praia da Luz, the Belavista lives up to its name. It is a stylish new hotel with Moorish elements incorporated into the pale pink exterior. Luz's beach is only a few minutes away, but you may prefer to take advantage of the hotel's good-sized heated swimming pool, kid's pool, tennis court, health club and children's playground. Dinner is served in the smart candlelit restaurant.

✚ 182 C2 ✉ Praia da Luz, 8600 Lagos ☎ 282 788655; fax: 282 788656; www.belavistadaluz.com

Hotel Lagos ££

The largest hotel in town, Hotel Lagos is modern and stylish, catering both for tourists and businessmen visitors. It is divided into zones that are linked together to create a series of pretty garden vistas. The clever design gives the hotel a light, airy atmosphere and makes it feel much smaller than it is (there are 315 rooms). Three restaurants suit every mood while breakfast, which is included in the room rate, is a veritable feast. Extensive amenities include outdoor and indoor pools, a games room and a health club. A convenient shuttle bus service links the hotel with the beach club at Meia Praia.

✚ 182 C2 ✉ Rua Nova da Aldeia, 8600 Lagos ☎ 282 769967; fax: 282 769920; email: reservas@hotelagos.pt

Where to...
Eat and Drink

Prices
Expect to pay per person for a meal, excluding drinks and service
£ under €15   ££ €15–23   £££ over €23

A Lagosteira ££

Under the same management since the 1960s, the Lagosteira remains a reliable, unpretentious fish restaurant, that has changed little over the years. Recommended dishes are the fish soup, shrimps flambéed, fried shrimps in garlic, fish *cataplana* and clams with shrimps and cream sauce. The bread and ice creams are homemade and a few international dishes are also available. The outdoor tables seat 30 but to secure one in summer, book in advance.

🕂 182 C2 ✉ Rua 1 de Maio 20, Lagos ☎ 282 762486 🕒 Daily lunch and dinner. Closed mid-Jan to mid-Feb

A Tasca ££

The spacious seaview terrace is a lovely spot to linger over lunch – or dinner on a warm evening. Converted from the old market, the restaurant overlooks the port where fresh fish is landed daily. The seafood theme is obvious. Choose a fish kebab or *cataplana*, or reserve in advance (two hours at least) for one of the house specials: sea bass, stone bass or bream baked in the oven, rice with crayfish or monkfish or stewed crayfish with potatoes.

🕂 182 A1 ✉ Praia da Mareta, Sagres ☎ 282 624177 🕒 Sun–Fri lunch and dinner

Beach Bar £–££

This longtime favourite, right on the beach, serves snacks all day and full evening meals. You can get king prawns in wine and garlic butter, grilled swordfish or turbot, chicken or steak, Banoffi pie or lemon cheese cake. It's popular in high season so you may need to reserve three days in advance for an evening meal.

🕂 182 B2 ✉ Burgau, Vila do Bispo ☎ 282-697553 🕒 Tue–Sat lunch and dinner, Sun lunch

Cangalho ££

Escape from the bustle of the coast and try this rustic restaurant in a farmhouse near the village of Barão de São João. Here, you can dine on quails' eggs, chicken liver pâté and flambeed slices of smoked sausages while your suckling pig, lamb or fillet of pork roasts in the brick oven. (Note, however, that for some of the roasts you need to order well in advance.) This is a great place for children – there's a fish pond inside the restaurant and a zoo with exotic birds and monkeys dashing about in natural surroundings.

🕂 182 B2 ✉ Quinta Figueiras, Sítio do Medronhal, Barão de São João, Lagos ☎ 282-687218 🕒 Daily lunch and dinner

Dom Sebastião ££

You can't fail to notice the Dom Sebastião in the heart of Lagos, with inviting tables laid out on the pedestrianised shopping street. The emphasis is on fish, particularly shellfish such as oysters, prawns, lobster or crayfish. There is no need for a starter here as delicious little dishes are included in the cover charge and main courses are generous. If that doesn't fill you up, end the meal with the homemade almond tart and, if you're lucky, a liqueur on the house.

🕂 182 C2 ✉ Rua 25 de Abril 20–22, Lagos ☎ 282 762795 🕒 Daily lunch and dinner

Escondidinho £

Join the locals here, hidden behind Hotel Lagos (▶ 132). Among the favourite dishes here are the charcoal-grilled mixed fish or the *cataplana*. If you're not a fish enthusiast, go for the no-frills steak or pork dishes. The setting is simple café-style, with a terrace.

⊞ 182 C2 ✉ **Lagos (opposite the GNR)** ☎ **282 760386** ⊙ **Mon–Sat lunch and dinner**

Florestal ££

For a change from the beach scene, try this restaurant in a forest above the village of Barão de São João. It's not easy to find (telephone for directions or ask in the village), but it's worth it for the breathtaking views from the bougainvillea-clad terrace and the wide range of snacks and meals. The owners are English and American, their menu featuring good soups and salads, homemade all-meat burgers, eggs Benedict, grilled rack of lamb, steaks and fish.

⊞ 182 B2 ✉ **Barão de São João, 3km west of Bensafrim** ☎ **282 687204** ⊙ **Tue–Sat lunch and dinner, Sun lunch**

Fortaleza da Luz ££

Save this one for a special night out. It's the most expensive restaurant in Luz with a splendid fortress setting and spacious seaview terrace. You can count on the freshly caught seafood and fish, either simply grilled or in a Mediterranean or creamy sauce. There's plenty of meat too. For a barbecue and live jazz, book for Sunday lunch.

⊞ 182 C2 ✉ **Rua da Igreja 3, Praia da Luz, 8600 Lagos** ☎ **282 789926** ⊙ **Daily lunch and dinner. Closed mid-Nov to mid-Dec**

Fortaleza do Beliche ££

The tiny stone fortress, reconstructed in 1632, perches dramatically on the cliffs between Sagres and Cape St Vincent. The sea crashes against the rocks below, but the dining room is inviting, with its beamed ceiling and log fire. Come for a lunch of soup, salad or omelette, served on the seaview terrace (winds permitting), or opt for the fish of the day or one of the Portuguese specialities. The *fortaleza* is also a *pousada*, with four simple but attractively furnished rooms.

⊞ 182 A1 ✉ **8650 Sagres (off the road to Cape St Vincent)** ☎ **282 624124; fax: 282 624225** ⊙ **Daily lunch and dinner. Closed one month in winter**

Piri Piri £

Cheap and cheerful, the busy, centrally located Piri-Piri caters for all tastes. There are around 90 dishes, and a choice of four tourist menus. Predictably, chicken *piri-piri* is a house speciality, as is the grilled fish and *cataplanas*. In summer tables are laid out on the street.

⊞ 182 C2 ✉ **Rua Lima Leitão 15 and Rua Afonso de Almeida 10, Lagos** ☎ **282 763803** ⊙ **Daily lunch and dinner**

Pousada do Infante £££

The *pousada*'s reputation for top-quality cuisine, combined with its clifftop setting and sea views, draws many non-residents. Firm favourites are fish soup, fried baby squid, grilled sole with almonds, fried tuna steak in an onion marinade and fish and shellfish *cataplana*. *Azulejos* decorate the walls of the elegant dining room, and tables are laid out on the terrace in summer. The weighty wine list offers an impressive range, from *vinho da casa* from Lagos to Lagoa to Bairrada and Dão vintages.

⊞ 182 A1 ✉ **8650-385 Sagres** ☎ **282 624222; fax: 282 624225** ⊙ **Daily lunch and dinner**

Reis £

This friendly, unpretentious restaurant in the centre of Lagos is one of the city's more notable restaurants. The dish of the day is usually excellent value. Specialities are tuna steak with cream sauce, fish soup (deliciously rich), swordfish with onions, monkfish *cataplanas* with shrimps, lamb cutlets and loin of pork with figs.

⊞ 182 C2 ✉ **Rua António Barbosa Viana, 21, Lagos** ☎ **282 762900** ⊙ **Mon–Sat lunch and dinner**

Where to...
Shop

LAGOS

This is the principal centre of western Algarve, with a lively morning market and an abundance of pavement cafés, craft shops and galleries. The main street is the pedestrianised Rua 25 de Abril, with shops selling ceramics, linen, basketware and antiques. **Caixote** (5, Rua 25 de Abril) has a large selection of ceramics from all over Portugal ranging from the ubiquitous pottery rooster (➤ 38) to large decorative pieces from the Alentejo. You'll also find the pottery **Olaria Nova** (➤ 25) on this street.

Antiques

At **Casa da Papagaio** (27, Rua 25 de Abril), a couple of loquacious parrots lure customers into a dark and fascinating treasure trove of Portuguese antiques – ranging from coins and cash tills to dusty religious artefacts and African statuary. A further source for antiques and *objets d'art* is the **Casa da Barroca** (Rua da Barroca, tel: 282 760893) to the east of Rua 25 de Abril, a large shop with a range of collectables.

Food and Drink

For delicious regional cakes, pastries and other edible gifts, try **Gelanel** (Rua Lima Leitão, 7/9, beyond Rua 25 de Abril, and also at Rua Marquês de Pombal, 7, tel: 282 760542).

Algarve desserts such as almond tart and Dom Rodrigo (with almond and egg) are their specialities. **The Wine Shop** on Praça Luis de Camões is the place to go for reasonably priced Portuguese wines and spirits. It's a small shop with a helpful owner who speaks good English.

Speciality shops

Off the Praça Luis de Camões, the Rua Cândido dos Reis is one of the main shopping streets, notable for leather boutiques selling jackets and bags. For African crafts try **Sirocco** at No 37, which sells leather lamps and mirrors from Morocco, or **The Africa Craft Shop** (Rua António Barbosa Viana 8, tel: 282 767736) off Rua Cândido dos Reis.

Over the river and accessed over the pedestrian bridge, **Lagos Marina** makes for a pleasant stroll and has a few shops among the cafés and restaurants, including the stylish **Terra a Vista** art gallery.

Markets

The covered food market in Lagos (Rua das Portas de Portugal, Monday to Saturday 8 am–1 pm) has a splendid display of fresh fish as well as fruit and vegetables. If you happen to be in the region on the first Saturday of the month, don't miss the colourful gipsy market.

Antiques markets and collectors' fairs are held at the **Cultural Centre Barão de São João**. Look for details in the free *Welcome to the Algarve* newspaper, which is available from the tourist office.

The **Centro Cultural de São Lourenço** (➤ 136, 154) also hosts art exhibitions, as does the **Mercado dos Escravos** (Slave Market) off Praça da República.

SAGRES

For all surfing gear, head for **Surf Planet** (N268, tel: 282 624815). Alternatively, there are often bargains to be found at roadside stalls selling handpainted pottery and souvenirs. Try **Amó** (Sitio do Tonel, tel: 282 624748), which sells very reasonably priced handpainted plates, cups and saucers and colourful vases.

Stalls at Cape St Vincent sell chunky woollen cardigans and fishermen's jumpers – useful for tourists caught unawares by the battering winds (➤ 125). Other stalls offer fossils from Morocco, pots of honey and small baskets of figs or almonds.

Where to...
Be Entertained

The tourist information centre in Lagos (inconveniently located on Rua Vasco da Gama, 20 minutes' walk from the town centre) has information on sports, boat trips and events. Detailed listings are given in English-language papers and magazines, available free from the tourist office, hotels and travel agencies.

OUTDOOR ACTIVITIES

Beaches are the big attraction, whether it's the spectacular west coast where surfers ride the Atlantic rollers or the less exposed sandy coves and bays further east. **Surfing and windsurf centres** with equipment to hire can be found at **Meia Praia** (Lagos, tel: 282 762091) and **Praia da Mareta** (Sagres, tel: 282 620209). Windsurfing, sailing, waterskiing and boat trips are available in Praia da Luz at the **Watersports School** (tel: 282 778581). Clear waters, caves and a couple of wrecks draw many divers to the coast. Courses are available at The **Sea Sports Centre** (Praia da Luz, tel: 282 789538), **Lagos-Sub** (the fishing port, Lagos, tel: 282 789538) and **Blue Ocean Divers** (Motel Ancora, Estrada de Porto de Mós, tel: 282 782718).

For **coastal cruises**, taking in the sandy coves and clear grottoes of Ponta da Piedade, contact **Bom Dia** (tel: 282 764670). **Speed Cruises** (tel: 282 764670) offer spins across the bay, cave cruises or dolphin safaris. **Big-game fishing trips** with the possibility of hooking blue, mako or hammerhead shark can be organised through **Pescamar** (Lagos Marina, tel: 966 193431).

Alternatively, see the bay from the sky in a **microlight** (Lagos aerodrome, tel: 282 762906).

Golfers have the choice of two 18-hole clubs: **Palmares** (tel: 282 762953) near Lagos or **Parque da Floresta** (tel: 282 690055) at Budens, 16km west of Lagos.

There are six **horse-riding centres** in the area, including **Tiffany's** (Almádena, tel: 282 697395) and the **Quinta do Paraíso Alto** (Bensafrim, tel: 282 687596), which can organise overnight treks to the west coast.

For tennis, squash, basketball, football and other activities for adults and children contact the **Burgau Sports Centre** (tel: 282 697350).

Bullfights occasionally take place on Saturdays at the Lagos bullring (tel: 282 763194).

MUSIC AND NIGHTLIFE

The **Centro Cultural de São Lourenço** in Lagos (Rua Lançarote de Freitas, 7, Lagos, tel: 282 763403) hosts music festivals, concerts and recitals featuring international musicians and choirs as well as local groups. In the centre of town Rua Cândido dos Reis and Rua 25 de Abril have the greatest concentration of late-night bars, several of which stage live music. Many bars are British or Irish-run, offering Boddingtons, Guinness and infinite cocktails, along with big sports events on Sky TV. Happy Hour, offered by many bars, tends to last four or five hours. Cafés and bars at Lagos Marina, overlooking the brasher establishments, are pleasant places to sit over a drink in the evening. The only disco, **Phoenix** (Rua 5 de Outubro 11), attracts the crowds and stays open til 4 am.

Out of Lagos, *fado* nights are held on Tuesday and Saturdays at **Adega do Papagaio** (Espiche, tel: 282 789423). A converted wine cellar, the Adega is open daily for lunch and dinner, and for a set price you can eat as much as you like from seven types of meat, all grilled on hot stones.

The Hills

Getting Your Bearings 138 – 139
In Two Days 140 – 141
Don't Miss 142 – 146
At Your Leisure 147 – 148
Where to... 149 – 152

Getting Your Bearings

Although the heart of the Serra de Monchique is a mere 24km from the coast, it's a different world from the nearby holiday developments of Carvoeiro and Praia da Rocha. Just beyond the N125 the pace of life slows perceptibly as you cross the border from the "International Holiday Zone" to truly rural Portugal.

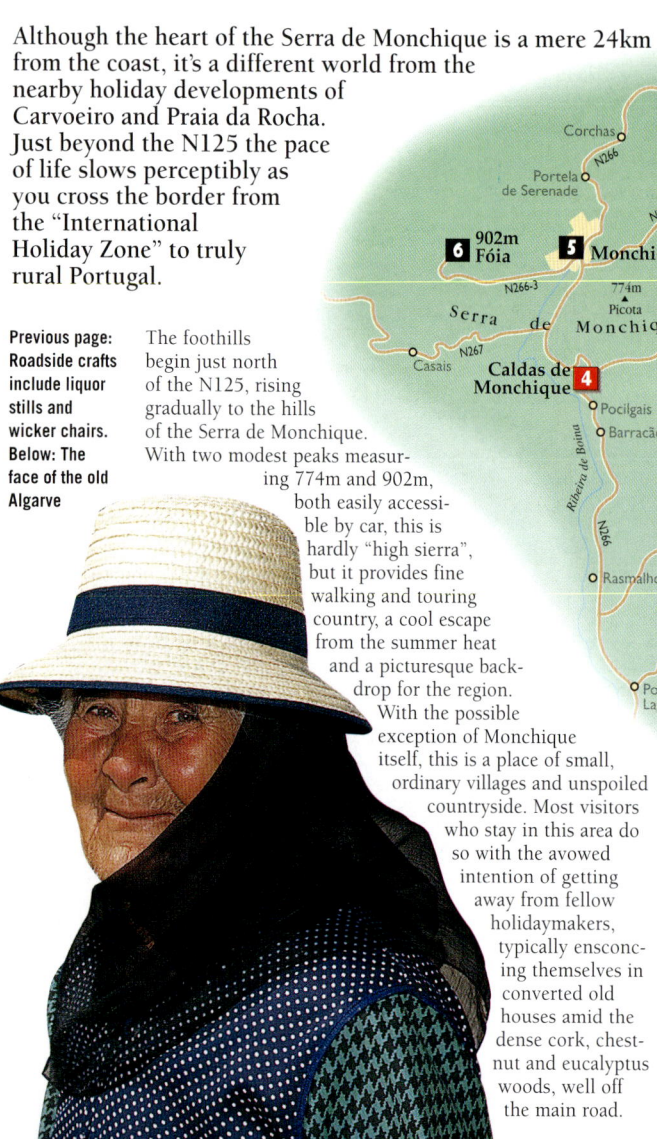

Previous page: Roadside crafts include liquor stills and wicker chairs. Below: The face of the old Algarve

The foothills begin just north of the N125, rising gradually to the hills of the Serra de Monchique. With two modest peaks measuring 774m and 902m, both easily accessible by car, this is hardly "high sierra", but it provides fine walking and touring country, a cool escape from the summer heat and a picturesque backdrop for the region. With the possible exception of Monchique itself, this is a place of small, ordinary villages and unspoiled countryside. Most visitors who stay in this area do so with the avowed intention of getting away from fellow holidaymakers, typically ensconcing themselves in converted old houses amid the dense cork, chestnut and eucalyptus woods, well off the main road.

Getting Your Bearings

★ Don't Miss
- **3** Silves ➤ 142–4
- **4** Caldas de Monchique ➤ 145–6

At Your Leisure
- **1** São Bartolomeu de Messines ➤ 147
- **2** Barragem do Arade ➤ 147
- **5** Monchique ➤ 147–8
- **6** Fóia ➤ 148

Right: Naive pottery

Day-trippers can cram in Silves, Caldas de Monchique, Monchique and Fóia in a few hours, but if you take your time to appreciate the area, your efforts will be rewarded.

The old bell tower of Monchique's parish church

The Algarve's most historic town, a quaint spa village and lunch amid the pines all beckon on this rural tour.

The Hills in Two Days

Day One

Morning
Drive to **Silves** (➤ 142–4) via Lagoa, for the lovely view. You should be able to fit in the cathedral (opposite page), municipal market, castle and archaeological museum before lunch. Silves has a good choice of places to eat (➤ 150–1).

Afternoon
Take the N124 towards Monchique and turn right onto the N266 to visit **Caldas de Monchique** (➤ 145–6). As it probably won't take long to browse around the little spa town, you could spend the rest of the afternoon on the walking tour (➤ 156–7). Have dinner at the Rouxinol (➤ 150) and either stay at the Albergaria do Lageado (➤ 149) or return to your resort.

Day Two

Morning
Drive north on the N266 to **Monchique** (pictured above, ➤ 147), stopping just before you get into the centre to look at the handicraft shops. See the famous parish church, walk up to the ruined monastery for the views then return to your car. Head a

little way out on the old Lisbon road, visit the shop of the "Chair Man of Monchique" (➤ 38; famous scissor chairs pictured above) and have lunch at nearby Albergaria Bica Boa (➤ 149).

Afternoon
Either take a tour (by bike or on foot) from the Bica Boa, or return to Monchique and head west on the N265 to Fóia or on the N267 (towards Alferce) to Picota. Both routes give great views, though the latter is the much less trampled of the two.

Return to Monchique and drive south on the N266 to Silves (turning off left on the N124), then spend the evening at the Fábrica do Inglês (➤ 144, 152).

Silves

If you are making your own way to Silves, come from the direction of Lagoa so that the beautiful panorama of the castle-topped city unfolds before you. It is a great sight and leaves you in no doubt that here is a town with a sense of history.

An attacker's view of the city's sturdy hill-top castle

In Moorish times Silves, or Xelb as it was then known, was the capital of the kingdom of Al-Gharb (Algarve). According to the Arab chroniclers it was a place of "shining brightness", "ten times more remarkable than Lisbon". Its wealth was renowned as far as Scandinavia and in 966 Viking longships ventured up the River Arade. In those days the Arade was the key to the wealth of Silves and, as unlikely as it may seem now, the town was once a thriving port, equipped with shipyards and exporting citrus fruit and cork oak. With the expulsion of the Moors, however, and the loss of their considerable knowledge and skills, the town deteriorated. Worse still, the river began to silt up, and by 1577 the once-great Arab town of over 30,000 people had become a forgotten backwater with a population of around 150. Thus it stagnated for three centuries, until the revival of the cork industry in the second half of the 19th century breathed new life back into the city.

Today Silves is thriving again, albeit on a smaller scale, thanks to the surrounding citrus groves, farming and tourism. The cork oak industry is commemorated by a museum, and "longships" once again come upstream in the shape of traditional Portuguese gondolas from Portimão (➤ 100–1).

Relaxing beside the câmara munipal (town hall)

Around the Town

Despite being reshaped after the Reconquest (➤ 30), the present **Castelo de Silves** (Silves Castle) retains its Moorish design. Today it is little more than a shell, but there are excellent views from the battlements and the huge vaulted cistern, which once provided the town with much of its water, is devoted to temporary exhibitions.

Adjacent to the castle is the atmospheric **Sé** (cathedral), some 700 years old, with fine Gothic architecture and ancient tombs of medieval knights and bishops. A headstone commemorates King João II (➤ 106), whose remains were buried here then later moved to Batalha monastery in northern Portugal.

The Moorish well is the centrepiece of the Archaeological Museum

Take the steep cobbled path downhill to the **Museu Municipal de Arqueologia**, which traces regional history back through Moorish, Roman and Phoenician times.

Adjacent is part of the old city walls, most notably the 12th- to 13th-century **Torreão da Porta da Cidade** barbican (see "Hidden gem"). This gives onto the pretty square of **Praça do Município**, one side of which is occupied by the old town hall. Its foyer, now home to a self-service café, is covered in *azulejos* and worth a look inside. In the corner of the square a pillory has been rebuilt from 16th-century stones and the tourist office is a few metres off the square on Rua 25 de Abril.

Make your way downhill – any street will do – to the river, the bustling municipal market and the medieval bridge. One of the town's newest attractions, the **Fábrica do Inglês** (➤ 152), is a five-minute walk, left, along the main road. This impressively restored complex occupies the grounds of the old cork factory that operated here between 1894 and 1995 and its name derives from a period of English ownership. It was reopened in 1999 as a leisure complex, featuring a **Museu da Cortiça** (Cork Museum), high-quality restaurants, bars and cafés, plus various entertainments by night.

Dark Deeds

The heroic, oversize statue of Dom Sancho I in Silves Castle is a reminder of a treacherous event that took place in 1189. After a four-month siege, the Moors surrendered to the king's Christian forces – including many English crusaders – on guarantee of safe passage. Instead, Dom Sancho's men turned the castle into a "blaze of hell", slaughtered around 6,000 inhabitants and tortured others into revealing the whereabouts of their treasures.

TAKING A BREAK

For coffee and cakes in a great location you can't beat **Café Inglês** (➤ 150), and for good cheap local food try **Casa Velha** on the Praça do Municipio, or **Tasca do Bene** on Rua Policarpo Dias. Fish lovers should head for the renowned **Rui Marisqueira** (➤ 151).

Classic view of Silves from the main Lagoa road

Castelo de Silves
- 183 E3
- Daily 9–7, Sep–Jun; 9–8, Jul–Aug
- Inexpensive (with exhibition moderate)

Sé
- 183 E3
- Mon–Sat 8.30–6.30   Free

Museu Municipal de Arqueologia
- 183 E3
- Rua das Portas de Loulé
- 282 444832
- Daily 10–6
- Inexpensive

Fábrica do Inglês
- 183 E3
- 282 440440
- Daily 9 am–11 pm   Free unless a special event is taking place in the evening

Museu da Cortiça
- 183 E3
- 9.30–1, 2–6.30
- Inexpensive

SILVES: INSIDE INFO

Top tips Opposite the grand front entrance to the cathedral note the classic **Manueline doorway** of the 16th-century Igreja de Misericórdia. This doorway is in fact above the ground, at cart level, so that coffins could be moved into the church.
• Park by the river on busy days; at quiet times you can drive almost to the castle.

Hidden gem For many centuries the room at the top of the ancient **Torreão da Porta da Cidade** barbican was the home of the municipal council. Today it's a public library (open Tue–Sat 9.30–1, 2–5.30).

Caldas de Monchique

4

Nestling in a steep wooded valley full of chestnut, cork, eucalyptus and pine trees, the quiet little spa of Caldas de Monchique is the antithesis of the Algarve's brash seaside resorts. It has been used since Roman times when it was called Mons Cicus, from which the name Monchique was derived. *Caldas* simply means spa. In the 19th century Caldas became a favourite of the Spanish and Portuguese bourgeoisie and took on the appearance that we see today. The old casino building, with its mock Moorish windows, is a notable survivor from this period.

Hidden among the hills, Caldas de Monchique is a good starting point for country walks

Caldas de Monchique, caught in an Edwardian time warp

Taking the Waters

The spa gushes out approximately 20 million litres of water per year, which emerges at a temperature of around 32 degrees centigrade. Visitors can taste the waters for free – though few enjoy the sulphurous experience, preferring the more palatable product from the commercial plant below the village. This is an ugly brute of a building, spoiling the immediate view down, though on the positive side it provides local employment and gives publicity to Monchique by distributing its bottled waters all over the country.

Below the tasting area and above the factory is the thermal hospital where visitors come for treatment of rheumatism and respiratory illnesses, among other ailments.

A New Look

During 2000, Caldas de Monchique received a major makeover. Deciding that its peeling patina of age and neglect had crossed over from the point of being charmingly faded to being just plain scruffy (and in some cases dangerously decrepit), the local council voted to spend some 1.8 billion escudos (about €90 million or £53 million) on making it fit for the new millennium. The end result is not only a spruced up village but new and improved accommodation and restaurants. Happily, despite fears that Caldas might lose its rustic down-at-heel charm and atmosphere, now the dust has settled it has more or less turned out to be business as usual.

Relax in the sun or cool off inside

TAKING A BREAK

For a snack try a *pão com chouriço* (spicy sausage in a roll), baked in an old-fashioned outdoor oven. You can enjoy it alfresco in the wooded picnic area by the stream, immediately above the village.

CALDAS DE MONCHIQUE: INSIDE INFO

Top tips **Visit early or late** in the day. During the summer tour buses arrive *en masse*.
• For **spa treatments** at Caldas de Monchique, tel: 282 910910 or go to www.monchiquetermas.com.

At Your Leisure

For Kids
- **Sail to Silves** up the River Arade by Portuguese gondola (➤ 142–4).
- Explore **Castelo de Silves** (➤ 143) but beware unguarded drops.
- Go to the **Fábrica do Inglês** (➤ 144, 152), by night to see clowns, street entertainers and dancing fountains.

The traditional town of Monchique

❶ São Bartolomeu de Messines
A typical small market town in the foothills of the Serra do Caldeirão, São Bartolomeu is reached from Silves along a road brimming with almonds, carob, figs and pomegranates. At its heart is the attractive 16th-century Igreja Matriz with a baroque façade and chapels decorated with *azulejos* and statues spanning the 16th to 18th centuries. Next door is the handsome 19th-century Casa Museu João de Deus, former home (now museum) of the eponymous local poet whose works were widely used to teach Algarvians to read and write around a century ago. It's worth a quick look inside just for the period interiors.

🞤 184 A3
Casa Museu João de Deus
✉ Next to Igreja Matriz ☎ No telephone ⏰ Mon–Fri 10–1, 2.30–6.30
💰 Inexpensive

❷ Barragem do Arade
A *barragem* is a reservoir or man-made dam but this picturesque stretch of water, interspersed by a series of low, hump-backed hills, 9km east of Silves, looks quite natural. The beauty spot is popular for picnics and family outings, and in summer a watersports centre operates here (➤ 152).
🞤 183 F3

Serra de Monchique
The Serra de Monchique is prime walking territory and a variety of guides advertise their services here. Ask in the tourist office for details. A cycling tour is offered by Alternativ (sic) Tour, led by a local man, tel: (mobile) 965 004337. Tours depart from the Albergaria Bica Boa on the old Lisbon road just out of the centre. If you decide to go it alone pick up a copy locally of the *Trilhos de Bio-Park Monchique* map, which covers 300km of trails in the Serra de Monchique.

❺ Monchique
Not to be confused with the tiny spa of Caldas de Monchique (➤ 145–6) 7km to the south, the small town of Monchique is the main settlement of the area, sitting at a height of 458m. It is known for its handicraft shops – mostly on the edge of town (➤ 151) – and parish

church. A good starting point is the tourist office in the square of Largo dos Chorões. Next to it is a spring-fed fountain – a modern interpretation of the traditional Algarvian *nora*, or well. From a corner of the square cobbled steps lead up to the village centre and the 16th-century parish church with its Manueline portal (➤ 21), *azulejos* and wooden ceiling.

Monchique can become busy, but to escape the crowds follow the signed footpath above the town hall to the ruins of the monastery of Nossa Senhora do Desterro (Our Lady of Exile). It's an easy 20- to 30-minute stroll and you will be rewarded with fine views. Note the magnolia tree in the monastery garden, claimed to be the biggest in Europe – possibly!

Just above Monchique on the road to Fóia is good rustic accommodation and a host of restaurants specialising in chicken *piri-piri* (➤ 17).

Another option for exploring the region is to take the picturesque N267 towards Aljezur, a route that offers some lovely views.

🞤 183 D4
Monchique Tourist Office
✉ Largo dos Chorões 8550
☎ 082 911189

A striking detail from the interior of Igreja Matriz in Monchique

❻ Fóia

At an altitude of 902m, Fóia is the highest point in the Algarve and also journey's end – the road goes no further, so you have to turn around and come back down. Topped with radio transmitters, a souvenir shop, and a café-restaurant, it's not the most inspiring location, but on a clear day is worthwhile for the views: almost the whole western Algarve is spread out before you, from Faro to Cape St Vincent. There are also some interesting walks nearby (➤ 152)

🞤 183 D4

Twin Peaks

For more spectacular views (and with far fewer people around) try Fóia's twin peak, Picota, at 774m, just east of Monchique. You can drive here – follow the Alferce signs out of Monchique – but this is also good walking territory and you should be able to get a guide (➤ 152) to take you up on foot.

Where to... Stay

Prices
Expect to pay per double room per night:
£ under €50   ££ €50–125   £££ over €125

Albergaria Bica Boa ££
The warm welcome and first-class food ensure many regulars at this romantic spot on the edge of the village, set back from the road in the wooded mountainside and surrounded by flower-filled gardens. Accommodation is limited to four rooms so in season book well ahead. The restaurant, one of the best in the region, features Monchique dishes as well as fish specialities and vegetarian dishes. The terrace is delightful for summer dining.

✚ 183 D4 ☒ Estrada de Lisboa 266, 8550 Monchique (1km north of Monchique, on the Lisbon road) ☎ 282 912271; fax: 282 912360

Albergaria do Lageado £
Set amid luxurious vegetation in the spa of Caldas de Monchique, this hotel offers comfortable, reasonably priced rooms with tiled floors, floral fabrics and good-sized bathrooms. The food – snacks and simple meals – is excellent value too. The garden has an attractive terrace and a swimming pool with thermal water.

✚ 183 D4 ☒ Caldas de Monchique, 8550 Caldas de Monchique ☎ 282 912616; fax: 282 911310 ⏰ May–Oct only

Colina dos Mouros ££
The "Hill of the Moors" on the outskirts of Silves is now a comfortable, modern hotel with superb views across the River Arade to the mighty walls and turrets of the Moorish fortress. Facilities are good for the size and category: there's a restaurant, a circular pool with bar and gardens, as well as landscaped 57 bedrooms, all with private showers, TV, safe and air conditioning. A room with a view is worth the small supplement – the fortress looks particularly dramatic at night when the battlements are floodlit.

✚ 183 E3 ☒ Pocinho Santo, 8301 Silves ☎ 282 440420

Estalagem Abrigo da Montanha ££
Standing on the road from Monchique to the summit of Foia, this inn enjoys sweeping views over the Serra de Monchique. The front garden and paved terrace are full of sweet-smelling camellias and citrus trees. Inside, stone walls, fireplaces and woodwork predominate. The 11 double rooms and four suites have wooden floors, pretty fabrics and balconies with mountain views. The six newer rooms are larger, smarter and more expensive though each room is charming in its own way. Amenities include an excellent restaurant (▶ 150) and a small pool with a terrace.

✚ 183 D4 ☒ Estrada da Fóia, 8550 Monchique ☎ 282 912131; fax: 282 913660; email: abrigodamontanha@hotmail.com

Quinta do Rio £
Enjoy the quiet rural life at this guesthouse, 5.5km northeast of Silves. There are six spotless guest rooms, all with shower and four with private terraces. There is no bar or official restaurant but with advance notice delicious meals can be provided. Assets of the rural setting are the freshly squeezed orange juice for breakfast from December to August and even strawberries in season.

✚ 183 E3 ☒ Sítio S Estevão, Apt 217, 8300 Silves (well signed off the N124 Silves to São Bartolomeu de Messines road) ☎ 282 445528

Where to...
Eat and Drink

Prices
Expect to pay per person for a meal, excluding drinks and service
£ under €15 **££** €15–23 **£££** over €23

Abrigo da Montanha ££
This mountain restaurant belongs to the Estalagem Abrigo da Montanha (▶ 149). In summer, meals are taken on the open-air panoramic terrace, or across the road at the Esplanada, which has equally staggering views. On cooler days, meals are served inside the rustic restaurant where a log fire blazes. Regional dishes dominate the menu: shellfish soup, razor fish rice, monkfish *cataplana*, grilled pork with garlic and parsley and kid *cataplana*. The speciality sweet is *bolo de frutas*, a sponge cake filled with fresh fruits and cream. Some of the most prized dishes need to be ordered in advance.

☐ 183 D4 ☒ Estrada da Fóia, Monchique ☎ 282 912131 ⓒ Daily lunch and dinner

Café Inglês £
After a morning's sightseeing in Silves, the Café Inglês is the perfect place to take a break. Located behind the cathedral and close to the castle entrance, it has been converted from a handsome 1920s town house. English-run, it combines café, restaurant, handicraft shop and rooftop bar. Sit inside or outside for coffee and delicious homemade cakes, good value meals, fresh salads or traditional Portuguese fare.

☐ 183 E3 ☒ Escadas do Castelo 11, Silves ☎ 282 442585 ⓒ Sun–Fri all day and evening, Sat dinner

Jardim das Oliveiras ££
Re-creations of mountain fare are served in this rural restaurant. The specialities are spicy red and black sausages, grilled pork, suckling pig, pork roasts and game, all prepared in an ancient wood oven. Traditional vegetable dishes include beans with rice or carrots, and Monchique cabbage stew. The atmosphere is relaxed, with woodburning stoves, a pretty terrace and an olive grove with swings and slides.

☐ 183 D4 ☒ Sítio do Porto Escuro, Monchique ☎ 282 912874 ⓒ Daily lunch and dinner

Paraíso da Montanha ££
The name says it all. Sit on the terrace for magnificent views over the mountains down to the coast. One of the first of Fóia's mountainside restaurants, this family-run establishment has been here for over 30 years. A typical meal starts with smoked mountain ham, followed by charcoal-grilled meats or casseroled rabbit, and ends with regional desserts such as *doces de amêndoa* (marzipan sweets) or Dom Rodrigo – almond and egg dessert wrapped in silver foil. Walk off the calories on the summit of Fóia (▶ 148).

☐ 183 D4 ☒ Estrada da Fóia, Monchique ☎ 282 912150 ⓒ Daily lunch and dinner

Rouxinol ££
Escape the coachloads in Caldas de Monchique and enjoy the rustic Rouxinol, a Swedish-owned café/restaurant just up the hill from the spa on the road to Monchique. Stop for coffee and homemade cakes and desserts (raspberry pie and ice cream is the speciality but the others are delicious too) or stay for a full meal. The menu changes according to the season but always features

Where to...

pasta, meat, fish, a buffet salad and a Swedish dish or two. Sit inside by log fires or out on the terrace overlooking citrus trees and mountains.

➕ 183 D4 ✉ Caldas de Monchique (on the road to Monchique) ☎ 282 913975 ⓘ Tue–Sun noon–10. Closed Jan and Dec

Rui Marisqueira ££

Book well in advance or be prepared to queue, for the restaurant's reputation extends far beyond the town of Silves. The setting is basic and the service can be brusque, but don't let this deter you. The food is great, particularly the shellfish, ranging from lobsters and crabs (which await you in the tank at the entrance) to whelks, oysters and barnacles. Starters can be followed by turbot, bass, bream or various *cataplanas*. Wild boar, rabbit or partridge feature on the menu in season.

➕ 183 E3 ✉ Rua Commendador Vilarinho, 27, Silves ☎ 282 442682 ⓘ Wed–Mon lunch and dinner. Closed 2 weeks Nov

Where to... Shop

MONCHIQUE

Monchique is known for its wooden handicrafts, cork and basketry. The main regional market is held on the second Friday of each month; on the third Friday farmers trade their livestock at a huge agricultural fair.

In Caldas de Monchique, 7km south of Monchique, try the famous spa waters or a nip of *medronho*, the local firewater. It's made from the distilled fruits of the arbutus trees that grow in the surrounding hills (▶ 157). *Medronho*-tasting takes place at the handicrafts centre in the old casino, which also has a good choice of ceramics. Roadside *artesanato* stalls between the spa and the town of Monchique sell pottery, rugs, woollens and basketry.

Coming into the town, on the left-hand side, **Casa J A Maio** (Estrada Velha 28, tel: 282 911000) offers handicrafts from Monchique and beyond. The baskets and the collapsible X-shaped wooden chairs (also sold across the road by the "Chair Man of Monchique") are made locally; the ceramics and slippers come from the Alentejo, the jerseys and rugs from the Fátima area in central Portugal. In the centre of Monchique, **Ardecor** (Largo dos Chorões 2) has a collection of stylish ceramics, rugs and handpainted wooden furniture. There are more handicrafts, as well as port and wine, at **Garrafeira de Monchique** on the same square. For an interesting selection of traditional pottery, ceramic sculpture, panels and fountains, visit the studio of Leonel Telo at the **Casa da Nogueira** (Rua do Côrro, 2; tel: 282 911377). On the windswept summit of Fóia above the town, stalls sell thick woollen sweaters, Monchique honey, ceramics and other souvenirs.

SILVES

In the centre of the town **Pandora** (Rua Samora Barros, 16, tel: 282 441246) is a good source for creative Portuguese artwork: woodcarvings, silver jewellery, handpainted glass, sculpture, silk scarves and paintings. Temporary art exhibitions are held here. More handicrafts and souvenirs can be found at **Coisas Loiças** (Rua 25 de Abril, near the main square, Praça do Municipio). In the square to the north (Large Jerónimo Osório), in a 16th-century building just below the castle, you'll find the **Estúdio Destra**, the studio-gallery of Kate Swift (▶ 15). On the same square **Peter Liesegon** (tel: 282 445233) has an elegant antiques and art shop specialising in glassware, ceramics, tiles and furniture. Further up on Largo do Castelo, by the entrance to the castle, **D Sancho** combines a café and handicraft shop where you can sample almond and orange cakes and browse amid lace, linen and painted pottery.

Where to...
Be Entertained

OUTDOOR ACTIVITIES

The wooded scenery of the mountains and the sweeping views from the summits make the Serra de Monchique an ideal place for walks and gentle strolls.

For the best views walk from the summit of Fóia to Picota, the Algarve's second highest peak (774m), which takes several hours. If you prefer to be guided by a local, contact **Alternativ Tour** (tel: 965 004337), which organises guided treks and cycle tours through the mountains. The guide is an expert on the flora, fauna and geology of the region, and the traditions of the local people. For more ideas, see the box ➤ 147, and the Caldas de Monchique area walk ➤ 156–7.

Northeast of Silves, the **Barragem do Arade** (➤ 147) is a peaceful reservoir with walks and plenty of good picnic spots. Level of the lake permitting, pedaloes and canoes can be hired and visitors can take a trip across to the island for swimming and sunbathing.

To the northeast of the reservoir, **Quinta Penedo** (Vale Fuzeiros, São Bartolomeu de Messines, tel: 282 332466) is a horse-riding centre in a picturesque valley. It offers gentle lakeside treks around the Barragem do Arade and more challenging routes for experienced riders.

NIGHTLIFE

The mountain towns are quiet by night and there are few of the types of entertainment that are found along the coast. However, Silves' evening scene has been enlivened by the addition of the **Fábrica do Inglês** (Rua 25 de Abril, tel: 282 440440, ➤ 144). Originally a cork factory with an English owner (hence the name), it reopened in 1999 as a complex of restaurants, featuring day and night entertainment. To remind you of its origins there is also a small and informative **cork museum** (➤ 144). In the evenings street artists provide colourful entertainment and the central plaza becomes the stage of a special show featuring dancing, singing and poetry, which is based on local history and legend. At midnight floodlit fountains provide the backdrop for a multimedia show that combines laser beams and music. Late-opening restaurants and cafés include the **Cervejaria** or Seafood Restaurant (serving Portuguese specialities and seating 700), **Churrasqueira** (Grill House), **Pizzeria**, **Tapas Bar**, **Tea Rooms** and the **Café da Fábrica**.

During the summer months, after 6pm, a convenient free shuttle-train service running every 15 minutes links the two main car parks to the Fábrica do Inglês.

MUSIC

In the centre of Silves, the cathedral hosts occasional choral music and recitals, while jazz can be heard in the **Cine-Teatro Silvense** (tel: 282 442413), which also shows films in their original language. For a lively place to eat in the evening try **Tasca do Bene** (tel: 282 444767), popular with the locals for stews, duck or fish dishes, washed down with wine from the barrel. The **Café Inglês** (Rua do Castelo 11, tel: 282 442585) has occasional live music on its roof terrace and a Brazilian band on Sunday afternoons in summer.

On the edge of Silves on the N124, the **Quinta Pomona** (tel: 282 416350) hosts regular *fado* and folklore evenings.

Walks & Tours

1 Lagos Town 154 – 155
2 Caldas de Monchique 156 – 157
3 Boca do Rio 158 – 160
4 Villages and Countryside of the Barrocal 161 – 163
5 Tavira 164 – 165
6 Rio Guadiana 166 – 168
7 Quinta do Marim 169 – 170

LAGOS TOWN
walk

The streets of Lagos are full of historical curiosities – you just have to know where to look. This short, circular tour of the town shows you the good, the bad and the downright odd. To understand the historical context and personalities, take a couple of minutes to read ▶ 6–8 before you start.

DISTANCE 1.5–2.5km
TIME 1.5 hours including museum visit
START/END POINT Statue of Prince Henry the Navigator, Avenida dos Descobrimentos ✚ 182 C2

1–2
In the **Praça da República**, behind the statue of Prince Henry, a modern mural represents King Sebastião's disastrous North African venture. Look directly opposite to see an ancient window, formerly on the Governor's Castle (now part of Lagos Hospital), from where it is said the boy-king rallied his troops. Leave the square from the left, following the castle walls past the statue of **Gil Eanes** (▶ 7).

2–3
Go through the arch between the 16th-century walls, past the shrine of São Gonçalo, the city's patron saint, and turn right, passing the hospital on your right. You emerge back into the Praça da República. On the corner directly opposite you is the **Armazém Regimental** – formerly a military magazine, dating from 1665. It is now used for art exhibitions. Turn left into Rua de São Gonçalo and continue for 50m to the **Igreja de São António**, on the left.

King Sebastião's statue is unmissable

Take time for a leisurely window shop while you're exploring the town

3–4
The church entrance is around the corner via the **Museu Municipal** (▶ 119–120). After looking round, you will exit the church onto Rua Silva Lopes and from here make a brief detour left into Rua Lançarote de Freitas to see what's on at the **Centro Cultural de São Lourenço** (▶ 136).

4–5

Return to Rua Silva Lopes, which leads into Lagos's main street, **Rua 25 de Abril**. This top end of the street, now mostly devoted to bars, was once the home of wealthy 19th-century merchants and many handsome stone door surrounds and balconies still survive. Continue up the street and look into the delightful **Casa da Papagaio** antiques shop on the right for an idea of the sort of paraphernalia that may once have filled these houses.

5–6

Either fork of Rua 25 de Abril leads to the square, **Praça Gil Eanes**, where you will find the strangest statue ever to commemorate a king. Unveiled in 1973, this modern take on the boy-king Sebastião – who made Lagos capital of the Algarve – is the most talked-about statue in the region (▶ 6–8).

6–7

To the left of the Caixa Geral de Depositos bank, leading off the square, is **Rua da Barroca** – this is a quiet alleyway with a pavement decorated with marine life. Opposite Antik & Velharias antiques shop is the old Lagos lifeboat house. Continue round the corner and turn left into Rua da Senhora da Graça, a small alley with some attractive restaurants that finishes back in the **Praça da República** by an arcade and some railings. Traditionally, this is the site of the very first European **slave market** (▶ 119). A less savoury by-product of Portugal's voyages of discovery, it was established in Lagos during the rule of Henry the Navigator, who, so it is chronicled, "reflected with pleasure on the salvation of these souls which would otherwise have been lost". Many of the slaves came from Nigeria, from the place that we now know as Lagos, (it was named after its trading partner in the Algarve). The statue of Henry, the man who facilitated it all, still sits just a few metres away.

2 CALDAS DE MONCHIQUE
walk

DISTANCE 7.5km
TIME 2–3 hours
START/END POINT Caldas de Monchique ✚ 183 D4

This rural ramble will take you through the countryside south of Caldas de Monchique into the foothills of the Serra de Monchique, with wonderful views south to the coast.

1–2
Start from the red telephone box in Caldas (▶ 145–6) and walk downhill until you reach the end of the village. Go past the water-bottling factory on your left, then turn right off the road onto a track that leads downhill, lined on either side by mimosa trees. The river runs below on your right. Follow the track until you come to a bridge crossing the river.

2–3
Cross the bridge and turn immediately left onto a narrow path that follows the river. Eventually you come to another bridge – ignore this and continue straight ahead. The path at this point may be a little overgrown. On your left, on the banks above the river, you will see tiny fields

planted with citrus trees. Soon a large house comes into view on the opposite bank and the path then forks. Take the right branch that leads slightly uphill, away from the river.

Guided Walks
If you would like a guide to accompany you on this walk, Julie Statham is an expert on the area and leads regular walking tours in the Algarve, tel: 282 698676 or (mobile) 096 575 3033; www.portugalwalks.com.

3–4
The path drops a bit before widening considerably into a track that leads uphill quite steeply. At the top you will meet another wide track. Turn right and follow this track for about 25 minutes, enjoying the wonderful views to both right and left.

The red telephone box is the starting point of the walk

4–5

Eventually you will come to a turning off to the right that climbs slightly before levelling off. Take this and soon you will have a panoramic view of Caldas de Monchique down below to your left. Continue on this track, which bends quite sharply left before leading steeply downhill. At the bottom of the hill you will pass a small white house on your left. The track bears right, leading you back to the first bridge you crossed at the beginning of the walk. Cross the bridge and continue straight ahead to get back to Caldas de Monchique.

The small arbutus fruit, from which fiery *medronho* is made

Algarve Moonshine

In many places along this walk you will see a small bush with a pretty little red fruit that vaguely resembles a strawberry. This is the arbutus fruit, *Arbutus unedo*, prized as the ingredient for *medronho*, the Algarve's *aguardente*, or firewater, spirit. The fruit is fermented in wooden barrels then distilled in copper alembics, or kettles, and can eventually reach a brain-numbing 70–90 degrees proof. *Medronho* is legally produced (at around 40 degrees proof) and sold throughout the Algarve, but there is a parallel illicit cottage industry of which Monchique (*not* Caldas de Monchique) is the capital! If you go along to one of Monchique's back-street shops with an empty bottle you may well be able to buy some of the real *caseiro* (homemade) moonshine. If you do, be careful – it is potent stuff.

3 BOCA DO RIO
Walk

This is a very rewarding and easy walk with great clifftop views and quite a few surprising features en route, including an ancient fort, Roman remains and freshwater wetlands where rice was once grown.

DISTANCE 8km **TIME** 2–2.5 hours
START/END POINT Boca do Rio beach (signposted off the N125 close to Budens Wetlands)
✚ 182 B2

1–2
Park your car by the beach but walk inland to the river (Boca do Rio is the Portuguese for "Mouth of the River") on your right. Cross it by the small concrete bridge then walk back towards the sea. Just before the path reaches the beach you will see another path on the left that leads uphill. Take this and, as you climb, look back to enjoy the view over the **Budens Wetlands** (see box ▶ 160). On reaching a wide track at the top of the hill turn right and then follow the winding path to find the still fairly substantial remains of a 16th-century fortress – these are not visible from the beach so come as something of a surprise. There are wonderful views along the coast from here.

2–3
Take any of the paths to the left of the fort; they all lead parallel with the coast towards a large white house that lies directly ahead, on top of the cliffs. Pass behind and around the house and take the wide track that leads downhill to the left of the garages.

At the bottom of this path is a choice of routes. The path to the right will take you to the beach of **Cabanas Velhas** (▶ 129), but unless you are desperate to sunbathe, or to get a drink at the beach bar, carry on straight across to take the path that climbs gently uphill. Follow this and soon you will be back on top of the

Handicrafts for sale at the Boca do Rio

3 Boca do Rio

cliffs with an even better view than before, this time of the beach at Cabanas Velhas. The sight of these inviting sands may well make you wish you had opted to turn right to the beach, but press on!

3–4

The track heads downhill and soon you meet another track coming in from the left. Turn left

here and pass through a cutting in the rocks as you begin once again to head uphill. There is a turning off to the right just before reaching the brow of the hill, but ignore it and continue ahead. On the brow you have a fantastic panorama of the coastline from the headland of Carvoeiro in the east to Sagres in the west.

4–5

The path now runs parallel with the clifftop for a short while before forking left and heading inland through a grove of umbrella pines. Take this left fork and continue along the track, which will soon bring you

to the old (surfaced) road that runs between **Burgau** and **Salema** (▶ 129).

Turn left onto the road (it's normally very quiet) and

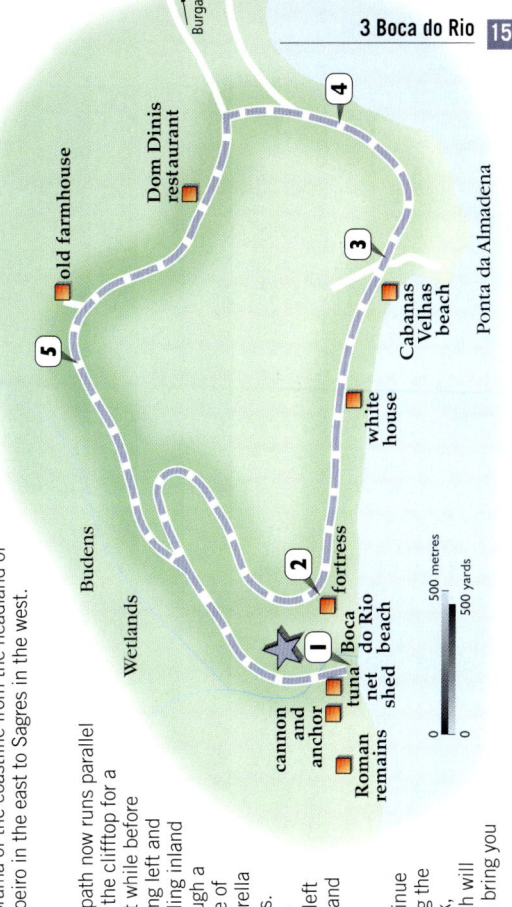

Echoes of the Past

Although there are no longer boats on Boca do Rio beach, the sheds that were built to hold large tuna nets in the days when sizeable tuna catches were made off here still stand. By the sheds you can see the large anchor and cannon that came from *L'Ocean*, a French warship sunk by the British some 300m offshore in 1759, during the Battle of Lagos. The wreck is now a popular site for divers.

A little further along the beach are the scant remains of a Roman villa and you can see how the sea has encroached right up to the villa in the 2,000 years since it was built. More Roman remains lie buried on the hillside in the area fenced off behind here.

This walk offers plenty of spectacular coastal views

continue for about five minutes, passing the Dom Dinis restaurant on your right. Just beyond this, you'll see a turning on your right marked by two old cartwheels and various handmade signs. Turn, and follow this track until it bends to the right towards an old house. Don't go down here – instead go straight on, passing between almond and fig trees and heading downhill. As you descend you see the Budens Wetlands ahead.

5–6

At the bottom of the slope turn left to follow a well-trodden path along the edge of the wetlands until it meets a wide unsurfaced road. Cross the road and keep straight on along a less clearly defined track below the hillside. This follows the river bank and takes you back to the small bridge at the start of the walk.

Finally, before you return to your car, take a brief stroll to the right-hand side of the beach to explore a little more of the area's rich history and current habitat (see box).

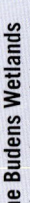

Birds, such as this heron, thrive in the Budens Wetlands

The Budens Wetlands

This marshy area is home to many species of birds, the Egyptian mongoose, otters, terrapins and other wildlife. In the years between the two world wars it was used for growing rice, but as development increased near by and wells were sunk for water the freshwater table of the Budens Wetlands was depleted and filled by rising seawater. In the end the marshes became too salty for any type of cultivation.

4 VILLAGES AND COUNTRYSIDE OF THE BARROCAL

Drive & Walk

DRIVE – **DISTANCE** About 50km
TIME 3–4 hours (including walk)
START/END POINT Loulé ✚ 184 C2
WALK – Around Fonte de Benémola (➤ 163)

This tour explores the central Barrocal region, an area of rolling hills north of Loulé. Because of its fertile soil and abundant produce (including almonds, oranges, carobs and figs), it has been called the Garden of the Algarve. Salir and Querença are two of the Algarve's prettiest and lesser-known villages.

An optional, easy walk around the beauty spot of Fonte de Benémola will take you right into the region's unspoiled rural heart.

1–2

Start at the town landmark, a Roman-style column (Duarte Pacheco monument) in the centre of **Loulé** (➤ 79–81). With the column behind you, turn left onto the main road and follow it around to your left, picking up signposts to Querença/Ameixial. After around 8km you'll reach a handsome, arched bridge and an old *fonte* sign. Turn left (signposted "Querença 2km") then almost immediately left again up to the village square. This is a lovely unspoiled village with an attractive baroque church, an ancient cross, two cafés, a good restaurant, a little shop selling locally produced gifts and a red telephone box.

2–3

Go back down the hill and turn left at the bottom. Pass through a number of small hamlets and after around 3km turn left to the **Fonte de Benémola** (signposted). See box (➤ 163) for optional walk at this point.

3–4

If you have stopped for the walk, turn left out of the parking area and continue for around 1km.

You might see an orange tree in fruit if you go at the right time of the year

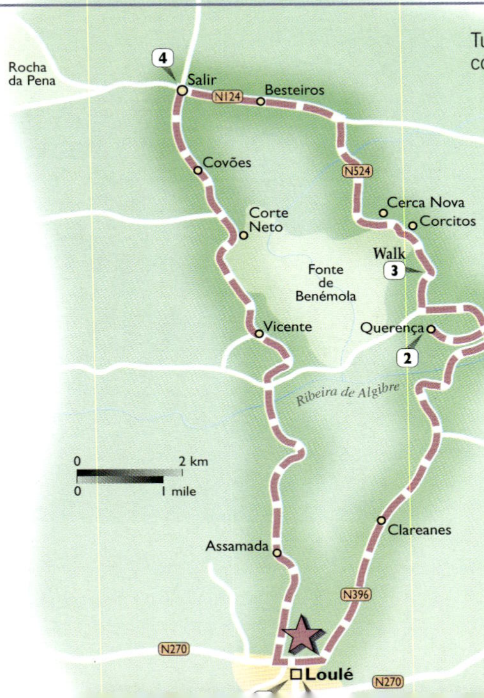

Turn left towards Salir (signposted) and continue straight ahead for around 7km, passing though typical Barrocal countryside and several tiny hamlets, including Cerca Nova and Corcitos. Turn left onto the main N124 road (signposted for Salir and Alte) and after around 3km (below a water tower) turn left to **Salir** (▶ 84) then almost immediately right to go up a steep hill to the village centre. To get to the castle remains go back down the hill, turn right to go through a narrow gap, turn left, follow the road round to the right, then opposite the post office (CTT Correio) turn right. Turn right again then either left or right will take you to the *castelo* (both ways are signposted). Park your car by the former church (now converted into domestic dwellings) and walk up the hill.

4–5
Head back down the hill, turn right by the restaurant bar and then at the triangular "roundabout" go left to get onto the road back to Loulé, which is a 16km drive away.

Farmers such as these live and work in the rural **Barrocal** area

WALK – **DISTANCE** 5km **TIME** 1 hour
AROUND Fonte de Benémola ✚ 184 C3

Fonte de Benémola Walk

1–2

Leave your car by the ruined house just inside the turn off and begin the walk. A sign says "Círculo Pedestre 5km". Initially there is only one track so it is impossible to go the wrong way. (You can actually drive most of the way to the *fonte* (spring) – some locals may well do so – but the track is narrow and this is not recommended.) Note the red, white and yellow splashes on trees and walls that indicate the correct way to go.

2–3

After about 1km of walking, fork left and cross a small bridge (a sign to the *fonte* reassures you at this point) to reach the start of the *fonte* area in another 1.5km. This is a lovely leafy beauty spot where a small babbling river strewn with boulders and stepping stones rushes through a quiet little valley. To get to the *fonte* you must walk for another five minutes or so, past some floodgates and a dam. Past the spring is a rest area with picnic tables, where the path ends.

You can usually cross the river at this furthest point by stepping stones, unless the river is in flood. Wherever you decide to cross, turn left immediately on the other side of the river. The path climbs up and away from the river – but don't be tempted to wander down through the fields by the river as there are no pathways. After a few minutes you will pass a small house where a basketmaker plies his trade, selling baskets of varying sizes to walkers.

Carry on, past a small stand of part-stripped cork trees, and eventually you emerge back onto the N524. Turn left, cross the bridge, and after around five minutes of walking you are back at the car-parking area.

• There are free guided tours of the Fonte de Benémola each Thursday, courtesy of the local Querença tourist office. Reservations are required: tel: 289 422495.

The tranquil Fonte de Benémola

5 TAVIRA
Walk

The most beautiful town in the eastern Algarve, Tavira is a quiet, civilised place in which to stroll, especially if you are a lover of architecture and churches. This walk crosses over the bridge to visit its lesser-known east bank.

1–2
Start by the riverside (car park) square, Praça da República, and walk back up the hill about 100m to the steps leading up (right) to the tourist office and the **Igreja da Misericórdia** (Church of Mercy, ➤ 50). If this lovely church is open take the opportunity to see inside.

2–3
Pass to the left of the church, along the Rua da Galeria, then turn left. Straight ahead, up a narrow cobbled path, is the **Igreja de Santa Maria do Castelo** (➤ 50, 51), another of Tavira's fine churches. To the left of the church is the castle garden and below it, the **Igreja de Santiago**

DISTANCE approx 2–3km
TIME 1–2 hours
START/END POINT Praça da República ✚ 186 A2

Unspoilt Tavira has changed little since the 19th century

(Church of St James, normally only open for Mass: Sat 4.30 pm, Sun 6 pm). Note above the church door the classic Iberian portrayal of Santiago as the slayer of the Moors.

3–4
Return to the Igreja de Santa Maria do Castelo and follow the path down to the river. At the river turn right and you will soon be back in the square where you started. Turn left to cross the **Ponte Romana** (Roman Bridge, ➤ 51). The inscription on it refers to the brave citizens of Tavira who fought against the Spanish in the War of Independence from 1383 to 1385.

4–5
Cross the bridge and bear left along Rua 5 de Outubro, which leads into the pretty garden square of **Praça Dr Padinha**. Here there is a statue of Dom Marcelino Franco, a local man who became Bishop of the Algarve. At the far side of the square is the **Igreja Parroquial de São Paulo** (Parish Church of St Paul) – occasionally open outside Mass times (➤ 51).

5–6

Turn right opposite the statue into Rua Almirante Cândido dos Reis, then take a detour right into Rua António Cabreira to see a small metal workshop producing tulips, boats, weathervanes and other portable items. There are some good backstreet restaurants around here too.

To visit the **Igreja do Carmo**, go along Rua Almirante Cândido dos Reis for around 200m and turn left into Rua 1 de Dezembro. If the church is not open ask for the key at No 22 (opposite).

Turn right off Rua Almirante Cândido dos Reis (left if you have been to the Igreja do Carmo) into the narrow Travessa do Carrasção, right again, and then left into Largo da Caracolinha, by the river.

6–7

Cross the river by the road bridge. On the left is the old fish market, now converted into a **cultural and shopping centre**, and on the right are the riverside gardens with an elegant, silver-painted wrought-iron bandstand. Turn left to see the fishing boats at anchor by the fish auction house and dock.

7–8

By the cultural and shopping centre head for one block along Travessa das Cunhas, into **Rua Dr Parreira**, a busy street of handsome buildings, shops, cafés and a cinema. Mooch along here then take any one of the side streets back to the riverfront and turn left to return to the Praça da República.

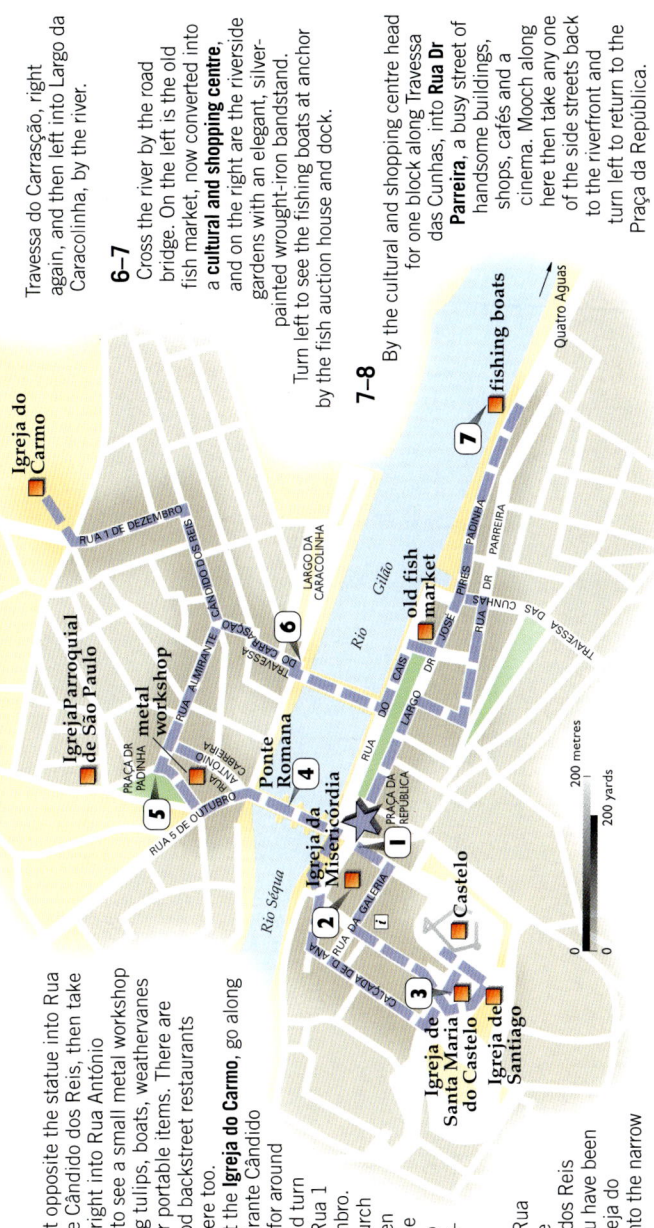

RIO GUADIANA
Drive

DISTANCE approximately 111km
TIME driving: 3–4 hours; **visits:** 1–2 hours: so allow a full day
START/END POINT Tavira ✚ 186 A2

This is perhaps the most unusual and one of the least travelled drives you can make in the Algarve. It begins along the pastoral banks of the Rio Guadiana – in complete contrast to traditional Algarve holiday scenery, but no less beautiful for that. It then takes in the moor-like northern frontier and the fascinating Parque Mineiro Cova dos Mouros (the Moor's Cave Mining Park), isolated in one of the Algarve's loneliest spots. Make an early start so you can explore Alcoutim and enjoy the spectacular final part of the journey in daylight.

1–2
From Tavira (➤ 49–51) head north, cross the N125, and turn onto the E01 motorway heading east towards "Espanha". Turn off to the left, just before the border, onto the N122 towards Beja/Mértola.

Sanlúcar de Guadiana viewed across the river

6 Rio Guadiana

2–3

After only a few kilometres the scenery becomes very rural. Go through Junqueira and Azinhal and eventually turn right towards Alcoutim, where the road forks onto the N507. Just past Azinhal, look over to your left for views of the Barragem de Beliche.

Beyond two landmark white castellated towers, look right for your first glimpse of the Rio Guadiana. As you continue down the hill a wonderful panorama of the river unfolds before the road crosses another river, the Ribeira de Odeleite, and reaches the grassy banks of the Guadiana.

3–4

The small village of **Foz de Odeleite** is a picturesque stop with a small quay, a café, a couple of restaurants and, occupying the old schoolhouse, the tiny **Museu do Rio** (open Tue–Sat 9–12.30, 2–5.30). The museum comprises little more than a few display panels but it does have some interesting facts about the history of the river. This region once had trade links with Carthage, Rome, Athens and Tyre, and salted fish, cereals, mercury, gold, silver, iron and copper were all shipped along the Guadiana.

4–5

At Alamo the road swings briefly away from the river. Follow the signs at the mini-roundabout towards Alcoutim to rejoin the Guadiana at Guerreiros do Rio where yachts and catamarans lie at anchor.

The name "Warriors of the River" recalls its history as a strife-torn border settlement. A couple of kilometres further on stop at the *miradouro* (lookout) and enjoy the view. The castle you can see on the horizon is actually on the Spanish side of the river, at Sanlúcar de Guadiana. Continue on to Alcoutim (▶ 53–4), an attractive and interesting little town.

5–6

Turn right out of Alcoutim back onto the main

Walks and Tours

Parque Mineiro Cova dos Mouros

✚ 186 A4 ✉ Vaqueiros
☎ 289 999229 or 281 498505,
http://minacovamouros.sitepac.pt
🕙 10.30–6, Mar–Oct; 10.30–4.30,
Nov–mid-Dec, late Jan–Feb. Closed mid-
Dec–late Jan 💰 Moderate

road and go left at the next crossroads, sign-posted to Parque Mineiro Cova dos Mouros. At the next crossroads, after around 6km, go straight over, signposted to Cachopo. Continue on for another 30km through sparsely populated countryside with views of the plains of the Alentejo to your right. At the small settlement of Martim Longo look for a sign left to Vaqueiros. Follow this road for 6km and the Cova dos Mouros park is signposted off the road, though you have another 2km of bumpy dirt track to negotiate before you get to the gates.

The **Parque Mineiro Cova dos Mouros** describes itself as an experimental archaeological station and tells the story of 5,000 years of mining on this site. It began life as an ancient copper and gold mine, first worked in the neolithic period and exploited throughout the Bronze and Iron Ages. The Romans established a slave mine here and legend has it that the Moors hid both themselves and their treasure in it after the Reconquest (▶ 30). It then lay forgotten for centuries and was only rediscovered in 1865. The mine reopened with over 370m of galleries, up to 100m deep, and although copper, iron and sulphur were yielded, the operation was uneconomical and shut permanently in 1930. Today the main historical periods of its operation are illustrated on a 1km open-air circuit including re-creations of huts and a fort from the Calcolithic Age (2500 BC), Bronze-Age furnaces, a Roman crane and actual mine shafts. Hand-held audio guides provide an excellent commentary to the exhibits.

Donkey rides are also provided and there are natural swimming pools. Planned new ventures and facilities include underground mine tours, a bird recovery centre and an animal sanctuary.

6–7

Retrace your journey to Martim Longo and go left (signposted Barranco Velho). After 16km you'll arrive at Cachopo, where there is a restaurant. From here it is a spectacular, twisting turning descent of 43km back to Tavira.

Ancient techniques brought to life at Cova dos Mouros

7 QUINTA DO MARIM

Walk

Quinta do Marim is the visitor centre for the Reserva Natural da Ria Formosa (▶ 57) and a well-signposted visitor trail and information boards give a good introduction the reserve. This peaceful stroll takes you through pine woods and along the seashore.

The letters below, in brackets, correspond to the signboards.

DISTANCE 3km
TIME 2–3 hours
START/END POINT Quinta do Marim reception ✠ 185 E1

1–2

Stop at the reception (by the entrance gate) where you will be given an excellent map/plan of the area. Walk on past the car park, turn right past the dormitory block and you'll see the white building of the **visitor centre** ahead. After having a look inside, turn left out of the visitor centre to reach the *salinas* (saltpans).

2–3

The **salinas** (C) of the Ria Formosa contribute substantially to the national production of salt. Those nearest to the sea have been used for centuries as **fish farming tanks** (D). Walk down to the shore and onto the jetty, from where the island of **Armona** is virtually within swimming distance. Look out for fiddler crabs scuttling across the shore, and the seagulls pursuing them. Flamingos are frequent visitors here alongside Kentish plover and black-winged stilt.

A regular boat service ferries visitors to and from the island in the summer from here and you may also be able to take a ride in a restored traditional tuna fishing boat; tel: 289 704134 and expect to speak a little Portuguese.

3–4

Walk back, to the right of the hut, and fork right past the **rush beds** (G). Cross the **dunes** (H) by the boardwalk to get to the **tidemill** (J). This is a fascinating building, restored to use the power of the tides to produce flour. It is one of only three mills in the country that are still working. In the large lagoon behind the mill shellfish are farmed.

The interior of the tidemill has been retained as it was

4–5

Follow the route away from the tidemill and turn right past the **saltmarsh** (L). There is a bird-watching hide here and another a little further on by the freshwater pond. You might spot herons, grebes, coots, moorhens, mallards and purple gallinule (recognisable by their dark purple colouring, bright red beaks and oversized feet).

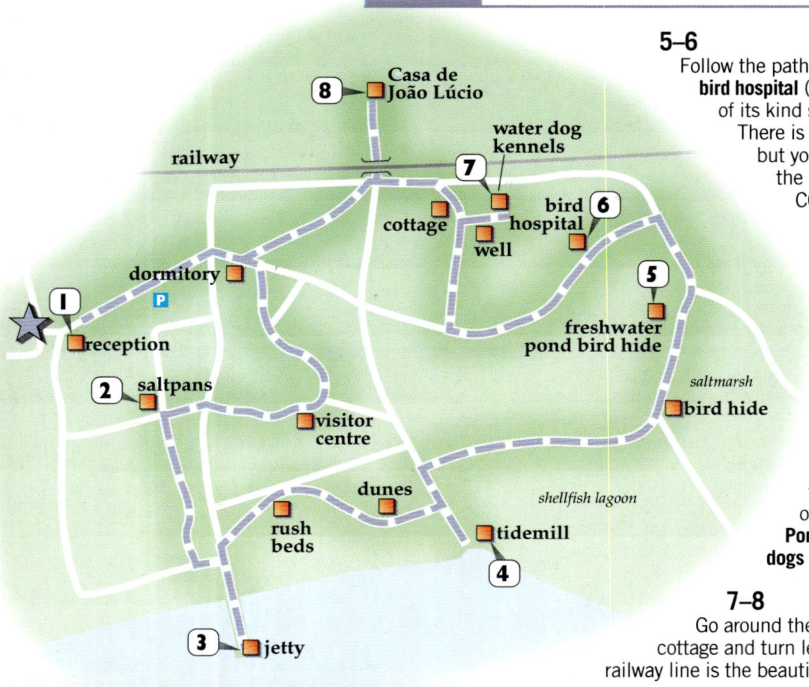

5–6

Follow the path around to the **bird hospital** (P), the only one of its kind south of Lisbon. There is no admission but you can check on the inmates by CCTV monitors.

6–7

Take the next right, which leads to a fine example of a *nora*, a traditional well. Behind the well you'll find the kennels of the Algarve's **Portuguese water dogs** (▶ 28).

7–8

Go around the back of the cottage and turn left. Across the railway line is the beautiful **Casa de João Lúcio** (not accessible to the public), built by a famous local poet at the turn of the 20th century. It is now used for environmental education purposes. The dormitory and car park (see 1–2) are 50m behind you.

Ornithologists can spot freshwater birds on the ponds

185 E1
Quinta do Marim, N125
289 704134
Daily 9–12.30, 2–5
Inexpensive

Practicalities

GETTING ADVANCE INFORMATION

Websites
- www.algarvenet.com
- www.thealgarve.net

Two comprehensive Websites, with everything from accommodation databases to town tours, currency conversion and weather forecasts.

- www.essential-algarve.com Leisure and lifestyle magazine covering what's on, nightlife and restaurants.

In the UK
Portuguese National Tourist Office
22–25a Sackville Street
London W1X 1DE
☎ 020 7494 1441

BEFORE YOU GO

WHAT YOU NEED

- ● Required
- ○ Suggested
- ▲ Not required
- △ Not applicable

	UK	Germany	USA	Canada	Australia	Ireland	Netherlands	Spain
Passport/National Identity Card	●	●	●	●	●	●	●	●
Visa	▲	▲	▲	▲	▲	▲	▲	▲
Onward or Return Ticket	○	○	○	○	○	○	○	○
Health Inoculations (tetanus and polio)	▲	▲	▲	▲	▲	▲	▲	▲
Health Documentation	▲	▲	▲	▲	▲	▲	▲	▲
Travel Insurance	○	○	○	○	○	○	○	○
Driver's Licence (national)	●	●	●	●	●	●	●	●
Car Insurance Certificate	●	●	●	●	●	●	●	●
Car Registration Document	●	●	●	●	●	●	●	●

WHEN TO GO

Faro

High season Low season

JAN	FEB	MAR	APR	MAY	JUN	JUL	AUG	SEP	OCT	NOV	DEC
15°C	16°C	18°C	21°C	24°C	30°C	35°C	37°C	33°C	28°C	19°C	17°C

☀ Sun   ⛅ Sunshine and showers

Temperatures are the **average daily maximum** for each month. Average daily minimum temperatures are 8 to 10° C lower. The best time of year for weather is May to June and September to October when it is warm and dry without being uncomfortably hot. July and August are very hot, with the temperatures pushing into the mid-30s, and at other times of year there is the risk of rainfall. April and November can still be very pleasant in terms of temperature. To miss the crowds, avoid the school holidays, particularly July and August when half of Lisbon as well as countless north European holidaymakers clog up the roads and beaches. If you are here for sport rather than sunbathing, the Algarve is an all-year destination.

In Ireland
Portuguese National
Tourist Office
54 Dawson Street
Dublin 2
☎ 01 670 9133

In the USA
Portuguese National
Tourist Office
590 Fifth Avenue
4th Floor
New York NY 10036
☎ 212/719-3985

In Canada
Portuguese National
Tourist Office
60 Bloor Street West
Suite 1005
Toronto, Ontario M4W 3B8
☎ (416) 921 7376

GETTING THERE

By Air The Algarve has only one international airport, at Faro. There are direct flights from major UK airports, Dublin, and most major European cities but transatlantic flights usually change at Lisbon. The majority of flights arrive in, and leave from, Faro on Thursdays and Saturdays. The main portuguese airlines are **TAP-Air Portugal** and **Portugália Airlines**.
Ticket prices are highest in summer and during school holiday periods, but inexpensive last-minute deals are also most common at these times.
Approximate flying times New York 6.5 hours, Toronto 10 hours, London and Dublin 2 hours.
By Rail and Bus Trains are generally unreliable and slow, but there are several coach and long-distance bus companies offering reasonable fares to the Algarve from northern Portugal and other part of Europe. **Inter Centro** (the Portuguese franchise holder of the Europe-wide Eurolines coach service) serves international routes to Porto and Lisbon and **Express** coaches make the journey from Lisbon to Faro in just four hours. **EVA** (www.eva-bus.com) runs the "Linha de Huelva" route across the border from Huelva and Ayamonte in Spain, with some coaches continuing as far as Lagos.
By Boat Most people travel from Spain to Portugal by driving over the motorway bridge over the Rio Guadiana, but ferries still operate between the two countries. The car and passenger ferry from Ayamonte to Vila Real de São Antonio departs at regular intervals.

TIME

The Algarve observes Greenwich Mean Time (GMT) during the winter; during the summer, from late March to late September, the time is GMT plus one hour. British visitors, therefore, don't need to adjust their watches.

CURRENCY AND FOREIGN EXCHANGE

Currency Portugal is one of the 12 European countries to use a single currency, the **Euro (€)**. Euro notes and coins, issued on 1 January, 2002, replace the escudo ($), the former unit of currency. Coins are issued in denominations of 1, 2, 5, 10, 20 and 50 Euro cents and €1 and €2. Notes are issued in denominations of €5, €10, €20, €50, €100, €200 and €500. The exchange rate is set at 100 escudos = €0.5.
Exchange bureaux generally offer a better deal than the bank when charges are taken into account, but there are so many variations that the best advice is to shop around.
Never change in shops despite the deals they appear to offer and note that **banks** can take an age to serve you. Never wait in a queue that is not dedicated to *cambio* (foreign exchange). Typically you will wait and wait then simply get passed on to another line!
Travellers' cheques in sterling or US dollars are widely accepted.
Credit cards are accepted in the resorts and ATMs are common. Elsewhere it's usually cash only, and when in the countryside it is advisable to have small denomination notes to hand. It is easier and no more expensive (depending on your credit card charges) to rely solely on plastic, rather than taking travellers' cheques or buying cash in advance. Pay larger bills with your card and withdraw petty cash locally from a cash machine.

TIME DIFFERENCES

GMT 12 noon	Portugal 12 noon	USA (East) 7 am	USA (West) 4 am	Germany 1 pm	Australia Sydney 10pm

WHEN YOU ARE THERE

CLOTHING SIZES

UK	Italy	USA	
36	46	36	Suits
38	48	38	
40	50	40	
42	52	42	
44	54	44	
46	56	46	
7	41	8	Shoes
7.5	42	8.5	
8.5	43	9.5	
9.5	44	10.5	
10.5	45	11.5	
11	46	12	
14.5	37	14.5	Shirts
15	38	15	
15.5	39/40	15.5	
16	41	16	
16.5	42	16.5	
17	43	17	
8	34	6	Dresses
10	36	8	
12	38	10	
14	40	12	
16	42	14	
18	44	16	
4.5	38	6	Shoes
5	38	6.5	
5.5	39	7	
6	39	7.5	
6.5	40	8	
7	41	8.5	

NATIONAL HOLIDAYS

1 Jan	New Year's Day
Feb	Shrove Tuesday/Ash Wednesday
Mar/Apr	Good Friday/Easter Monday
25 Apr	Day of the Revolution
1 May	Labour Day
Jun	Corpus Christi
10 Jun	National Day
15 Aug	Feast of the Assumption
5 Oct	Republic Day
1 Nov	All Saints' Day
1 Dec	Restoration of Independence Day
8 Dec	Feast of the Immaculate Conception
25 Dec	Christmas Day
26 Dec	St Stephen's Day

OPENING HOURS

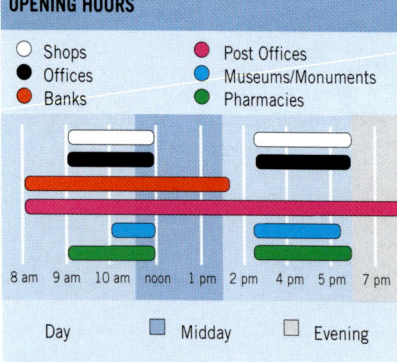

Shops catering for tourists are open all day during high season until 9 or 10 pm, even on Sundays and holidays. Large stores and supermarkets are open continuously from about 9 to 7. Some supermarkets stay open until 10 (5 on Sundays).
Museums and churches Opening times vary greatly and often seem unpredictable so it's best to check individual opening times.
Banks may open late to offer exchange facilities.
Post offices in smaller towns may close for lunch and not open at all at weekends.

EMERGENCY

POLICE 112

FIRE 112

AMBULANCE 112

PERSONAL SAFETY

- Petty theft is the only crime that is likely to concern visitors to the region.
- Theft from parked cars is not uncommon so try to take all personal belongings out with you. If you must leave anything in the car, hide it in the boot.
- Beware of pickpockets in crowded markets.
- Portugal is the least macho of Europe's Latin countries and generally women travellers will find few problems.

Police assistance:
 112 from any phone

TELEPHONES

There are phone kiosks on street corners almost everywhere. To prevent having to fiddle with mountains of small change buy a *telecarte* from a tobacconist or a newsagent displaying the credifone sign.
Don't phone home from a hotel. Portuguese telephone charges are among the highest in Europe and with the added hotel premium, your total bill can be astronomical.

International Dialling Codes
Dial 000 followed by
UK:	44
USA/Canada:	1
Irish Republic:	353
Australia:	61
Germany:	49

POST

The postal service is good, and most postcards to Europe arrive in a few days. Allow around ten days to North America. Stamps are available at post offices, gift and souvenir shops, tobacconists and newsagents, but outlets other than post offices often run out or may only sell them if you buy their postcards.

ELECTRICITY

The power supply in Portugal is 220 volts AC. Sockets take two-pronged continental plugs, so visitors from the UK and USA need an adaptor for non-continental appliances, and a transformer for 100–120 volt devices.

TIPS/GRATUITIES

Tipping is not expected for all services and rates are lower than those elsewhere. As a general guide:

Restaurant bill	(service not included) 10%
Taxis	small change
Tour Guides	half day €3
	full day €5
Porters	50 cents per bag
Chambermaids	€1–€2 per night
Toilet attendants	small change

Practicalities 175

CONSULATES and EMBASSIES

UK
☎ 282 417800

USA
☎ 217 273300

Ireland
☎ 221 3929440

Australia
☎ 221 3404666

Canada
☎ 289 803757

HEALTH

Insurance It is advisable to take out full travel insurance but EU citizens can reclaim medical expenses if they travel with the E111 form. Most doctors will treat you in your hotel if you have adequate insurance cover.

Dental Services The standard of dental care is generally excellent. Dental practices advertise in the free English- or German-language magazones and newspapers you can pick up at hotels.

Weather The sun is intense at all times of year, and it is possible to burn very quickly, even on cloudy days. Put sunscreen on all exposed parts of the body, wear a hat and drink plenty of water, especially if walking in the hills or along the coast.

Drugs Chemists (*farmâcia*) are open Mon–Fri 9–1 and 3–7, and Sat 9–12.30. Some open through lunch and the late night duty rota is posted in pharmacy windows. Pharmacists are highly trained and can sell some drugs that require prescriptions in other countries. However, take adequate supplies of any drugs you take regularly as they may not be available.

Safe Water Tap water is safe but its mineral content makes it taste unpleasant. Ask for fizzy (*água com gás*) or still (*água sem gás*) bottled water.

CONCESSIONS

Young People Museums often have lower rates of admission for students (and entry is usually free for children) on production of a passport or student identity card as proof of age.

Senior Citizens Senior citizens from many European countries come to the Algarve for its year-round warmth and discounted long-stay low-season rates.. However, there are few concessions specifically for older people and if mobility is impaired then getting around anywhere other than in the newer resorts can be a bit of a trial (see Travelling with a Disability).

TRAVELLING WITH A DISABILITY

Away from modern resorts such as Vilamoura, Quinta do Lago and Vale do Lobo, steep slopes, narrow pavements, cobbled streets and a lack of ramps or lifts all conspire to make life difficult. For information in Britain contact RADAR (12 City Forum, 250 City Road, London EC1V 8AF, tel: 020 7250 3222). In the USA contact Mobility International (PO Box 10767, Eugene, OR 97440, tel: 503/343-1284; www.miusa.org) or SATH (347 Fifth Avenue, Suite 610, New York, NY 10016, tel: 212/447-7284; www.sath.org).

CHILDREN

Most hotels and restaurants are geared towards families. Outside the resorts the Portuguese are tolerant of children but there are few facilities such as high-chairs or baby-changing areas.

TOILETS

Use toilets in cafés or hotels as public toilets are rare. Plumbing is easily blocked, so put paper in the bin provided.

WILDLIFE SOUVENIRS

Importing wildlife souvenirs sourced from rare or endangered species may be illegal or require a special permit.

USEFUL PHRASES

There are two distinctive Portuguese sounds: firstly, the nasalised vowels written with a til (~, like the tilde on Spanish ñ): (so "bread", *pão*, is pronounced "pow!" with a strong nasal twang; secondly, "s" and "z" are often pronounced as a slushy "sh" (so "banknotes", *notas*, is pronounced "not-ersh").

GREETINGS AND COMMON WORDS

Yes / No **Sim / Não**
Please **Se faz favor**
Thank you **Obrigado** *(male speaker)* / **obrigada** *(female speaker)*
You're welcome **De nada / Foi um prazer**
Hello / Goodbye **Olá / Adeus**
Welcome **Bem vindo/a**
Good morning **Bom dia**
Good evening / night **Boa noite**
How are you? **Como está?**
Fine, thank you **Bem, obrigado/a**
Sorry **Perdão**
Excuse me, could you help me? **Desculpe, podia ajudar-me?**
My name is... **Chamo-me...**
Do you speak English? **Fala inglês?**
I don't understand **Não percebo**
I don't speak any Portuguese **Não falo português**

EMERGENCY! Urgência!

Help! **Socorro!**
Stop! **Pare!**
Stop that thief! **Apanhe o ladrão!**
Police! **Polícia!**
Fire! **Fogo!**
Go away, or I'll scream! **Se não se for embora, começo a gritar!**
Leave me alone! **Deixe-me em paz!**

I've lost my purse / wallet **Perdi o meu porta-moedas / a minha carteira**
My passport has been stolen **Roubaram-me o passaporte**
Could you call a doctor? **Podia chamar um médico depressa?**

DIRECTIONS AND TRAVELLING

Airport **Aeroporto**
Boat **Barco**
Bus station **Estação de camionetas**
Bus / coach **Autocarro**
Car **Automóvel**
Church **Igreja**
Hospital **Hospital**
Market **Mercado**
Museum **Museu**
Square **Praça**
Street **Rua**
Taxi rank **Praça de táxis**
Train **Comboio**
Ticket **Bilhete**
  Return **Ida e volta**
  Single **Bilhete de ida**
Station **Estação**
I'm lost **Perdi-me**
How many kilometres to...? **Quantos quilómetros faltam ainda para chegar a...?**
Here / There **Aqui / Ali**
Left / right **À esquerda / À direita**
Straight on **Em frente**

NUMBERS

0	**zero**	16	**dezasseis**
1	**um**	17	**dezassete**
2	**dois**	18	**dezoito**
3	**três**	19	**dezanove**
4	**quatro**	20	**vinte**
5	**cinco**	21	**vinte e um**
6	**seis**	30	**trinta**
7	**sete**	40	**quarenta**
8	**oito**	50	**cinquenta**
9	**nove**	60	**sessenta**
10	**dez**	70	**setenta**
11	**onze**	80	**oitenta**
12	**doze**	90	**noventa**
13	**treze**	100	**cem**
14	**catorze**	101	**cento e um**
15	**quinze**	500	**quinhentos**

DAYS

Today	**Hoje**
Tomorrow	**Amanhã**
Yesterday	**Ontem**
Tonight	**Esta noite**
Last night	**Ontem à noite**
In the morning	**De manhã**
In the afternoon	**De tarde**
Later	**Logo / Mais tarde**
This week	**Esta semana**
Monday	**Segunda-feira**
Tuesday	**Terça-feira**
Wednesday	**Quarta-feira**
Thursday	**Quinta-feira**
Friday	**Sexta-feira**
Saturday	**Sábado**
Sunday	**Domingo**

MONEY: Dinheiro

Bank **Banco**
Banknote **Notas**
Cash desk **Caixa**
Change **Troco**
Cheque **Cheque**
Coin **Moeda**
Credit card **Cartão de crédito**
Exchange office **Cámbios**
Exchange rate **Cámbio**
Foreign **Estrangeiro**
Mail **Correio**
Post office **Agência do correio**
Traveller's cheque **Cheque de viagem**
Could you give me some small change? **Podia dar-me também dinheiro trocado, se faz favor?**

ACCOMMODATION

Are there any...? **Há...?**
I'd like a room with a view of the sea **Queria um quarto com vista para o mar**
Where's the emergency exit / fire escape? **Onde fica a saída de emergéncia / escada de salvação?**
Does that include breakfast? **Está incluido o pequeno almoço?**
Do you have room service? **O hotel tem serviço de quarto?**
I've made a reservation **Reservei um lugar**
Air-conditioning **Ar condicionado**
Balcony **Varanda**
Bathroom **Casa de banho**
Chambermaid **Camareira**
Hot water **Água quente**
Hotel **Hotel**
Key **Chave**
Lift **Elevador**
Night **Noite**
Room **Quarto**
Room service **Serviço de quarto**
Shower **Duche**
Telephone **Telefone**
Towel **Toalha**
Water **Água**

RESTAURANT: Restaurante

I'd like to book a table **Posso reservar uma mesa?**
A table for two please **Uma mesa para duas pessoas, se faz favor**
Could we see a menu, please? **Poderia dar nos a ementa, se faz favor**

What's this? **O que é isto?**
A bottle of... **Uma garrafa de ...**
Alcohol **Alcool**
Beer **Cerveja**
Bill **Conta**
Bread **Pão**
Breakfast **Pequeno almoço**
Café **Café**
Coffee **Café**
Dinner **Jantar**
Lunch **Almoço**
Menu **Menú / ementa**
Milk **Leite**
Mineral water **Água mineral**
Pepper **Pimenta**
Salt **Sal**
Table **Mesa**
Tea **Chá**
Waiter **Empregado/a**

SHOPPING

Shop **Loja**
Where can I get....? **Em que loja posso arranjar...?**
Could you help me? **Pode atender-me?**
I'm looking for... **Estou a procura de...**
I would like... **Queria...**
I'm just looking **Só estou a ver**
How much? **Quanto custa?**
It's too expensive **Acho demasiado caro**
I'll take this one / these **Levo este(s) / esta(s)**
Good / Bad **Bom / Mau**
Bigger **Maior**
Smaller **Mais pequeno**
Open / Closed **Aberto / Fechado**
I'm a size... in the UK **Na Grã Bretanha o meu número é...**
Have you got a bag? **Tem um saco?**

TOWN PRONUNCIATION GUIDE

Armação de Pêra **arma-sow** (as in female pig) **der pear-uh**
Carvoeiro **carve-where-ooh**
Faro **far-oo**
Lagos **lah-goosh**
Loulé **l-ow-lay**
Monchique **mon-chic**
Olhão **ool-yow**
Portimão **porteem-ow**
Praia da Luz **prior da loozh**
Quarteira **quart-air-ah**
Sagres **sar-grersh**
Silves **sill-versh**

178 Useful words and phrases

Atlas

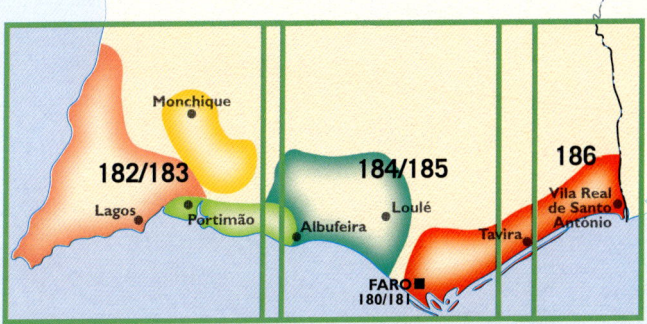

To identify the regions, see the map on the inside of the front cover

Regional Maps

—··—	International boundary
—·—	District boundary
▬▬	Major route
= = =	Motorway under construction
▬▬	Main road
▬ ▬	Main road under construction
▬▬	Other road

- Natural park, Nature reserve
- Built-up area
- ☐ City
- ▫ Major town
- ○ Other town
- · Village
- ◼ Featured place of interest
- ▪ Place of interest

City Plan

▬▬	Main road
▬▬	Other road
▬▬	City wall

- Important building
- Featured place of interest
- ⓘ Information

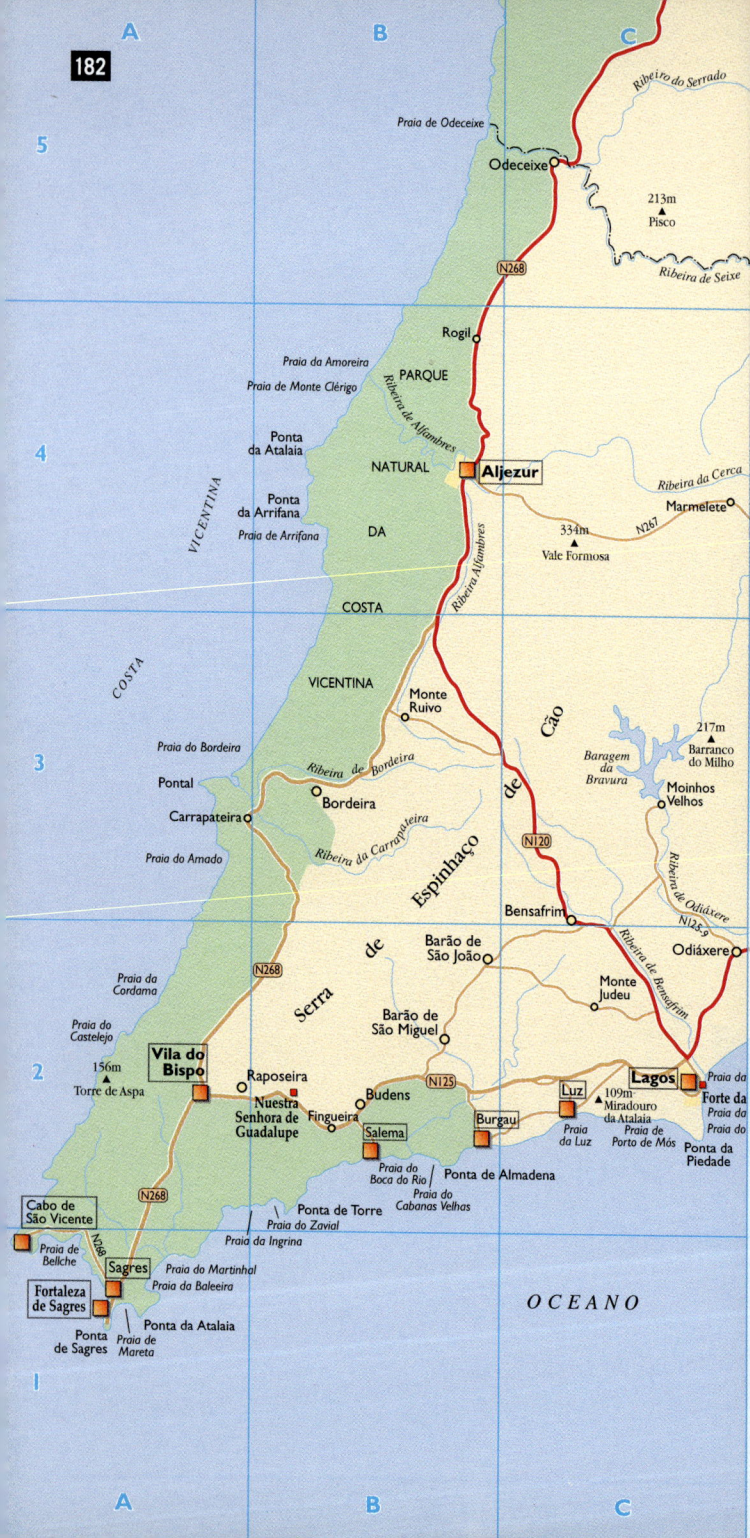

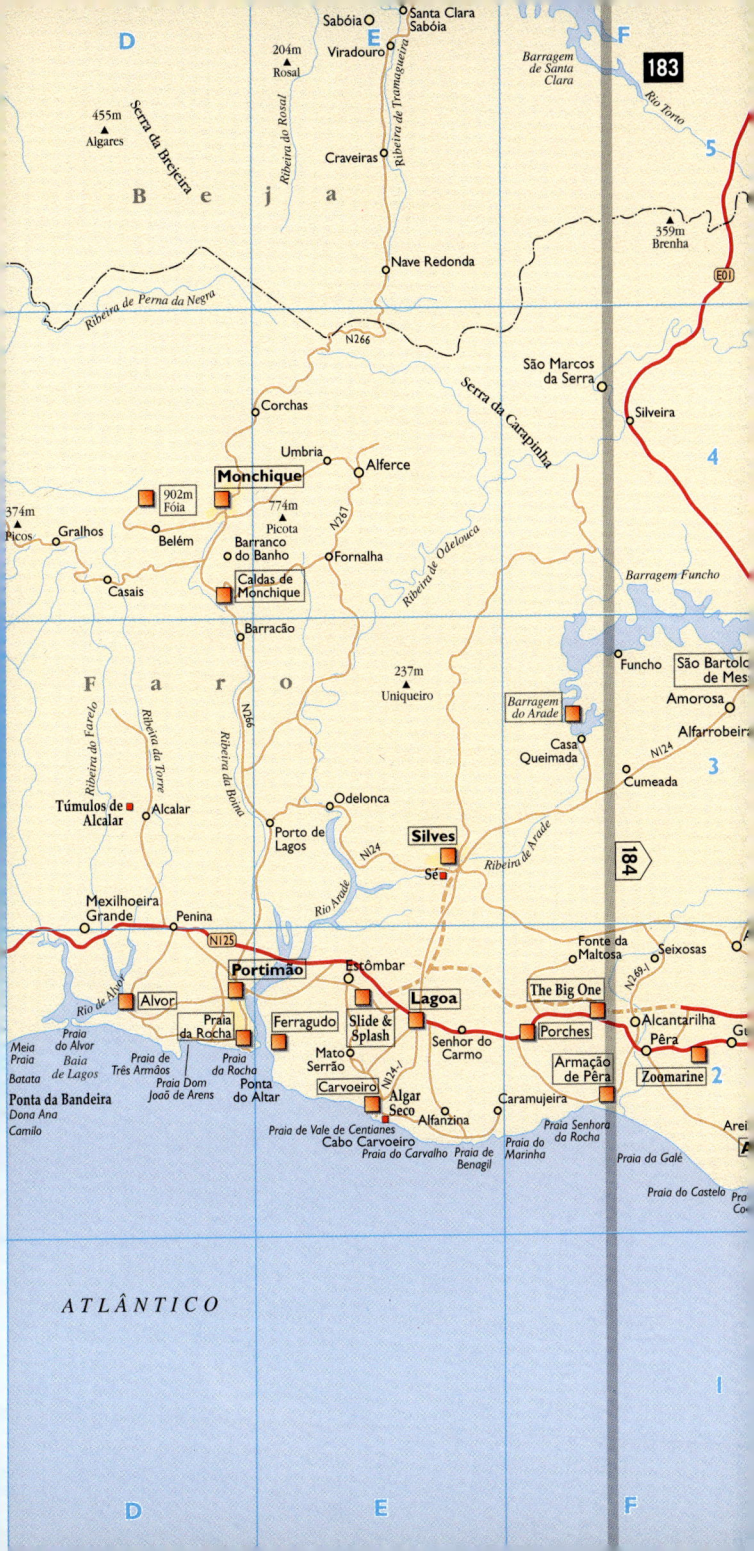

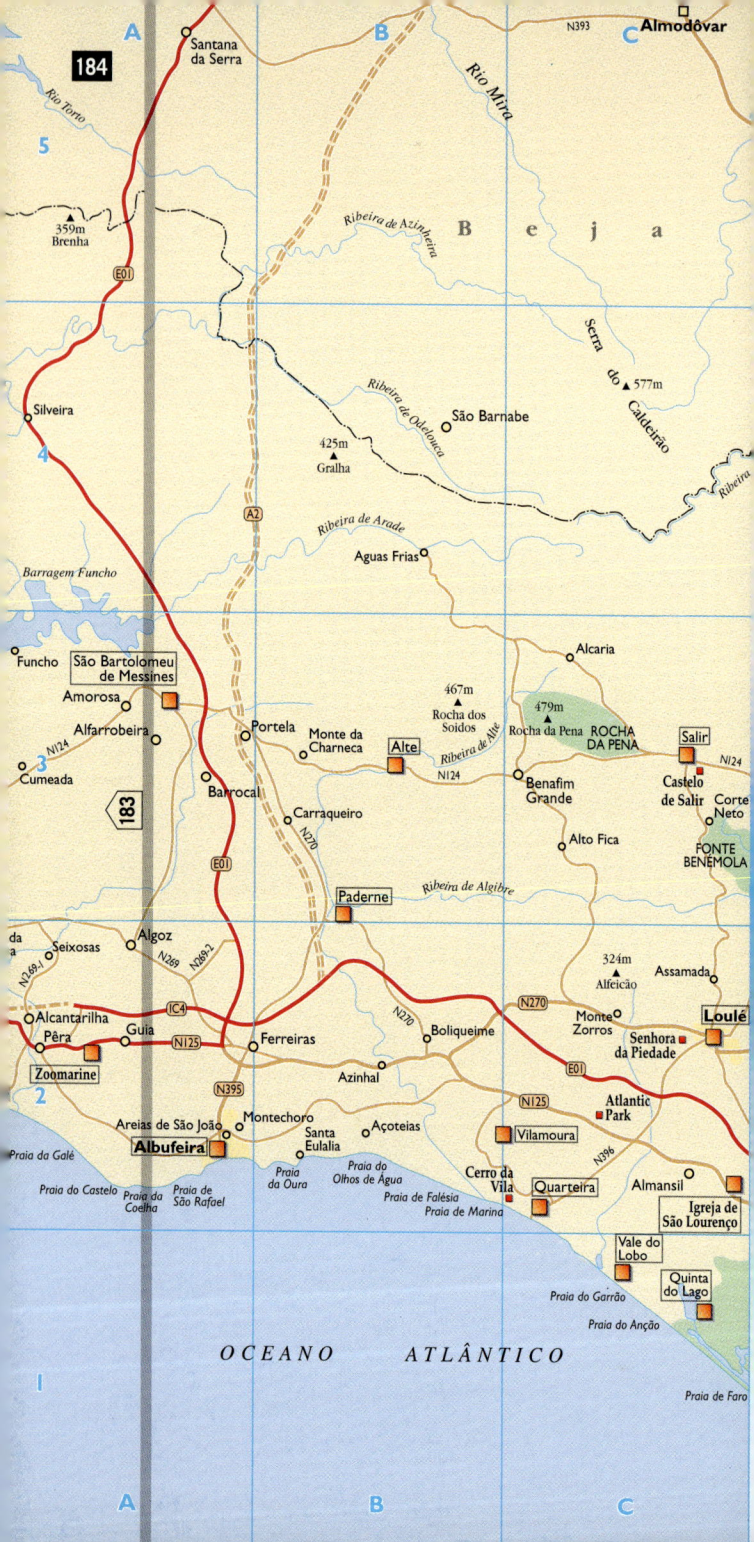

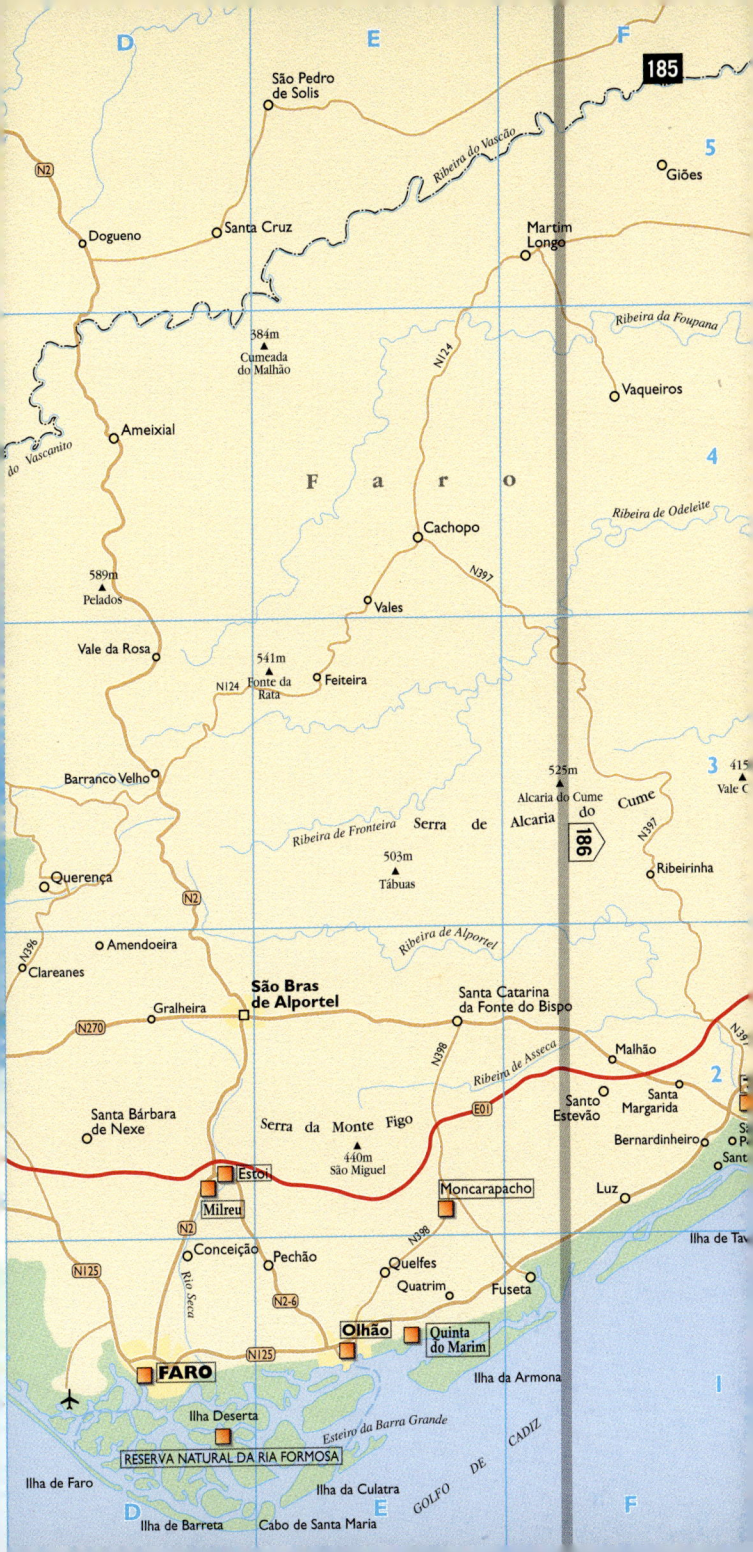

accommodation 35–6, 178
see also individual areas
airport and air services 32–3, 173
Albufeira 24, 68, 72–4, 90, 92
  beaches 82
  Museu Arqueológico 73
  Old Town 73
  walking tours 74
Alcalar 21, 101
Alcantarilha 22, 29
Alcoutim 22, 53–4, 167
  Núcleo Museológico Arte-Sacre 54
Algar Seco 95, 102–3
Aljezur 131
  Casa Museu José Cercas 131
  Museu Municipal 131
Almancil 90
Alte 84–5
Alvor 94, 104, 106
Alvor Estuary 104
architectural heritage 20–2
Armação de Pêra 106
Armona 169
Atlantic Park 83, 92
Ayet, Jacinto d' 74
azulejos 20, 77, 84, 101

bacalhau (dried salt-cod) 17, 29
banks 173, 174
Barlavento 94–5
Barragem do Arade 147, 152
Barrocal 161–3
beaches 24
  Algar Seco 95, 102–3
  Alvor 104
  Amado 24, 126
  Armação de Pêra 106
  Arrifana 23, 24, 127
  Baleeira 131
  Batata 121
  Beliche 131
  Benagil 24, 103
  Bordeira 24, 126
  Cabanas Velhas 24, 129
  Cacela Velha 24, 55, 60
  Camilo 122

beaches (cont.)
  Castelo 24, 82, 84
  Carvalho 103
  Castelejo 126
  Central East Algarve 82
  Central West Algarve 102–3
  Coelha 82
  Cordama 23, 126, 127
  Dona Ana 24, 122
  Eastern Algarve 55
  Estudantes 121
  Galé 82
  Ilha da Armona 55
  Ilha Deserta 55
  Ilha de Tavira 55
  Ingrina 24, 131
  João de Arens 104
  Manta Rota 55
  Mareta 131
  Marinha 24, 103
  Martinhal 131
  Meia Praia 8, 118 121, 122
  Monte Clérigo 127
  Nossa Senhora da Rocha 106
  Odeceixe 127
  Olhos de Água 82
  Ponta da Piedade 23, 122
  Porto de Mós 122
  Praia Grande 105
  Praia da Rocha 98–9, 105
  Santa Eulalia 82
  São Rafael 82
  Smuggler's Beach 103
  Três Irmãos 104
  Vale de Centianes 103
  The West 121–2, 126–7, 131
  Zavial 131
The Big One 105, 107
boat and river trips 66, 91–2, 94–5, 100, 112, 136
Boca do Rio 158–60
bone chapels 28–9, 47, 56
bridges 20
Budens Wetlands 158, 160
bullfighting 40, 136
Burgau 10–11, 129
buses 32, 34, 173

Cabanas Velhas 24, 129
Cabo de São Vicente 23, 115, 124–5

Cabral, Pedro Alvares 7
Cacela Velha 24, 55, 60
Caldas de Monchique 145–6, 156–7
camping 36
cão d'agua (water dog) 28, 170
Cape St Vincent 23, 115, 124–5
car hire 32, 34
Carvoeiro 94, 102–3
Casa Grande 10–11, 132
Casa Museu José Cercas 131
casinos 40, 112
Castelo beach 24, 82, 84
Castelo dos Mouros 51
Castelo de Silves 143
Castro Marim 53, 54
  archaeological museum 53
  Fort of São Sebastião 53
  wetlands 53
Central East Algarve 67–92
  accommodation 86–7
  Albufeira 24, 68, 72–4, 90, 92
  Alte 84–5
  beaches 82
  children's entertainment 84
  eating out 88–9
  entertainment 91–2
  four-day itinerary 70–1
  Igreja de São Lourenço 77–8
  Loulé 79–81, 90, 161
  map 69
  Paderne 85
  Quarteira 22, 83
  Quinta do Lago 12–13, 68, 83–4, 90
  Salir 84, 162
  shopping 90
  Vale do Lobo 22, 83–4
  Vilamoura 22, 75–6, 91–2
Central West Algarve 93–112
  accommodation 108–9

Central West (cont.)
  Alvor 94, 104
  Armação de Pêra 106
  Barlavento 94–5
  beaches 102–3
  Carvoeiro 94, 102–3
  children's entertainment 105
  eating out 105, 109–10
  entertainment 112
  Ferragudo 20, 94, 104–5
  Lagoa 105, 111
  map 94–5
  Porches 14–16, 24, 25, 105–6, 111
  Portimão 24, 95, 100–1, 111
  Praia da Rocha 24, 94, 98–9
  Praia da Vau 99
  shopping 111
  three-day itinerary 96–7
  waterparks 107
Centro Cultural de São Lourenço 78
Cerca Nova 162
Cerro da Vila 76
children 176
children's entertainment
  Central East Algarve 84
  Central West Algarve 105
  Eastern Algarve 48, 59
  The Hills 147
  The West 128
chimneys 20, 24
churches
  bone chapels 28–9, 47, 56
  Ermida de Nossa Senhora de Guadalupe 129–30
  Faro cathedral 47, 48
  Misericórdia 50, 164
  Nossa Senhora da Conceição (Our Lady of the Conception) 80
  Nossa Senhora da Piedade (Our Lady of Piety) 80
  Nossa Senhora dos Prazeres (Our Lady of Pleasures) 47

Index 187

churches (cont.)
Nossa Senhora da Rocha (Our Lady of the Rocks) 106
Nossa Senhora do Rosario (Our Lady of the Rosary) 57
Santa Maria do Castelo 50–1, 164
São António 119
São Clemente 80
São Francisco 48
São Lourenço 77–8
Sé, Faro 47, 48
Sé, Silves 143
Silves cathedral 143
Ciência Viva 56
climate and seasons 172
clothing sizes 174
Coelha 82
concessions 176
consulates and embassies 176
Convento de Nossa Senhora da Assunção 24, 47, 48
Convento de São José 105
Corcitos 162
Cork Museum 144
cork industry 142
Costa Vicentina National Park 127
crafts 65, 81, 90, 111, 135, 151
credit cards 37, 173
crime and personal safety 175
currency 173
cycling 66, 147, 152

dental services 176
disabilities, travellers with 176
diving 39, 122, 136
Drake, Sir Francis 124
drinking water 176
driving 32, 33–4, 172
driving tours
  Barrocal 161–2
  Rio Guadiana 166–8
drugs and medicines 176

Eanes, Gil 7
Eastern Algarve 41–66

Eastern Algarve (cont.)
accommodation 61–2
airport 32
Alcoutim 22, 53–4, 167
beaches 55
Cacela Velha 24, 55, 60
Castro Marim 53, 54
children's entertainment 48, 59
eating out 63–4
entertainment 66
Estói Palace 20, 58–9
Faro 42, 46–8, 65
four-day itinerary 44–5
map 42–3
Milreu 58
Moncarapacho 59
Monte Gordo 60
Olhão 21, 24, 42, 57, 65
Quinta do Marim 21, 42, 57, 169–70
Rio Guadiana 52–4, 166–8
shopping 65
Tavira 21, 22, 42–3, 49–51, 65, 164–5
Vila Real de Santo António 60
eating out 23, 25, 37
  mealtimes 37
  useful phrases 178
  see also individual areas
electricity 175
emergency telephone numbers 175
entertainment 39–40
  see also individual areas
Ermida de Nossa Senhora de Guadalupe 129–30
Estói Palace 20, 58–9

fado 39, 66, 136, 152
Faro 42, 46–8, 65
  Capela dos Ossos 28–9, 56
  cathedral 47, 48
  Chapel of Nossa Senhora dos Prazeres 47

Ciência Viva 56
Convento de Nossa Senhora da Assunção 24, 47, 48
eating out 56, 63, 64
Faro New Town 56
Faro Old Town 46–8
Igreja de São Francisco 48
Igreja do Carmo 28–9, 56
modern art galleries 48
Museu Arqueológico 47
Museu da Marítimo 56
Museu Regional 56
Paço Episcopal 46
Ferragudo 20, 94, 104–5
festivals 40, 81
fishing 76, 91, 112, 136
Fóia 148
folk singing and dancing 39, 92
Fonte de Benémola 163
Fonte Grande 85
Fonte Pequena 85
food and drink 17–19, 29, 37
  see also eating out
foreign exchange 173
Fortaleza do Beliche 131
Fortaleza de Sagres 123–4
Forte da Ponte da Bandeira 118
Foz de Odeleite 167

Galé 82
Gama, Vasco da 7, 99
gifts and souvenirs 38
golf 26–7, 39, 66, 75, 76, 83–4, 91, 112, 136
Great Earthquake (1755) 78, 130
Guerreiros do Rio 167

health 176
Henry the Navigator 6–7, 119, 124, 125, 129–30

The Hills 137–52
accommodation 149
Barragem do Arade 147, 152
Caldas de Monchique 145–6, 156–7
children's entertainment 147
eating out 150–1
entertainment 152
Fóia 148
map 138–9
Monchique 147–8, 151
Picota 148
São Bartolomeu de Messines 147
Serra de Monchique 138, 147
shopping 151
Silves 22, 25, 142–4, 151
two-day itinerary 140–1
horse-riding 39, 83, 91, 112, 136, 152
hot-air ballooning 76
hot-chestnut sellers 30
hotels 35

Ilha da Armona 55
Ilha de Tavira 55
Ilha Deserta 55
Ingrina 24, 131
inoculations 172
insurance 172, 176

jeep safaris 66
João II 106, 143
João de Arens 104
João de Deus Museum 147

Lagoa 105, 111
Lagos 25, 115, 118–22, 135
Armazém Regimental 154
beaches and coves 121–2
Ciência Viva 56
Forte da Ponte da Bandeira 118
Igreja de Santo António 119
map 155
Museu Municipal 24, 119–20
slave market 119, 155
walk 154–5

language guide 177–8
Lisbon 21
Living Science 56
Loulé 24, 79–81, 90, 161
  crafts 81
  festivals 81
  market 79
  Municipal Art Gallery 80
  Museu Municipal 80
  Nossa Senhora da Conceição 80
  Nossa Senhora da Piedade 80
  Old Town 80
  São Clemente 80
Luz (Praia da Luz) 128

Magellan, Ferdinand 7
Manta Rota 55
Manuel Cabanas Museum 60
Manueline architecture 20, 21, 84
Maritime Museum 56
markets 24, 38
  Central East Algarve 79
  Eastern Algarve 65
  The Hills 151
  The West 135
medical treatment 176
Meia Praia 8, 118, 121, 122
Milreu 58
Miradouro da Atalaia 128
Miradouro da Cordama 23
Moncarapacho 59
Monchique 147–8, 151
money 173, 178
Monte Gordo 60
Moorish architecture 21
Moorish legends 29–30
museum and church opening times 174
museums
  Casa Museu José Cercas 131
  Casa Museu João de Deus Museum 147
  Cerro da Vila Museum 76
  Ciência Viva 56

museums (cont.)
  Convento de Nossa Senhora da Assunção 24, 47, 48
  Living Science 56
  Museu Arqueológico, Albufeira 73
  Museu Arqueológico, Faro 47
  Museu da Cortiça 144
  Museu Manuel Cabanas 60
  Museu, Moncarapacho 59
  Museu Municipal, Aljezur 131
  Museu Municipal, Lagos 24, 119–20
  Museu Municipal, Loulé 80
  Museu Municipal, Portimão 101
  Museu Municipal de Arqueologia, Silves 143
  Museu Regional, Faro 56
  Núcleo Museológico Arte-Sacra 54

national holidays 174
Nossa Senhora do Desterro 148
Nossa Senhora da Rocha 106

Obelisk Lookout 128
Olhão 21, 24, 42, 57, 65
Olhos de Água 82
opening hours 38, 174
ostrich ranch 66

Paderne 85
palheiros 21
Parque Mineiro Cova dos Mouros 21, 168
Parque Natural da Costa Vicentina 114
passports and visas 172
pensões 35
pharmacies 174, 176

picnic spots 85
Picota 148
police 175
Ponta da Piedade 23, 122
Porches 14–16, 24, 25, 105–6, 111
port 18
Portimão 17, 20, 21, 24, 95, 100–1, 111
  Alcalar 21, 101
  boat trips 100
  Museu Municipal Portimão 101
  Sardine Dock 100
Porto de Mós 122
postal services 175
pottery 14–16, 24–5, 105, 111
pousadas 35
praia see beaches
Praia de Alvor 104
Praia do Amado 126
Praia de Arrifana 23, 24, 127
Praia da Baleeira 24, 131
Praia da Batata 121
Praia do Beliche 131
Praia do Benagil 24, 103
Praia da Bordeira 24, 126
Praia do Camilo 122
Praia do Carvalho 103
Praia do Castelejo 126
Praia da Cordama 23, 126, 127
Praia Dona Ana 24, 122
Praia dos Estudantes 121
Praia Grande 105
Praia da Mareta 131
Praia da Marinha 24, 103
Praia da Martinhal 131
Praia de Monte Clérigo 127
Praia Nossa Senhora da Rocha 106
Praia de Odeceixe 127
Praia da Rocha 9–10, 24, 94, 98–9, 105
Praia da Vau 99
Praia de Vale de Centianes 103

Quarteira 22, 83
Querença 24, 161
Quinta do Lago 12–13, 68, 83–4, 90
Quinta do Marim 21, 42, 57, 169–70

radio 25
rail travel 34
Raposeira 129
Reserva Natural da Ria Formosa 57, 60, 84, 169
Reserva Natural do Sapal de Castro Marim 53, 54
residenciais 35
Rio Guadiana 52–4, 166–8
road systems 33

Sagres 6–7, 115, 123–4, 130–1, 135
Salema 129
Salir 84, 162
salt pans 169
Sanlúcar de Guadiana 166, 167
Santa Eulalia 82
São Bartolomeu de Messines 147
São Rafael 82
Sardine Dock 100
Sé, Faro 47, 48
Sé, Silves 143
Sebastianismo 8
Sebastião 7–8
self-catering 36
senior citizens 176
Serra de Monchique 138, 147
shark- and dolphin-watching 91, 130, 136
shopping 38, 174, 178
  see also individual areas
Silves 22, 25, 142–4, 151
  Castelo de Silves 143
  cathedral 143
  Fábrica do Inglês 144, 152
  Museu da Cortiça 144
  Museu Municipal de Arqueologia 143
  Torreão da Porta da Cidade 143, 144
slave market 119, 155

Slide & Splash 105, 107
Smuggler's Beach 103
Solar Penguin 9–10, 99, 108–9
solares de Portugal 36
spa 145–6
sport and leisure activities 39
star-spotting 12–13
students and young travellers 176
sun safety 176
sunsets and views 23
surfing and windsurfing 39, 127, 136
Swift, Patrick 14–16, 102

Tavira 21, 22, 42–3, 49–51, 65
Castelo dos Mouros 51
Igreja da Misericórdia 50, 164

Tavira (cont.)
Igreja de Santa Maria do Castelo 50–1, 164
map 165
Ponte Romana 51, 164
walk 164–5
taxis 32
telephones 175
tennis 39, 83, 112
time differences 173, 174
tipping 37, 175
toilets 176
tourist information 32, 172–3
travellers' cheques 173
Três Irmãos 104

Vale do Lobo 22, 83–4
Vila do Bispo 129–30
Vila Real de Santo António 60

Vilamoura 22, 75–6, 91–2
Cerro da Vila 76
golf 75, 76
watersports 76

waterparks 83, 105, 107
watersports 39, 76, 91, 112, 136
Websites 172
The West 113–36
accommodation 132
Aljezur 131
beaches 121–2, 126–7, 131
Burgau 129
Cape St Vincent 23, 115, 124–5
children's entertainment 128
eating out 133–4
entertainment 136
Fortaleza do Beliche 131

The West (cont.)
Lagos 25, 115, 118–22, 135, 154–5
Luz (Praia da Luz) 128
map 115
Sagres 115, 123–4, 130–1, 135
Salema 129
shopping 135
three-day itinerary 116–17
Vila do Bispo 129–30
wildlife 53, 57, 160, 169
wildlife souvenirs 176
wines and spirits 18, 105, 111, 151, 157

youth hostels 22, 36

Zavial 131
Zoomarine 105, 107

Picture credits

Abbreviations for terms appearing below: (t) top; (b) bottom; (l) left; (r) right; (c) centre.

The Automobile Association wishes to thank the following photographers and libraries for their assistance with the preparation of this book:
ARDEA LONDON 28 (John Daniels); ART DIRECTORS & TRIP PHOTO LIBRARY 48 (S Grant), 98t (S Grant), 104b (T H - Foto Werburg), 120t (F Bradbury), 128b (J Bartos), 140 (F Bradbury); AXIOM PHOTOGRAPHIC AGENCY 8t (Peter M Wilson); MICHELLE CHAPLOW 3(i), 29t, 93; MARY EVANS PICTURE LIBRARY 6/7, 6; GOLF PICTURE LIBRARY 26/7, 27; PAUL MURPHY 9b, 10, 15t, 16t, 16b, 19tr, 21, 30b, 53b, 59b, 72, 81t, 107, 141t, 157, 158, 160l, 163, 166, 169, 170; NATURE PHOTOGRAPHERS LTD 53t (P R Sterry), 160b (P R Sterry); PHOTONONSTOP Front & back/Cover (ct) (J-Marc Blache); PICTURES COLOUR LIBRARY 18/19, 30t, 82, 131; POPPERFOTO 9t, 13; REX FEATURES LTD 11t, 12tl (Sinead Lynch), 12tr (Ray Tang), 12b; TRAVEL INK 130 (Ronald Badkin); THE TRAVEL LIBRARY 14, 17t, 20b, 47c, 85, 123, 126/7; WORLD PICTURES 23.

The remaining photographs are held in the Association's own photo library (AA PHOTO LIBRARY) and were taken by Caroline Jones with the exception of the following:
Malcolm Birkitt 58, 96b, 98b; Michelle Chaplow 3(iii), 19b, 22t, 44b, 45l, 45r, 52, 54, 59t, 71t, 79b, 84, 103t, 117, 121, 122, 125, 126, 128t, 129t, 129b, 137, 138, 139t, 139b, 141c, 143t, 143b, 144, 146t, 147, 161, 162, 168, 175r; Jerry Edmanson 3(v), 15b, 18tr, 19tl, 70, 124t, 145, 156, 171, 175t; Alex Kouprianoff 3(ii), 7, 8b, 24/25, 29tr, 29b, 60, 74, 101t, 113, 114, 120b, 127, 141b, 142, 146b; Peter Wilson 14/5/6 b/ground, 16c.

Acknowledgements

Paul Murphy would like to thank the following individuals and organisations for their help during the research of this book:
Sally Vincent of Casa Grande, Dorothy Boulter of the Solar Penguin, and Julie Statham of Portugal Walks for their hospitality and expert advice. Thanks also to Josè Aragão of the ICEP Portuguese Trade and Tourism office for his help with general queries, and particularly with golfing advice.

SPIRAL GUIDES

Questionnaire

Dear Traveler

Your comments, opinions and recommendations are very important to us. So please help us to improve our travel guides by taking a few minutes to complete this simple questionnaire.

Send to: Spiral Guides, MailStop 66, 1000 AAA Drive, Heathrow, FL 32746–5063

Your recommendations...
We always encourage readers' recommendations for restaurants, nightlife or shopping – if your recommendation is added to the next edition of the guide, we will send you a FREE AAA Spiral Guide of your choice. Please state below the establishment name, location and your reasons for recommending it.

_____
_____
_____
_____
_____

Please send me AAA Spiral_____
(see list of titles inside the back cover)

About this guide...
Which title did you buy?

_____ AAA Spiral

Where did you buy it? _____

When? m m / y y

Why did you choose a AAA Spiral Guide? _____
_____
_____

Did this guide meet your expectations?

Exceeded ☐   Met all ☐   Met most ☐   Fell below ☐

Please give your reasons _____
_____
_____

continued on next page...

Were there any aspects of this guide that you particularly liked?

_____
_____
_____
_____

Is there anything we could have done better?

_____
_____
_____
_____
_____

About you…

Name (Mr/Mrs/Ms) _____

Address _____

_____ Zip _____

Daytime tel nos. _____

Which age group are you in?

Under 25 ☐ 25–34 ☐ 35–44 ☐ 45–54 ☐ 55–64 ☐ 65+ ☐

How many trips do you make a year?

Less than one ☐ One ☐ Two ☐ Three or more ☐

Are you a AAA member? Yes ☐ No ☐

Name of AAA club _____

About your trip…

When did you book? m m / y y   When did you travel? m m / y y

How long did you stay? _____

Was it for business or leisure? _____

Did you buy any other travel guides for your trip? ☐ Yes ☐ No

If yes, which ones? _____

Thank you for taking the time to complete this questionnaire.

All information is for AAA internal use only and will NOT be distributed outside the organization to any third parties.